Give Me Back My Glory

by

Connie E. Curry

authorHOUSE®

AuthorHouse™
1663 Liberty Drive, Suite 200
Bloomington, IN 47403
www.authorhouse.com
Phone: 1-800-839-8640

This book is a work of non-fiction. Unless otherwise noted, the author
and the publisher make no explicit guarantees as to the accuracy of
the information contained in this book and in some cases, names of
people and places have been altered to protect their privacy.

First published by AuthorHouse 4/3/2008

ISBN: 978-1-4343-3317-9 (sc)

Library of Congress Control Number: 2008900974

Printed in the United States of America
Bloomington, Indiana

This book is printed on acid-free paper.

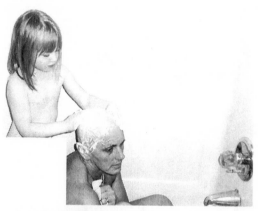

A child's love heals.
Dedicated to Allie Dawn Etgen, who always gives me
unconditional love.

Special Thanks:

Thank you to Dr. Houser, Dr. Rhoades, Delaware Radiation Oncology and Dr. Linda for making me well again. Thanks to Dr. Schissel, my family doctor who gave me great advice when I was misdiagnosed. His concern and quick action to help was appreciated. Thanks to Ben Romero, Vickie Miller, Shirley Link, Daughter Amber and Naoma Van Brimmer (my mom) for the extra eyes and opinions as I wrote my book. Thank you Melissa and Phil Mercer for your time and support. Jessica Crooks, thank you for your belief in me and your expert opinion. My Delaware Writer's group always gave me drive to finish my book. They listened and critiqued honestly for me many evenings as we sat at the library. Judy Falter, thanks to you. You put people back on track when they are low. You are an inspiration and validate that being handicapped is really not a handicap if you choose. Thanks to Sara Risley, a pro in photography who offered me much advice. Aussie Michelle Ludlow, my writing friend from down under always has been there for me. Thanks Mate. To Margi, who stood by me even when my opinion seemed clouded and selfish. Thanks to Vicki Maggard at Grady Memorial who helped me in many ways. From words of comfort and hope to my blonde bombshell wig, thanks. Nora White, fight hard, girl! I thank you for coming back into my life and supporting and reading each chapter of my book. Thanks to Ken Reed and Rudy Pamintuan who gave me the confidence to write professionally. Thanks to Tammy Williams for the countless things she did for me, including my breast cancer scrap book which I'll cherish forever. Teresa Evans gave me fight back on the day of the Susan Komen Race for the Cure. Thanks for always being my friend, Teresa and knowing just the right time to call and check on me. To Ryan who ran with me in hope, spirit and loyalty of me. He left me in the dust but waited at the finish line for me. Rowena Wycoff and Viv Curry thanks for running with us. Thank you to Kate and Jack Curry, my in laws who showed such concern. Kate, you are the best in a mother-in-law. Thanks to all my friends for the cards, food, flowers, inspirational gifts and donations for the Relay for Life in my honor. I have the best in friends and I am blessed. To Mom and Dad, I thank. I am ranked in the top 5 for great parents. To David, who was tolerating of all my mood swings, and changes in body and soul, thank you. Amber, Ryan and Katie, thank you for caring and loving me unconditionally. To Allie most of all who gave me reason to fight hard. A child is special. A granddaughter is golden.

Table of Contents

1
The Verdict Was In

His voice was compassionate. With sorrow, he spilled the words we all fear: "Your pathology report is not good, Connie. You have cancer."

My carefree life was shaken. I was scared to the core of my being. I don't recall much more that he said. I heard words like lumpectomy, mastectomy, chemo, radiation, clear margin, and he paused and then apologized to me.

I tried to convince myself that this could not be true. It had to be a mistake. Breast cancer is not in my family. Immediately, I felt sad thinking of my two daughters and my granddaughter and what would now be included on their family medical history.

My kids tell me I have a sixth sense. I know things before they happen. I am almost always on target when I meet someone and I am a good judge of character. I love people! I try to find the good in everyone.

I am an early riser, jumping out of bed ready to begin a new day. Invigorated by the thoughts of fresh-brewed coffee, I am anxious to experience everything life has to offer. The sun radiating the promise of a new day and birds chirping warm my heart. I don't want a minute of life to pass me by.

I am a free spirit. I love big crowds of people and having everyone's attention, telling funny stories. Laughter makes life smooth and easy.

All of a sudden, I couldn't find laughter. I cried each morning and wanted to curl up in a fetal position, not wanting to deal with my breast cancer. Would I ever have the desire to get out of bed? I buried myself under the comfort of warm blankets and wished the world would go away. I wanted to die.

At age forty-eight, I was struggling with feeling that life was moving too fast, and my youth was truly gone. Menopause was knocking at my door. I denied looking and growing older. I wanted to put the brakes on to stop the aging process.

It seemed David, my husband and I had grown apart, Mom and Dad were soul mates. They couldn't comprehend or didn't want to understand my need to live for me for the first time in my adult life. I was not losing my mind; I was sure I was not in midlife crisis, although I often wondered what the signs and symptoms were for this overused terminology.

David and I met when we were kids. His family lived next door to my favorite aunt. I played hide-and-seek with him when we were innocent children with only summer mosquitoes to worry about. He went off to the navy as a young seventeen-year-old. We corresponded and wrote many letters. We were friends and nothing more.

He arrived home, discharged with an honorable mention. He'd grown up and into a much taller, good-looking man without acne. He was still very shy, but his childhood crush on me had flooded over into love. I broke off my engagement with another man, and we started dating. Within five months, we married. We did everything right in the beginning. We saved money, bought yard sale items to decorate our simple, rented first home, and wore thrift-store clothes in an effort to save money. We drove junk cars as we saved for our first home. David always hurried home after work. Life was good as we settled into the simple ranch home that we'd bought.

Four years later, my water broke in Lamaze class and Amber, born five weeks early, came into our lives. She was a beautiful redhead as Mom had predicted, and we loved her more than life.

Nineteen months later, Ryan was born. What more could a couple want? We had a perfectly healthy son, too. He was beautiful, with chubby cheeks and brilliant blue eyes.

As toddlers, it was obvious that Amber and Ryan's personalities were extremely different. Amber was talkative and loved everyone. She did not know a stranger. Ryan was very shy. As people leaned down to greet him, he'd hide behind me. He loved toy tractors, combines, hay wagons, and any kind of ball. Sports became his passion, and soccer was his favorite.

We sold our first home and bought a beautiful, bigger home closer to town with three bedrooms and a mortgage payment that doubled, but the kids filled our home with love.

Like two careless teenagers, without planning I became pregnant just months after our move. "This baby was meant to be," Mom said as I cried about being pregnant. "You need to change your attitude, both of you," Mom said to David and me. Slowly I grew excited about the birth of another child. Secretly I wanted another daughter. My wish came true. Katie, born seven years after Ryan's birth, was easily accepted in our hearts and home. Her fingers were so long, I noticed as I looked at her for the first time. Mom declared, "She'll be a piano player." As she grew, her personality was similar to Ryan's. Her shyness and hiding between my legs was a rerun of her big brother. And as she grew older, it was obvious she was going to be tall, and she turned into a six-foot-tall beauty. She never learned music with her long fingers but excelled in every sport she played.

It seemed that so many changes and adjustments had taken place over a span of many years. It was easy to parent when the kids were little. I was on overdrive from stress. Our innocent, sweet babies had grown into teens and, although born beautiful and healthy, they lacked angel wings. I felt alone as I watched them making bad decisions. David tended to leave discipline and worrying to me.

I felt burned out by being a mother and wife. I had grown tired of feeling unappreciated, taken advantage of and fighting battles alone, and I wanted to think of myself. I was spent and tired.

The lump that I had discovered one night while shaving my arm pits caused me horrific mental torture. I waited and feared the worse. October 15, 2004 was a day I will never forget. It was a dreary, damp fall evening. I had returned home from work and was rushing to head out to a school function for my daughter. I turned on the coffeepot for the added energy to keep me going into the evening. I began filling the bathtub to take my half bath. I was home alone, since David was going to the game from work and would meet me there.

I thought about Shelley, my niece who always laughed at me when I talked about taking half baths.

"What the hell is a half bath?" she asked me once when she heard my phrase. I was a senior in high school when she was born. Shell was the apple of all of our eyes, the first baby in years to enjoy. Mom remembers finding comfort in Shelley. Grandma was dying and Mom would visit Grandma daily after a hard day of work. Two blocks away, she would go hold her new granddaughter to lift her spirits. Shell was born a redhead like Mom and Wayne, my brother.

I take a half-bath when I am in a big hurry and time is too short to wash, comb, and blow-dry my hair. I wash my face, carefully avoiding water near my eyes to prevent having to redo my eye makeup. I can be in and out of a tub, dressed and ready, heading out the door in fifteen minutes. Sometimes, I'd just throw on a ball cap.

As the water rushed into the tub, I played the answering machine as I jumped out of my clothes. The football game was an away game, and forty-five minutes from home. Time was a-wastin'! When I heard my doctor's voice come over the answering machine, I stopped … dead in my tracks. My heart raced, and fear grew inside me like I had never felt before. Being one with an almost-always positive attitude, I immediately felt overwhelmed with negative assumptions about Dr. Schumer's call. The night before, I had gone to bed, snuggling up with a good book, almost forgetting about the lump I had found. As I routinely do each night, I read until my eyes couldn't stay open, turned the light out, and immediately fell asleep. I recall being awakened from what I thought was a hard, peaceful sleep.

A sick feeling had come over me, and my first thought as I forced myself awake, was the biopsy results that I had been waiting for. My sixth sense had awakened me and left me shaken in a semi-panicked state. I felt pessimistic. Somehow, I knew the awaited phone call would bring me sadness.

For three days, this was the news I had anticipated and yet didn't want to know. My gut wrenched. His message was evasive and simple, and I knew the news could not be good, or he would have just happily announced the verdict. He wanted me to page him at the hospital. This also set my worries in motion. It was early evening, his office was closed, and he was like anyone on a Friday night … wishing to go home after a long, hard workweek.

I already knew and I couldn't cry. I was in shock. As I sat down to call him at the hospital, I impatiently waited for him to come to the phone. The house seemed so quiet, and the fall temperature crept into my bones. All of a sudden, the autumn colors were not so beautiful to me. My mouth felt very dry when I hung up the phone. His words played in my head. *You have cancer. I'm sorry. You will probably need to do chemo. I recommend a mastectomy.*

I also remembered that I had a daughter to watch play a unique high school varsity sport: football! And time was flying by. I needed a bath and needed to muster strength. As I walked into my bedroom after my bath, grabbing clothes to put on, I reached for my bath-and-body lotion. I felt nauseated. I stood looking at my well-rounded 36C perky breasts in the mirror and began rubbing the lotion across my face, down my neck, and across my chest. I ran my hands over my breasts as I looked at them in the mirror. At forty-eight, a mother of three and grandma to one, I was proud of them. I cupped them in my hands as I rubbed the lotion in. They were warm and soft. I broke into tears, unable to control my fear. I began to sob uncontrollably.

Mechanically, I continued to dress, putting on my shoes, grabbing my coat, purse, and a travel mug of freshly made coffee, turned out the lights, and headed to Friday night football. I felt empty inside.

I decided not to wear my seatbelt, and I drove erratically fast, heading out of my county and into what felt like a world unknown. Why bother using the Whitestrips to brighten my teeth? Who the hell looks at teeth anyway? I decided I would cancel my dentist appointment to have my capped tooth redone. Piss on it, piss on my teeth, my tits, and my life. We live in a bosom society. How could I have a breast removed?

Katie is special, and my motherly instincts had to kick in. No matter how my news affected me, I knew I could forget my problems when I reached the football field. What I felt at the time seemed like a death sentence. It had to wait.

Katie, a football kicker, was about to do what few females even dream about. She was doing the unthinkable, beating the odds, and succeeding with style, bravery, and stardom every Friday night, among and against all male athletes. She didn't need to know ... yet.

I also was about to test my strength and bravery. Just in another way. And I would see my husband, who would be at the game, and I'd have to find the right time to tell him. It would have to wait.

2
A Friend To Tell

As I drove across country roads, I picked up my cell phone. I needed to talk to someone. Friends are abundant, and without much hesitation, I dialed Margi, my best friend of almost forty years.

Margi and I grew up together. We were neighbor children, rode the same school bus and spent countless weekends in each other's homes. We were what country folks call neighbors. Our homes were two miles apart on the same county road. Our road was what many city kids called the boonies.

We have been through thick and thin together. We shared weddings and the births of our babies, exchange recipes, vacation together, and still wear each other's clothes. We laugh, we argue, we sing, and we give each other advice, whether it is welcomed or not. We fall right back into place ... our friendship always more solid then the day before.

I was with her, supporting her and helping her to heal, when she divorced. I cried for her when her young daughter became pregnant. She cried with me when I shared the same unexpected news a year later about my daughter, Amber.

When she answered her telephone, I blurted it out immediately, without even a hello, "Margi, I have breast cancer." And I wailed, crying and wanting her advice and thinking she would know what to do. I drove on, not paying much attention to the country roads. She could find a way to fix this and make me laugh. "What am I going to do, Margi, what? What? Oh my God!" I screamed into the phone.

Margi, so strong, independent, and with so much common sense, broke. Her voice cracked, and I recall her words, "Connie, we can win this; you can beat this. I will help you."

Oh how I wish we were away on one of our many girl trips. "Chicks only, no cocks allowed," we would announce as we would head out of town, windows down, music blaring, on another adventure.

New York, Put-in-Bay, Ohio, Florida—anywhere we went, we laughed! We turned trips into total chaos at times, and sometimes had barely enough money between us to know if we'd make it back home.

We took a trip to New York several years ago. Our plans were to tie in some pleasure, sightseeing in New York, and also do some official business while on Long Island. Oh, not work-related stuff for me, certainly. It was her business trip, and I was along for companionship. Wow, what a ride!

We journeyed out in our rental car and headed south, leaving Long Island. In my lap were the directions to Freeport given to us by a Long Islander. Margi was behind the wheel! I think of her as the experienced driver, because she lives in the big city now. I am still residing in the county we grew up in.

The directions looked simple. We had two major interstates, a couple right turns and a left, and our destination would be reached. The casino boat called *Majesty* would head out at 7:30 PM and we would have an entertaining evening dropping coins in the slot machines. We had plenty of time on our hands. Freeport was twenty minutes away, so we looked forward to time for shopping and walking along the pier. We couldn't wait to see the ocean.

Something went haywire. One New York minute, we were making good time, excited about going out on the boat, and in another minute, we were at a tollbooth, traffic stopped, creeping bumper to bumper, and with policemen everywhere. It seemed that every other car was a cab. No one told us we had to go through a tollbooth to get to Freeport. We never did find Freeport and it was the scariest ride ever for two country girls.

We still laugh about that trip. But as I turned my cell phone off as I approached the football game, I knew Margi truly would be there for me.

I blew my nose, wiped my smeared mascara, parked my car, and got out.

3
Being Brave as Katie

I walked into the football game, cold, sad, and trying to concentrate on each step as I walked. My legs felt weak and the cold made me shiver. I immediately scanned the football field for number 49 and I looked up in the stands for David.

As I walked toward the stands, looking up to the crowd, it occurred to me that no one had a clue that I was sick. I didn't look ill, and I felt well. My skin color was good, my hair shone, and I was in relatively good shape for my age. I also realized that good health had spoiled me. Other than a worn-out back from twenty-five years of lifting patients on the job, I had been blessed and had taken good health for granted.

I also knew that I would remain silent, put a smile on my face, and watch the game, my biggest interest always with number 49.

I recalled how Katie accidentally became the first girl in our county and possibly one of only a handful in the nation to be part of a high school varsity football team.

It was late summer of 2003. Katie was about to start her sophomore year. Summer was about to end; football season and school days were approaching quickly.

She walked toward the football field, apprehensive and shy— her typical character. As the players finished practice, they watched her approach the field. The football team at Buckeye Valley High School, located in rural Delaware, Ohio, had heard rumors.

"There's no room on a football team for a girl," one player outspokenly said.

"A girl? We are going to have a girl on our team?" another player sarcastically asked Coach Gray.

"Give her a chance. Watch her kick before you form such a negative opinion," Coach Gray fired back.

Most of the players were skeptical, some were supportive, and others wanted to see it to believe it. Curiosity got the best of them. Many stayed after practice on this humid, late summer day to watch her. The placeholder and a select few were asked to help assist in retrieving and holding the ball as she tried out.

Katie, a gentle, timid girl of fifteen at the time, excels in sports. Her shyness and comfort zone are hidden when she competes. She doesn't like attention but loves to play sports at the competitive level. Katie is a team player and prefers someone else being the star.

This sudden opportunity happened because Coach Condit had faith in her and saw her talent for several years when she played soccer. He was amazed at the distance and accuracy she had when she kicked soccer balls.

That evening our telephone rang and Coach Condit told me his intentions of asking Katie to try out for the team. I instantly replied, "She isn't home, but you'd better call back and talk to her yourself. If I tell her what you want, she will instantly tell me she is not interested and probably won't return your call."

Coach Condit, a father, coach, and man with gentle but great coaching skills, was well known among the students. Katie had played some summer softball for him and respected and liked his coaching style.

I suspected that if Coach Condit spoke to Katie directly, she would not be able to turn him down. She adored him!

When he called back, I listened and hoped she would try out for the team. I didn't want to pressure her, but I knew this was a wonderful opportunity that might open many doors for her.

Coach Condit assumed she might start out kicking on the junior varsity team, gaining experience kicking off the tee, and maybe move up to the varsity level her junior or senior year.

I remember that day as I pulled into the parking lot to let Katie out of the car. I heard her nervous sigh. Getting out of my car to walk toward the football field was probably one of the most difficult and courageous things she had ever done. She held on to the door, trying to get the courage up to open it. She hesitated again as her hand held on to the door, sighing.

I sigh constantly, and I can't seem to be as brave as Katie when I think of letting doctors, nurses, and an anesthesiologist be in charge of my body. I worked full time for so long in the medical field, as an emergency medical technician. Unfortunately ... like any line of work, there are good and bad in the medical field. I knew I would have trouble trusting my future team of doctors.

I heard her take another deep breath that day, looking over to me as I gave her a reassuring smile and said, "It will be OK, Katie. You are good; you know you can do this and can do it well. Show those boys what you are made of."

The boys stared, looking her up and down. Katie's name and face were not well known. Being tall can draw attention in a crowd, but her shyness held her back socially in school. She struggled when she began high school. It seemed that her only comfort zone was when she competed in sports. Self-assurance and high self-esteem radiated during competition.

Katie shines when she walks onto a softball diamond, a soccer field, or a basketball court. By the fall of her sophomore year, she had already earned two varsity letters in soccer and softball and was also playing basketball at the junior varsity level.

I remember that day like yesterday. The place-kick holder picked up a football and placed it on the tee. The assistant high school coach stood, arms folded, and watched as Katie kicked the football toward the uprights. Through the middle of the goal post it soared.

She kicked several more, and the coach was amazed.

"Wow, she is good! Jeremy, you have lost your job, and she hasn't hit my fingers or hand yet," the holder said to his friend, a football comrade.

"Good, I don't want the job anyway. She is better!"

Coach Condit smiled.

She was asked to return the following evening so the varsity coach could observe her and see if she truly had the skill and ability to play on the junior varsity high school football team.

The news had spread throughout the school. More students and players stayed after school to watch Katie kick for the head coach. Girlfriends came to cheer her on and offer their moral support.

Coach Tinkler, the head coach, snickered as he stared to read her T-shirt, which read "P.M.S." in big, bold letters, and he probably wondered what he had gotten himself into by even thinking of putting a girl on a boys' football team. Play More Softball was translated at the bottom of the T-shirt.

He had her stand back at the thirty-five-yard line, and she made one goal after another, through the middle of the posts. For accuracy, he had her move to the far side of the field to see if she could hit the goal from an angled shot. She did!

"Well, how do you feel about playing football on Friday nights instead of sitting in the stands with your girlfriends?" Tinkler asked.

"Ya know, I am not crazy about wearing those tight, spandex football pants," she said.

"Be at practice Monday morning," Coach Tinkler told her.

It seemed she had jumped from junior varsity football to varsity in two evenings of kicking a football.

She picked up the football and tee he had offered her to practice with during her free time and walked home.

Seemed he had her answer.

Coach Tinkler and Coach Truex of the soccer team talked and had a mutual understanding to share her, allowing her to play both sports. They would understand about the practice time she had to split. Friday night football would not interfere with varsity soccer games.

Katie spent the rest of the summer juggling soccer and football practice. Sometimes she literally ran into the house, pulling soccer shin guards off and grabbing her football pads and practice jersey as she headed to school for the next practice.

I wondered if she would be able to keep up with homework, once school began. My biggest fear was the harassment she might endure among the football players.

As she practiced, the football players slowly became more friendly and accepting of her.

Jeremy, the senior kicker, was the most supportive. How ironic and amazing! This senior who loved football was being challenged by a female and might possibly lose his position.

Adam, the place-kick holder, instantly saw promise and talent as he held one ball after another for her at each practice.

"C'mon, girl. You can do it," he would say as she kicked one after another, always backing up, testing her strength and accuracy.

School began, practices continued, and the season was about to begin.

"Mom! I can't believe all the kids that walk up to me at school, telling me how awesome it is that I am kicking on the football team. Kids are saying hi to me that I don't even know."

Classmates approached and made comments such as:

"Hey, you are the kicker, aren't you?"

"I just want you to know that I think what you are doing is so cool."

"You go, girl!"

"Are you Katie, the kicker?"

"MAN! I saw you kick, you are sooo awesome."

I watched Katie blossom from one shy girl to a girl who finally had confidence in herself socially.

The cheerleaders made up a Katie the Kicker cheer. Students signed up to take turns wearing her jersey on game day.

The first pep rally was held, and when Katie's name was announced to walk out to join the football team, the students' cheering amplified throughout the gymnasium. Katie, a girl who rarely showed emotion, was overwhelmed and shocked at the stir she had created among her classmates and teaching staff.

I could hardly wait for the game opener. Katie was as excited as I was, and she wasn't even nervous. She just wanted the chance to prove herself.

I recall watching the football players along the sideline and wishing one would stand next to her, talk to her, or notice that she was a team member. It appeared that they didn't ridicule her; they just ignored her existence.

The first two games came and ended. Jeremy, the senior kicker, was called in several times to kick field goals and the extra points. He struggled and missed all of them. Each week we returned home, hoping soon that Katie would get the opportunity to kick. She was growing impatient, but continued to hope the next game would be her chance.

The third game was about to end. Two minutes remained, and Jeremy had again attempted many failed extra points earlier in the game. Buckeye Valley was on the twenty-five-yard line, about to score another touchdown.

David, our oldest daughter and son, and I sat in the stands, planning another trip home without seeing Katie make an appearance on the football field.

"KATIE, KATIE, KATIE!"

"KATIE, KATIE, KATIE!"

The chanting from the stands grew louder. The distracted players and coaches turned around to see fans standing, cheering, and stomping the floor of the bleachers.

I looked down at Katie, standing with a tee in one hand, and saw the coach saying something to her.

"If we make this touchdown, you are going in to kick. Are you ready, Katie?" he asked her.

"Yep, I'm ready, and I can do this!"

"TOUCHDOWN!" The fans roared when they heard the announcer.

Katie hustled to the field, and the fans were elated, hollering, clapping, and whistling. It was obvious to me that my family members were not the only ones waiting for this opportunity.

"Katie Curry will attempt the extra point," boomed over the intercom.

It was at that moment that I knew the opposing team would know this player disguised in a football uniform was a girl.

"Ewww, a girl. A girl is kicking," laughed an opposing player.

I stood near the fence, my hands folded in a praying position. I remember talking and mumbling to myself. I knew everything had to work right. The snap had to be good, our offensive line had to hold the defensive line back, and Adam had to get the football on the tee at the precise, rapid time. Most importantly, Katie had to be strong and not choke.

Like clockwork, the ball was snapped and placed on the tee, and it soared down the middle, up high, and yards well beyond and past the uprights.

When I watched the football team run to Katie, giving her high fives and smacking her on her head, I knew she had truly been accepted.

I couldn't wait to pick her up after the game. I was so proud of her.

"Mom, I think this is the happiest day of my life."

That season ended, and as I remembered … it occurred to me that we were playing the same team as when she had scored her first extra point a year ago. My life was different now. I recall not having any worries in the world the year before, except maybe the thought of a big linebacker roughing up my kicker.

Katie was given more field goal opportunities her second year with the team. These two years of experience have been remarkable for her.

Katie broke school records, being the first girl to score so many points on a football team.

She attended her sports banquet and was recognized for earning two varsity letters in the same sports season (soccer and football). When the football coach announced her name to accept her varsity letter, she walked up to him, being her typical shy, humble self as she shook his hand. Coach Tinkler shook his head, and a big smile spread across his face. In his wildest dreams, I am sure he never thought he would be awarding a varsity football letter to a tenth-grade female.

The parents, football players, and classmates again gave her what has helped her to spread those wings to fly, and to dream big dreams ... respect, confidence, support, and love as they clapped ever so loudly for her accomplishment.

I was bursting with pride as I looked up at her. She looked just like one of the girls, without her pads, helmet, and the spandex pants that she hated so.

And there I was again, at another football game, waiting for number 49 to kick the ball with her ponytail hanging out of the bottom of her helmet. The thoughts of my days to come were briefly lost while I watched the game.

As I sat in the stands, among family, I hid my secret. I didn't want to ruin their evening, and the timing just didn't seem right. I wondered when the time would ever be right to tell my husband and three children about the cancer. I thought of Allie, my precious granddaughter of only four.

Katie had avoided any roughing of the kicker. It was me who got kicked in the gut.

4
Allie Girl

My marriage had been suffering. After twenty-eight years of marriage, two children of adult age, and Katie in high school, I found myself sucked dry emotionally.

Amber, my daughter of twenty-four and mother to Allie Girl, as I call her, had struggled with parenting, relationships, finances, and life. I felt pleasure but added burden and more responsibilities since the birth of Allie. I felt I had to watch out for her in order for Allie to have a somewhat normal childhood. It saddened me that Amber and Paul, Allie's dad, had divorced after only one year of marriage. Allie's life would not be that of a traditional family.

Shared parenting has been her lifestyle since she was six months old. I hoped that because this was the only life she has ever known, it was *normal* to her. I wondered if she knew where home was, and I worried about the different significant others who were coming in and out of Amber and Paul's lives. I prayed they would all be good to her and give her the attention and love she deserved. I tried to overcompensate for Allie. I woke up nights wondering if she was safe. Allie relied on me, adored me, and felt secure when she was in our home. I volunteered to watch her a lot, knowing that our home was her safe haven. I also knew that I was not teaching Amber to become a responsible mother. I was enabling her.

Amber and I are so alike in many ways, but yet different in many. The day she pulled into our driveway, with Allie just a baby, and a car full of her possessions, I knew that her marriage had failed. She needed us, and we would not turn our backs on this sweet grandchild who did not ask to be born.

I also knew that allowing Amber back into our home with a child would take much adjusting. It was the year 2000, and I was also struggling with my job. After twenty-four years working full time on an emergency squad, my back began to buckle under. My L-3 and L-4 discs were protruding in my lower lumbar, and I suffered a lot of pain. Therapy and many treatments were helping, but my back would not grow stronger.

My worries grew. I have always been a worrier, and tried hard to make everything right. I wished for peace of mind.

With Amber home and working, and Allie needing stability, love, and support, I opted to quit my job. I became a stay-at-home mom for the first time in my life.

Working in EMS was a rewarding, somewhat glorified job. I took maternity leave three times, always returning to EMS work. The public looked up to us. Saving lives was the ultimate feeling and reward. It was a great job and my partners and I meshed. I had some great partners, and we depended on each other on emergencies. Each day brought different challenges. I worked a twenty-four-hour shift and then would be off for forty-eight hours. My hours were good, giving me a lot of time home with the kids. David and I had a dependable babysitter, Pam, who came in each third day to baby-sit. She became my friend and was a gem. The kids grew to love her. I truly had much quality time at home to enjoy raising my babies.

My partners at work were my extended family. We bonded and worked well together, and I loved helping people in a crisis. My job was funded through taxes and many political people. County commissioners mostly dictated and were our bosses, even though they knew little about EMS work and patient care.

In my twenty-four years employed there, I saw many changes take place. Our county was bursting at the seams in growth. Jobs were created, more emergency squad stations were built, but the political arena was leaving a bad taste in my mouth.

Being outspoken, a fighter, and one who did not do well with changes, I was no longer happy going to work. I felt that taxpaying residents were being treated unfairly. I rebelled. I watched tax dollars being wasted and people being promoted who were not competent or worthy of these promotions. I was miserable and began thinking about my health. My back continued to plague me, and I thought it was time to take early retirement, since Amber and Allie were home.

These changes fulfilled me for a while, and I was enjoying watching my granddaughter full time. Much later, I started feeling like my life was not very important. I missed the work world. I had raised three children, and although Allie was the sparkle in my eye, I felt taken advantage of. I wanted the simple, quiet, long overdue life.

Our income had dropped drastically, and Amber seemed to decline in her responsibilities as a grown daughter and mother. She needed to move out, get her own place, and become responsible. I felt like a servant and had no breaks from childrearing. I found myself feeling resentful because I felt like I was raising another child. I wanted to be a grandma with the privilege of having her when *I* wanted her. I didn't want to childproof my house, pick up toys, do extra laundry, and have to look for a babysitter when I wanted to go out to a movie or lunch with David or a friend. I wanted to ground them all forever and love them without limits. But they tested me beyond patience.

I continued to write freelance, selling stories to various magazines, but I still wished to be back in the workforce of society. And most of all, I wanted Amber to thank me once or ask me to lunch just to show me she cared.

5
Back In The Work World

As luck would have it, a friend called me, looking for an employee. I seemed to be just the person she needed. Thompson Medical hired me, and as I began my training, I already knew this job was perfect for me.

Being back in the medical field, caring mostly for senior citizens, I was happy. Amber found a dependable babysitter. My job consisted of fitting patients for a special rehabilitation machine that was used after total knee replacement. Thompson Medical leased out various medical machines to patients.

My primary job was to fit post-surgery patients for the CPM (continuous passive motion) machine, instruct them on how to use it, and also pick the machines up after the patient's recovery. I traveled to various hospitals, nursing homes, and residences with the CPM machines. My patient care was short-term, much like my prior job. I loved taking care of the elderly, visiting all the hospital staff, and going to nursing homes all over Ohio.

It was not nearly as stressful as in EMS, and my back was not being constantly strained. I continued to miss EMS and my wonderful partners, but I was relatively content.

By this time, Amber and Allie had moved out and into an apartment. My hours with my employer allowed me two days a week to be able to care for Allie. This pleased me, because I did not want Allie to feel like I had abandoned her. She also began preschool and loved it. I looked forward to the days when I could watch her and have our special days. I had missed her.

I felt privileged to have spent twenty-four years working in such an exciting profession. I think about some of the emergency squad runs we responded to, and will always remember the special ones.

I helped delivered a baby in a resident's bathroom on a cold winter night in 1980. That same night, I responded to a DOA from a head-on car accident. A life was taken and one born all within two hours.

We hauled combative drunks to the hospital. We responded to overdoses, suicide attempts—those who attempted suicide and those who accomplished it before we could help. They were released to the coroner, who was also the anesthesiologist, the same man and friend to me who would intubate me for my breast surgery to come.

We extricated trapped victims from car wrecks. We picked up and life-flighted my cousin from a train/car collision; he died hours later. That squad run never left my mind, and tormented me for months. I questioned whether I wanted to continue working in the county where I had grown up, knowing that I had a chance of responding to many relatives or friends in need.

Victims died as we tried to save them. Victims holding on by a thread later thanked my crew and me for saving their lives.

I transported many cancer patients in and out of hospitals. I saw patients slowly dying after cancer had beaten them down.

I recall watching many parents running up the emergency room ramp, awakened at night by horrendous phone calls to be told their teen child was in the emergency room, not knowing if the child was dead or alive. I transported and treated spinal injuries, burn victims, brain-stem injuries, and abused children, and went to homes in the early mornings when parents found their infant cold and dead, a victim of SIDS.

There were rewarding times, stressful times, and some funny times while on squad runs.

We responded one night to a banker who was in town on business. He had recently had a bladder infection or kidney stones. I don't recall the entire scenario now. His problem had flared up, causing him pain while staying in a local motel.

Not wanting to go to the hospital, he decided to use a swizzle stick and try to "unplug it" (his words). He inserted a swizzle stick into his penis. The swizzle stick moved up into his penis and was lost!

We took him to the hospital, and when the X-ray was read, it was determined that he would have to go to surgery to remove it from his bladder. The man was in misery, humiliated, and seriously injured.

One particular night, as we worked our twenty-four-hour shift, a car squealed into the squad station parking lot. Our crew was preparing our evening dinner on this warm summer evening.

We heard a rapid banging on the door. "HEEEELLLLP!"

I ran to the door, and standing there was a frantic woman.

"I think my daughter is having an appendicitis attack; please help. I was trying to get her to the emergency room, but she is screaming in so much pain—please help!"

As I ran out to check the patient, my partners went out to the squad to retrieve the cot. An evaluation was done; the patient was in stable condition but appeared to be in severe pain and was holding her lower-right abdomen.

She was a young, big-boned teenager wearing a baggy pink sweat suit. I will always remember this particular squad run vividly. Between trying to calm the mother and daughter, emotions ran high.

I asked all the appropriate personal questions that pertained to a female patient with abdominal pain. She denied missing any menstrual cycles and insisted that her pain was on her lower right side.

Our squad station was about seven or eight minutes from the emergency room. We loaded her onto the cot, reassured the mother again that her daughter would be OK, and asked her to follow us in her private vehicle to the hospital.

A secondary exam was performed en route to the hospital. I palpated her stomach and I did not feel anything unusual. My report via our radio to the hospital was, "We are en route with a sixteen-year-old female with lower-right abdominal pain, possible appendicitis. Patient is stable, vitals normal, and patient has no medical history. Our ETA [estimated time of arrival] is about five or six minutes."

Just as I completed my report to the hospital, it occurred to me that the patient, who continued to hold her lower-right abdomen, had pains in regular intervals about two minutes apart.

I recalled hearing stories about hidden pregnancy and was always skeptical that someone could hide something so obvious. I had given birth to three children. My mind whirled in circles, thinking I had almost missed this as it hit me instantly what was truly not so obvious to the naked eye.

I leaned down to her and persistently asked, "Are you lying to me? Are you pregnant?"

In a whispered, secretive voice, she said, "Yes, but please don't tell my mama."

"Don't tell your mama? Your mama is behind us in her car! She is coming to the hospital! What do you mean, don't tell your mama?"

"It's comin'. I can feel it! It is comin'!"

As my partner and I pulled her sweat pants down, checking for possible crowning, I hollered up to our driver, "Light it up. GO! We are about to deliver a baby!"

Just as I expected, I saw a fuzzy, dark little head of hair. We were seconds from the hospital as she started crowning. We recalled hoping a train would not be crossing the track as we approached it.

"Look at me and blow! Do NOT push. Blow!"

In EMS, we are trained for a variety of emergency situations, and delivering babies is one of the many services we are trained and able to perform. I had already delivered one that was almost born in the toilet.

However, I did not have a strong desire to deliver a baby that was possibly premature, and I was sure this mother-to-be had not had prenatal care.

In all the excitement of reaching the hospital before she delivered, we forgot to radio the hospital with an updated report (after all, they thought we were bringing in a routine appendicitis).

As we pulled up to the emergency room dock, I recalled seeing the mother pull in and go past us in an effort to find a parking place.

We rapidly removed the cot from our squad, rolling our patient in as she screamed and thrashed around on the cot.

"Blow, blow. Don't push! We are here. Hang on."

As we came through the door, the emergency room staff all looked up as they heard the commotion.

"She is crowning! We need a bed, FAST!"

I laugh now as I recall the emergency room doctor reacting to my words. Her mouth dropped, and her eyes grew large in shock. (It is common knowledge in EMS that emergency room doctors do not like to deliver babies.)

The doctor said, "BABY! You said it was appendicitis! Holy SHIT!"

At the precise moment we placed the patient on the emergency room bed, she gave birth. The doctor had seconds to assist.

This young girl gave birth to a full-term, healthy, beautiful baby boy.

And Mom?

She was still circling the parking lot, looking for a place to park.

6
Emotional Turmoil

When the news of my breast cancer hit me, I immediately thought of all the things in my life I had done. I also thought of all I had not yet done or accomplished. I became very angry and depressed. I couldn't sleep, and sometimes I couldn't wake up. I just wanted to stay in bed, cover my head up, and never place my feet on the floor of a new day.

I'd skated though a relatively easy, exciting life with few sorrows. My childhood had been the best a kid could ask for, and I rarely had dull moments. I celebrated life and lived it like there were no tomorrows.

I have been fortunate in not having to deal with many personal tragedies. The deaths of Rodney, my dear cousin, Grandma Hawkins, Pam, Dan, and Nicole, a dear friend's daughter, woke me to how fragile life can be.

I'd been blessed with three healthy children, one beautiful, healthy granddaughter, and a husband who was a good man. My parents and siblings were all healthy and close to me geographically and in my heart.

The Saturday after Katie's football game and the first morning I had to get up and face the world, I continued to keep the news to myself. I looked at Katie and thought about my parents, David, the kids, and my siblings. I could not bring myself to find the right time to give them such horrid news. I was tempted to get on the Internet and start educating myself about breast cancer. I feared what I might read. I didn't want to know. All I could see was the mutilation of my body, and my funeral. I started thinking about my pallbearers. I have so many wonderful male friends—many co-workers from my days in EMS and firefighter friends who would be proud to carry me to my destiny.

So many people had heard me say many times, "I am going to write a book before I die." I had also joked about being buried in my 1974 VW Super Beetle. I drive it on pretty spring days or when I am in a bad mood, to lift my spirits. I drive it proudly in many local parades.

It grabs people's attention. When I am refueling it, at the car wash, or walking to it or away from it, someone asks about it. Many people want to buy it.

"Oh no, I am going to keep it forever. I will probably be buried in it," I tell them with a chuckle. It should be a crime the amount of money I have put in this old gem to get the glorified look that it has, but it was worth every penny to me. There isn't any amount of money that would change my mind. My Bug is with me until death do us part.

I tell all my girlfriends, "You buy your gold jewelry; give me my chrome wheels."

Instead of sitting idle in the house the Saturday morning after the football game, I jumped into the Bug. Telling Katie and David would have to wait. The weather was chilly but mild. The sun was shining, a promise of warmth to come. I needed my spirits lifted, and reality had hit me in the face when I woke up. *I have cancer.* I kept saying it over in my head, trying to believe it.

I drove to Tammy's house. She knew I was awaiting test results, and Tammy is the queen of worry. I knew that by Saturday, she would be in a frenzy wondering why I had not called her with the pathology report.

I knocked on her door, crying. Without a word, she knew. She immediately hugged me and kissed my cheek, and I couldn't stop crying.

27

"Where's Jen? I need to talk to Jen," I desperately said to Tammy.

Again, without even speaking words, she picked up the phone, called Jen, and simply told her that I had arrived and needed her.

No questions were asked or comment made about the emotional turmoil of my entrance. Jen arrived ten minutes after my request, nursing book in hand. Just like her mom, she clutched me to her chest and rubbed my hair and asked, "Does your family know?"

"No, God no. How can I tell them? Why does this have to happen to me now?" I asked as I blew my nose. I could not stop crying. Tammy began crying again with me, and for me.

I wiped my nose. "Katie had a game last night. How could I tell her when she had to concentrate on kicking? I dropped my head and sobbed in desperation. "How in the hell do I tell my family? David will handle it, I know but how do I tell them? When is the right time?"

It was then that I knew I needed Jen's expertise and advice in helping me to choose doctors, hospitals, surgeons, and an oncologist. Jen, being a full-time registered nurse and full of knowledge and love for me, would guide me. But I wasn't ready for all the information Jen had or wanted to read to me from her nursing book.

"You go home, try to calm down, and I will call you later," she said as she rubbed my arm. "We will all help you through this."

I remembered when she was just a child, and there I stood, listening to this woman who had grown up so fast. I thought about how life moves along so rapidly.

I composed myself to prepare for driving back home. I knew Katie would be up by then, and I still wasn't ready to tell her or David. I needed more information and some kind of optimistic news to tell her about this tough road I was about to travel.

7

Bug Heaven

As I drove home, my thoughts were about my good old 1974 VW Bug. I shifted gears and thought about how much I loved my car and how fun it was when I decided to have it restored. I love the attention it draws as I drive down streets. I grinned and almost forgot about the lump as I thought about the day I drove it home without a front window in it. Paul, the body shop guy wasn't quite finished with all the repairs and a few cosmetic things had not been done. We were waiting on a new window so I decided to drive it on home and take it back to him later. My hair flew everywhere as the wind swirled through the car on that cold spring morning. By the time I reached home, my fingers were numb and my cheeks were chapped. I didn't realize I had broken the law driving it without a window but I'd made it home without being caught. My God. The cops would have thought I was nuts if they'd seen me.

Those were wonderful, fun sunny spring days that year when my health was fabulous and my Bug turned more beautiful as each day improved its look. It became glorious bumblebee yellow with the most beautiful chrome wheels that added such flair and style.

I drove on as my bug caught the eye of many. I started to cry as I got closer to home. I kept thinking about my girls and Ryan. I am sure they had taken my life for granted. I was always so tough, full of energy and I realized my worry was more about protecting my kids and not giving them the horrible news.

I felt so lost and to not know what the future would bring ate at me. Being a Virgo, I was a planner, organized and I was in turmoil.

8
True Tammy

Jen called me later that day, as promised. She had worked full time in recovery for several years since receiving her nursing degree. I remembered when Jen was just a child, as her mom struggled in raising her and her sister Brittany. I knew that Tammy, a single mom with many health issues herself, had inspired Jen to become such a caring nurse.

Tammy and I had been through a lot together. We have spent many hours together, sharing secrets, laughing, going places together, and me consoling her when health issues or men sent her in a whirlwind of emotions.

Tammy, being a single mom on a fixed income and raised in an abusive home, was a survivor. I recall her sharing many stories with me. I think I was helping her to heal, and she didn't even realize it.

She would reminisce about her childhood. It would bring me to tears to hear how bad her childhood had been. I had gone to high school with her, and she and my other friend, Brenda, both kept their horrific childhood abuse secrets.

Tammy used to visit an aunt, a kind woman whose home brought her comfort. She remembered sitting on a deacon bench near the entry into the living room. Tammy would look through the

Sears and Roebuck catalog and notice the happy children posing in beautiful clothes.

She would say out loud to herself, "When I am old, I will have pretty clothes, and I will be a mom like those kids must have." Their happy faces in that book brought promise to Tammy.

And that promise was fulfilled. Jen and Brit, her daughters, became part of a cycle that was broken. Tammy vowed to never mentally or physically abuse them. She didn't, and I have always respected her for being such a fighter and wonderful mother. Jen and Brit are just fine ... independent, successful hard workers and respectful to their mom.

Many of us in life are blessed with good friends. Tammy, my friend, is what I consider the perfect friend. I don't recall a harsh word ever spoken between the two of us, and every conversation is full of laughter and love. She has never judged me, and I have shared my innermost private thoughts and concerns with her. Like Margi, she is also my golden friend. She has been through a lot in life, but always finds the strength, courage, and determination to continue on.

Tammy is very slender and petite. She talks with a cute little Southern drawl. She spent her youth in southern Ohio, just far enough south to pick up and keep her Southern twang. My little hillbilly friend is what I call her.

Tammy has Raynaud's syndrome, a disorder that affects the fingers, toes, ears and nose. Cold temperatures cause the blood vessels to constrict. This is a rare but awful disease. I also have it and working out in the winter in EMS had caused mine to get worse. We were dear friends before mine was diagnosed, but our friendship has grown and our common interest and disease has brought us closer. She has a big heart for a small woman and great determination to strive onward.

Several years ago, the medical field did not know much about Raynaud's Syndrome. Tammy was referred to several doctors in an effort to make a proper diagnosis. When she was finally sent to a specialist who knew immediately why her fingers were cold, dead, and lifeless, it was too late to save all her fingers. She had four fingers amputated over a series of two years.

Tammy adjusted well. She had rough days. Dealing with the loss of limbs has to be horrendous. She bounced back with humor. Her little stub index finger is rather cute when she mimics picking her nose. She talks fast with a lot of expression. I like to observe her movements when she points with her stub as she talks.

We go many places together. She is full of life and laughter. Our laughter is contagious. Her middle finger is a stub, too. She flips people off with it just so we can laugh as we drive by them, laughing like two banny roosters.

She found out about a place in Chicago that is known worldwide for prosthetics. Although she had adjusted to her lost limbs, she became excited with learning more about getting prosthetic fingers.

Off to Chicago she flew with so much enthusiasm. I couldn't wait to see the new look. After being measured, fitted, and taking two trips to Chicago, homeward bound she came with four new fingers.

They were very costly and durable, but not made to withstand daily use. Tammy treasured her new look and wore them on special occasions.

I was amazed. I visualized little hooks like the old prosthetic arms that were made years ago. These new fingers looked real! She could wear rings again, and they had fake fingernails on them. The joy of polishing nails again and never having to trim, cut, or remove hangnails excited her. Heck, she could polish them up and leave them on the table to dry as she finished applying her makeup. What more could a woman want?

We certainly had to celebrate! David encouraged us, and off to Atlantic City we headed to HIT the casinos! I wore my new Fashion Bug outfit (size fourteen) with a little glitter, and Tammy wore her new fingers. (She wore her cute little Abercrombie jeans, too … size one.) Her fingernails were painted to match her sweater.

We began playing the slot machines. Tammy felt whole again. No one batted a skeptical eye about her fingers. They truly looked real! She felt great. No one was staring at her not-so-perfect hands.

She became frustrated after a while. After all, they were not real fingers. They couldn't bend and flex like a real digit. She started dropping coins on the floor. We had purchased a twelve-hour junket deal for this celebration. Coins had to drop fast to acquire the thrills we wanted in a short period of time.

Tammy started talking trash. She would bend down to pick up the dropped coin to put in the slots, and start in with her sailor mouth. Tammy can swear like no man can! The angrier Tammy gets, the faster she swears. The words become more brutal and extreme. She loves to throw around the F-bomb. She became so aggravated and disappointed in her new fingers. They were so beautiful but were not as useful as she had hoped.

She jerked them off and decided playing slots with her stubs were much easier. "To hell with these damn fingers," she said. "Connie, would you put them in your purse?"

We continued playing the slot machines. Several hours had gone by, and I needed to cash in my bucket of coins. I walked up to the cashier's window and handed him my bucket in exchange for dollars.

He handed me my money and I opened my tiny little purse to put my money safely away. There, lying on top, were four forgotten fingers.

He gasped. I laughed. Tammy and I started our soul sister laughs as I told her about the shocked look on his face. Our laughter echoed through the casino.

We have reminisced about that day many times.

As I talked to Jen on the phone, I asked her to read me only the positive facts about breast cancer. I was not ready to hear the worst-case scenarios. Jen suggested I consider having a mastectomy on both breasts to decrease my chances of getting breast cancer again.

"Many women opt to do this, Connie. You might not have to have radiation. Another occurrence of cancer might be avoided," she said as she flipped through that damned nursing book. "They do reconstruction immediately," she said. "Heck, maybe you can get even perkier boobs!"

"Jen, I will NOT be mutilated. I like my tits. I want to keep them! I have worked hard to preserve their youth. I love my cleavage. Don't ask me to even consider this! And when they do a mastectomy, they take away your nipples! I love my nipples, and they have great sensation!" I listened for Katie. The music was blaring in her bedroom. I knew our conversation was safe.

"Damn it, Connie! Look at Mom's fuckin' ugly hands! If she can go out in public with four fingers gone, you can deal with this! I know it is tough, but you can decide later what your treatment will be. When you talk to your surgeon, he can help you. This is not a death sentence, and you have to fight. I need you in my life, and I know Mom needs you, too."

And we cried.

9
Game Plan

On Sunday, my coffeemaker and the worn-out vacuum cleaner broke. Off to the hardware store I went to replace both. I wondered why this had to happen now. I had enough flaws and broken things to deal with.

Monday morning, as Dr. Schumer advised me, I called his office. I was scheduled for a consultation in his office that same afternoon. And, like the dear and always dependable friends that they are, Jen and Margi came to be with me for my appointment. Jen had already made a list of questions for Dr. Schumer. She knew just what we needed answered. I had not formed a feeling of confidence in Dr. Schumer, whom I had only seen once when he'd done the biopsy. Of course, he had told me that one out of ten lumps is cancer, which reassured me. I felt mad at him for being wrong.

I truly believed the lump was benign like the lump that had surfaced on and off for two years. The lump was in the exact location as the one my prior mammograms had found, and that was ruled noncancerous.

As I walked out to schedule the biopsy, I joked with his staff. "My God, no one warned me the doctor was soooo damn good-looking. And I had never met the man. And what do I have to do? Whip my breast out for him to touch?" I told his staff. "Amazing!" The women looked at me and grinned.

"Dr. Schumer is so shy; he would be embarrassed if he heard you," one girl said as she was on hold, waiting to get the date of my biopsy surgery.

"Wait, I bet you are his wife. Look at you. You match. You are as cute as a button," I responded back.

"Yes, he is my husband," she said with a grin.

"My, my, my ... you lucky woman, YOU! Don't you dare get mad at me for noticing! You be proud." She winked and agreed. It was then that Dr. Schumer came out of another room, as we all were giggling like teenage girls.

"See you soon, and try not to worry," he'd said. And I did worry as I waited for the next appointment.

Dr. Schumer entered the room where Jen, Margi, and I sat, for my follow-up. His compassion, his time given to me, and his knowledge impressed me. When he walked out, we all commented about his good looks, and laughed like schoolgirls.

I told Margi and Jen how I had made silly remarks to the office staff when I had initially met him. His great looks did not make him cocky or arrogant. He was rather shy and very professional, and I liked him and his staff. That was when life seemed simple and I was happy and laughing and joking was easy.

His solution for the lump and to get me cured did not impress me. I panicked. I did not want to be taken to surgery, not knowing how much of my breast he would have to remove to get a clear margin. He suggested I get a second opinion if it would make me feel better.

I have always vowed that if a doctor ever suggested cutting me, I would always get another opinion. Working in the medical field, I had heard a lot of gossip about doctors and medical procedures. Hysterectomies, for example, are done many times when they may not be necessary. I just needed to be sure before I permitted a doctor to cut me. I decided to take his advice.

Jen, working in Columbus full time in a much bigger hospital, had not heard much about Dr. Schumer. She planned to do some homework to find out more about him. In the meantime, my plan was to call the James Cancer Clinic in Columbus. I knew people traveled from all over Ohio to go to the James Cancer Clinic in hopes of getting cured. Dr. Schumer was going to be put on hold, even if he was charming and professional.

Clear margin! I had never heard these two words until my ugly lump came. As it was explained to me by Dr. Schumer, I knew it was just what I needed…clear margin. Lumps are removed and the surgeon takes tissue beyond and around the tumor in hopes the extra tissue is cancer free. Jen knew quite well what clear margin meant, and she also knew what *evasive* meant in reference to my breast cancer. Evasive was not what I needed and was not great news. But I would learn this later.

Jen, Margi, and I went to a local sports bar for lunch. The weather was as dreary as my mood. Margi tried to lift my spirits. She teased me about how we would go to surgery on carts side by side on a buddy system, and have our busts worked on and come out with two pairs of twenty-year-old breasts. She had recently lost a friend to cancer. I knew her humor was a cover. Marsha, her friend, had started out with breast cancer. After many treatments, loss of hair, skin color, and energy, she went into remission, only to be struck again. The second time played havoc on her life. She died a young woman.

Margi could not fool me. I could read her like a book. I knew her almost as well as her mother knew her. I could finish sentences for her, and many times I did.

I also thought about how she had chosen to have a boob job years ago to boost her cup size. Don, her controlling ex-husband, had been behind this adventure, and constantly pressured her to have the surgery. At one time, Margi would do anything he demanded of her to try to save a marriage that was doomed from the start.

After Margi healed from her nasty divorce, she would numerous times joke about the boob job. "These are the only good things I got from that damn marriage, and come to think of it, I paid for them," she would announce as she put her chest out ever so proudly.

Unfortunately, the boob job was as flawed as her marriage. One breast had a slow leak, something like the slow leak on my VW tire, and it was becoming considerably smaller than the right breast. I was to be her excuse and opportunity to stop procrastinating and get a patch job.

"I'm serious, Connie. We can go together, maybe like an extreme makeover. We will be the belles of the ball when they finish with us," she said as the waitress came over to take our order. "We will have the perkiest boobs for two grandmas at our next class reunion," she said. "Maybe they will give us a deal, since it would be for a pair. One for you and one for me."

I could not find any humor or excitement in her attempt to cheer me. I just wanted to keep my breasts. I did not want chemicals dripping into me to kill the cancer. I just wanted to stay *me.* I wanted to go to my next reunion, happy, lookin' good, and knowing I was healthy.

As it was, our thirtieth reunion was in August, two months prior to my diagnosis. The lump had surfaced just a week before the reunion. I had worked hard on the planning committee. I ignored the lump as the reunion grew near.

And Margi and I? We *were* the belles of the ball, just as we confidently planned. And I sang with the rock-and-roll band. How cool is that? But I had a secret lump that would be dealt with later.

One of my fondest dreams-come-true was getting to sing solo with a reputable, local, kick-ass rock-and-roll band. My high school class of '74 was a special, tight-knit class. This class was also blessed with a true rock-and-roll band. The band, named Origin, began in 1971 and consisted of five passionate, musically talented students who became well known and played at many high school dances and special events. Jeff Warren, Dave Hickson, Tom Johnson, Gary Richardson, and Chris Hinshaw made up this fabulous band. Dave and Tom had graduated with me. I had not lost touch with them. With e-mail, we kept in touch even more. Dave was another golden friend.

With ideas about entertainment and lacking funds, we decided to utilize these talented musicians. Before we knew it, we had these loyal classmates offering to play at our reunion. Free! What luck and good fortune, since we lacked funds. We wanted to pull in a good crowd and get classmates to attend who had not come to prior reunions. These guys were the ticket that spiked interest. Fond memories and popularity of them from so many years ago would be the incentive to come.

Dave had been playing lead guitar since he was six years old. Jeff had played drums since eighth grade. Most Buckeye Valley alumni have vivid memories of Jeff with drumsticks in his hands and Dave carrying a guitar case.

Tom Johnson, a great vocalist and guitar player in his hometown of Chicago, was very successful in a blues band.

All three of them had never stopped playing professionally in all those years. I happen to be a karaoke fool. Dave had heard me sing off and on at various bars. I did not hang out at bars like a barfly. I went to socialize, sing my favorite songs, and hook Margi into this great, inexpensive hobby. Some nights we were the Supremes, and other nights we became the Dixie Chicks. We'd be the Supremes, minus one. Margi sang a great Sonny, and I would be Cher, without the long, lean body and hair. "I Got You Babe," we'd sing as we found comfort in the seventies songs from our teen years.

"Ya want to sing with the band at our reunion, Connie?" Dave asked me one night as I waited my turn to sing "These Boots Are Made for Walking."

It was at that precise moment when I about fell off my bar stool, sober as a minister on a Sunday morning.

"You are shitting me. ARE YOU SERIOUS? OH MY GOD!"

"Well, yeah. Let me ask the guys in the band. I know you can sing. You have a great voice. You'll have to practice some with us. Learn and know your lyrics. You can't have that cheat screen in front of you," he said as he took a swig of his German dark beer.

"My God. Lord have mercy," I said as I tipped my glass of Diet Coke to Dave.

"Cheers and thanks, Dave. You are a true gem. My dream come true. And, look … I promise, I will not embarrass you. I will do you proud," I said as we toasted.

After numerous practices, gigs, and four years of a musical connection, the five continued to be friends. Thirty years later, their passion for music connected and put them together again for this special reunion. "Band of the brothers," Tom Johnson says when he speaks of his old band.

With two months to prepare, and Tom Johnson living in Illinois, the friends had to find ways to practice. The anticipation brought excitement and the opportunity to relive their long-ago band days. Tom drove in from Illinois to cram in hours of practice. It was time to meet and get busy. And that they did for many weeks. I was thrilled to head to the garage every Wednesday night to practice my two tunes. I was a forty-eight-year-old wannabe rock-and-roll star. And I got their attention and did not embarrass them, and my classmates loved me. They stood, applauded me, chanted, and cheered as I finished "You're So Vain," and "These Boots Are Made for Walking." AND, I did not forget my lyrics. As Carly Simon's lyrics are, *"he watched himself gavotte,"* I gavotted off the stage, giving Dave a high-five as I handed him the microphone to finish their set.

Their hard work, generosity, and loyalty to old friends made the night special and an enormous success. People said it was the best class reunion they had ever attended. Alumni from other classes got wind about Legacy being reunited, and they showed up for our reunion also.

I will never forget that reunion, nor will I forget watching Dave Hickson take center stage for a solo with guitar in hand to sing the James Taylor song "Fire and Rain" as past pictures of the lost but not forgotten classmates came across the screen, *"But I always thought that I would see you again"* I recall hearing him sing when I heard his voice crack to the lyrics.

10
Reunion Rebel

Just a few months prior to my own class reunion, I attended another one. Oh, it wasn't a reunion from my school for another class. It wasn't even happening in my county.

Claire, my dear friend whom I worked with for many years on the emergency squad, was having her high school reunion. Her twenty-fifth! She called me in the afternoon, just hours before her big bash.

We'd kept in touch since I had quit working for the squad, but we certainly did not see each other like the good old EMS days. My crew came on duty at 6:00 AM every third day, relieving her crew. Claire's husband was on my crew. They said their goodbyes as she headed home, and our twenty-four-hour shift started.

The three of us were and still are good friends. I recall the births of both of her children. Alex, her son, always took Bug rides with me because he was so fascinated with my cool VW. I took him in the Fourth of July parade one year, and although it was a hot, humid day, he did the parade wave to each person as we Bugged by.

I recall him asking me to turn the air conditioning on. It occurred to me that this eight-year-old boy had never ridden in a car without the luxury of air conditioning.

"Why do you want me to go to YOUR class reunion, Claire?"

"Well, we need a girls' night out, and I don't want to go to it by myself. Tom is staying home to baby-sit the kids," she said. "And it is a nice summer night and a good excuse for you and me to do some catching up."

"I won't know a soul," I told her. I looked at the clock, and I truly did not have anything planned. As usual, Katie had plans to go to a movie with some friends, and David was couchin', watching sports on ESPN.

"Oh, why not. I'll ride along," I told her.

I started thinking about how much fun this might be as I took a bath and was picking out an outfit. Have you ever wished you could be someone else for just a day? Have you ever thought about how adventurous it would be to walk in on a huge wedding reception, all dressed up for the occasion, and appear to be a legitimate guest? You could wine and dine for free. People would probably whisper and ask one another who you are, but no one would assume you were crashing the party. Most would not have the courage to ask you, thinking they would offend Uncle John's grandniece that had flown in from Rhode Island.

I looked at the clock, knowing it was almost time for Claire's arrival. I decided this just might be one big blast.

We arrived; guests were abundant, and Claire immediately recognized some and was having fun, trying to identify others after twenty-five years. I noticed classmates looking at me inquisitively. I noticed some whispering and pointing, and I was sure they were having discussions, trying to decide what mysterious classmate I was. They probably thought I had changed a lot in my appearance, and they would figure me out soon enough. It certainly isn't unusual to attend a reunion after so many years and be unable to put a face with a name.

As I sat, watching Claire mingle among her old school friends, growing weary and feeling alone, in walked Todd, an old friend. I had not a clue this was his class and hometown, too.

"What are you doing here?" he asked me. I explained my friendship with Claire, thinking what a small world we live in, having mutual friends and discovering that Claire had gone to school with him.

Later, Todd approached me, "Connie, everyone's trying to figure out who you are."

"Well, give me a name. Heck, why not play along?" I laughed and said.

"Laura Meenan," he immediately said. "She came to our school in 1976, moved here from California, and just went to school with us for two years."

"Well, was she pretty, respectable, popular? If I am going be someone, let's make it good."

"Oh, she was hot," Todd said.

"Then, Laura Meenan it will be!" I said.

"There's Mark," Todd said, as he pointed across the room. "Go mess with him; tell him you are Laura."

I walked up to Mark, a man I had never seen in my life, and put my hand out to greet him.

"How are you, Mark? Remember me? I am Laura Meenan."

He studied my face as he continued shaking my hand. He held my hand as if our touch would jog his memory. His eyebrows wrinkled, and he squinted to study my face.

"Remember! We had math class together. Mrs. Um … um … um, what was her name?" I asked, as I waited in hopes he would produce a legitimate name of a math teacher from his school.

"Mrs. Martin! Yeah, Mrs. Martin. Wasn't she the tallest woman you have ever seen? I think she stood about seven feet tall," he reminisced aloud.

"Well, if you recall, she played basketball in college. She attended college on a full-ride scholarship," I said.

Claire and Todd listened, watched, and both fought back laughter to prevent blowing my cover.

As someone else approached Mark, Claire mumbled to me, "Man, you are good."

Yeah, my mama would be proud of how well I lie, I thought.

"Look! Here comes Mr. Willaby, our old principal," Todd said.

We all scanned the crowd and looked beyond Todd's finger. Mr. Willaby, another strange face to me, walked toward us.

He immediately recognized Todd and Claire. They all exchanged conversation as I stood quietly watching them all converse.

"Mr. Willaby, hi ... Laura Meenan, remember me?" I put my hand out to shake his.

"Laura Meenan, Laura Meenan ... hmmm. Laura Meenan? Hmmm, Laura Meenan," he said, shaking my hand, as he tried to recollect who I was.

"Where did you live?" he asked me.

"Hmmm. Maple Street," I said, hoping a Maple Street existed in this town. (All towns have a Maple Street.)

"Do you still live out off ...?" (I stopped and looked at Todd, hoping he would help me out of this daring question. I realized then that I might be pushing my luck.)

I read his lips as he said, "Route 245."

"245," I said.

"Oh Lord, yes. I will die there," Mr. Willaby said.

Todd and I talked about our children as Mr. Willaby quietly mumbled occasionally, "Laura Meenan, Laura Meenan?" He'd rub his forehead with the palm of his hand, thinking.

As my game started becoming fun and challenging, two familiar faces walked into the reunion (my cousin and his wife). I had totally forgotten that they had graduated from this high school. I thought my false identity was about to be discovered.

"Laura Meenan, hey ... remember me?"

Rick, my cousin looked at me, confused and baffled.

"Shhhh, I am Laura Meenan for the night. Don't blow my cover," I said.

They both snickered and, knowing me very well as a jokester, walked on, visiting and talking to old school friends.

The seventies rock-and-roll band played on as I continued socializing, enjoying the evening of fooling the crowd.

"Please come to the stage for a class picture. All those from the class of 1978, please come up," blared across the band's microphone.

People slowly gathered toward the stage. I stood back, watching, thinking, and grinning.

Just as everyone was standing in the appropriate places, with the tall ones in the back just like school days, I slithered up to the group.

It was amazing how no one seemed to notice me approach the group. I moseyed to the end of the front row, stood next to a gentleman, and smiled as the camera clicked and flashes went off.

Apparently, the gentleman standing next to me had heard from another classmate who I was.

"Laura Meenan, hi. Good to see you. You haven't changed a bit."

Flash went another camera.

I just smiled.

As the evening was about to end, a woman approached me.

"Could you please tell me what name I am supposed to put for you before I turn this in to the local paper? I know you are not Laura Meenan; she was in my wedding."

The game was over.

I later learned that the class did put their picture in the local paper. Thanks to technology and all the choppin' and croppin', my picture was sliced off for the publication.

Claire and I recall that reunion and still laugh at all the pranks in one fun evening on a hot summer night.

11
The Secret Is Out

Jen and I discussed my idea of getting a second opinion. She was returning to work the next day, and planned to call me after she accumulated information about Dr. Schumer.

As this horridly cold day turned into a horrid evening, Katie, David and I spent a quiet evening home. I got busy doing all the normal things around the house and would briefly forget I had a huge medical problem. I still did not feel sick. David and Katie didn't think to ask me if I had gotten my test results back. I doubt it crossed their minds. It wasn't that they didn't care. Katie was just busy being a teenager and the entire family was used to me not ever being ill. I was strong, and ran non-stop being the giver like many moms. I knew many of my girlfriends would be calling me to get an update about my tests. At some point, I had to come clean and confess.

Ryan, my twenty-three-year-old son, rarely came home to visit. This was a son who was so wrapped up in his social life that he put off family, responsibility, and his education. He showed very little interest in the family unity.

He had returned home from an out-of-state college two years ago, a dropout, promising to finish school in Ohio. Sleeping all day and staying up or out all night and leaving lights and the television on all night were new bad habits for him. College had changed him. I understood his need for privacy and to be independent and wanting to be treated like an adult, but I saw very little sign in the maturity department to give him this chance.

I grew resentful and disappointed in him. Ryan, an intelligent guy with so much talent, had thrown it away so he could party. He had squandered our money and let his education take the back seat. The door of opportunity was wide open for him when he left home a young boy of eighteen. He could have been a football kicker in a Division 1 school and gotten his education with scholarship money. Instead we became poorer, and each semester he promised to get his grades up. Football was never to be, because it required discipline that he wasn't ready for.

After many arguments and disagreements with David, I convinced him that Ryan needed to come home and work. The money being spent was not being used to pass classes with a degree at the end. The door of opportunity shut, and in the spring of his junior year, he returned home from West Virginia to learn a real wake-up call about reality and life's struggles as an adult. The party was over!

This, like many issues and chaos in our home, caused me to tire of my life. I was burned out as a mother and wife. My resentment grew as Ryan lay in bed, sleeping all day with no ambition to find a job. His evenings consisted of partying. I worried about him drinking and driving. I whined, I bitched, I warned! David did not have expectations and he wouldn't discipline like I did. The kids saw their father as the cool parent. I was the bad guy. Because I expected more, and disciplined them, I was the enemy. My unhappiness grew and my resentment skyrocketed. Ryan no longer had medical insurance or a desire to finish college. He drank entirely too much and did not come home many nights. There were no courtesy calls home, and I resented that David could sleep peacefully while I worried.

I tried many times to explain to Ryan that no matter his age, as a parent, I worried. We worry about their safety, health, and happiness. I worried about the possibility of him becoming an alcoholic. I reminded him of the alcohol abuse in our family and the genetics of it. He patronized me and thought I was overreacting. My father grew up in an alcoholic home.

David rarely corrected the kids or asked questions. I was the one feeling the burden as he watched TV on weekends.

Our daughter Amber's instability with a job, her finances, and relationships did not improve. She dated the same guy each time, just with a different name. I could not understand how a physically fit athletic female with such beautiful looks and personality wished to date controlling, abusive men. I felt the only time she came home was when she needed me for something. I always wished for the days when the two of us could just go have lunch. The talk could be casual, full of laughter, and with no pressure and worries about the issues of her life.

I just grew tired of parenting adult children. I was burned out! But I also knew that I had to tell the kids and David about my illness. I could not keep something so important a secret. They had every right to know.

I decided to invite Amber over for dinner knowing Ryan would soon be home from his new job.

"Dad is coming soon, and we all need to talk," I told them all as I called their cell phones to warn them. I dreaded the entire evening.

I am sure the kids thought it had to do with some new chaos about them. I had always been there for them, the one to fix everything, always putting them first. I was the super mom—or so they thought. All the problems we'd had often made me wonder if the excessive stress I'd had might have lowered my immune system. I wondered if it was some hidden message.

"I have something to tell you all. This is not easy, but ... I got my tests back and I have breast cancer," I said. And with that, I tried so hard to be strong and act brave. I failed. I could not be the strength and wall that they had lived with. My leadership in my family unit crumbled. I burst into tears.

Amber immediately starting crying and Ryan sat, showing no emotions. Katie walked away.

"I will help you with this, Connie. You need me, and I want to help," David said.

I dropped my head, and I knew I needed all the help I could get. I wished to fight it alone because I'd been so mad at all of them. It was scary not knowing what my battle might entail and maybe it was time they all thought about someone else besides themselves.

Amber just sat at the kitchen table that night and cried. I remember thinking and hoping she would find peace and understanding with me. We'd had many fights. Each one was because of the love and hope I had for her as a mother to Allie and a daughter to me. My intent was always to help her. Ryan seemed lost as his emotions were kept hidden away. Very few words were spoken as tears fell from many eyes.

I needed leadership and help. They'd have to step up to the plate. I knew David would. I could tell that he was concerned, and now maybe there was a chance for them to take care of me.

That very evening, I called another friend to vent and share my bad news. Teresa, my friend of twenty years, was waiting to hear from me. She knew I had a lump in my breast, and I knew I had to tell her.

We met when our two boys had started preschool together. Ryan and Derrick, two days apart in age and exactly the same size at three, were instantly drawn to each other. They met at Storks Nest, a preschool they attended for two years. I remember that they both wore 4T slims and loved their Levi's jeans. They walked arm in arm and always picked each other for partners in school. Derrick was Ryan's first stay-over in our home. Wow, they were both ornery as hell and fed off each other.

Teresa and I talked at preschool and realized we had met before. "Lamaze class! That's where I have seen you before," she said. A friendship grew, and twenty years later, Ryan and Derrick along with Teresa and I all share special friendships.

My friendship with Teresa is always full of laughs, excitement, and spontaneous adventures. She and I could turn heads in our younger days, and loved innocent flirting. Many times, people asked us if we were sisters, I presume because we both have blonde hair and blue eyes. It was rather silly that people see a similarity.

Shit, we both are *bottle blondes.* I am not even sure what my natural color is anymore.

Her marriage, an up-and-down roller coaster ride, continued to strive on and surpass many of our friends' marriages. I suppose years ago, if all of us would have predicted whose marriage might fail, we would have picked Teresa and Jeff's. My marriage would have been the one they all would have felt would survive, grow, and bloom into the golden years.

Teresa knew David and I had drifted apart and had struggled with many growing pains with the kids. I decided I needed to call her.

"I have breast cancer," I told her instantly when she answered the phone. I began to cry again. It seemed I would never stop crying.

"WHAT? No way ... you do? Oh, Connie."

And the flow of tears began again from me. Teresa, who never ever cries and who is always solid as a rock and never one to falter, continued to hold back tears.

"What will you do next? Well, you know you can get through this, and you just can't let it take you, Connie. "

I held the phone tightly to my ear, searching for Katie. I knew my conversation with Teresa might not be private and I didn't want Katie to hear me crying again. Katie was a room away. I wiped my eyes. I blew my nose. I scanned the room for Katie, knowing she was scared.   Katie loves me. Being a teenager and having a friend who had recently lost her mom to cancer probably brought fright to Katie, thinking she might lose me. Whitney and Katie had become very good friends while growing up together, with Pam babysitting.

"Teresa, let me call you later," I said in a soft tone. "Katie is confused enough. I'll call you tomorrow."

As I hung up the phone, I remembered what Mom had said when Grandma died. "When you lose your mom you have lost your best friend."

I thought of Whitney, who had lost her mom. Pam, my dear friend had died eight months prior. Diagnosed with a form of lymph node cancer, she was determined to beat it. She had gone through an aggressive chemo treatment, working almost to the end, and was very upbeat, even after losing her hair. She'd started a new job after my kids were old enough to not need a sitter, and shortly after, she lost her life when a bone marrow procedure failed and caused her lungs to be irreversibly damaged.

Even today, I can't believe Pam is gone. Many miss her, and I thought about how tough it was on Whitney, losing her mom her senior year of high school. I watched her enter the prom in her beautiful dress, and it saddened me that her mom did not see Whitney all dolled up for her high school prom.

News of my recent diagnosis had spread throughout Buckeye Valley, the high school Katie and Whitney attended.

Two weeks after my shocking news, my emotions still in an unpredictable turmoil, I remember standing in the kitchen, cooking dinner. As always in my crazy house, the phone rang, the pasta needed draining, and I had to go answer the door. I was not in the mood for company, and dinner needed my attention.

As I opened the door, standing holding a box was Whitney.

"Here. These are for you. They are Mom's scarves she wore when she lost her hair. I know she would love for you to have them."

I clutched the box to my chest, leaned over, and hugged Whitney. I thought about her still grieving the loss of her mom. As I hugged her, I looked up. *Yep, Pam, you are smiling down, and pleased as punch at the thoughtfulness of Whitney* was my thoughts as I released my arms and invited her in for dinner. I knew my head would be warm, and my heart, too. I wiped more tears and blew my nose.

Katie came in from basketball practice and greeted Whitney. Katie is a simple girl who loves all sports and dresses conservatively. Whitney is a girlie-girl who loves fashion and jewelry, hates sports, and likes long, polished fingernails. But their friendship stayed solid, even though they shared very few interests.

"Hey, Whitney! Mom, guess what? Oh, and what's for dinner?"

"Slow down, Katie. What? Guess what … WHAT?" I asked.

"Coach Fraker called me into his office after practice and asked me if it was true what he had heard about you," said Katie as she lifted the lid on the casserole and opened the oven door to smell the rolls.

"I told him yes, and he asked me if it was OK if he gave the team these bracelets," Katie said as she held out her arm to show me the pink breast cancer awareness bracelet. "Look," she proudly said.

"He told us that we are a team and we are family, and he offered to help you, Mom if you ever need it. He even told me that I could have time off practice to spend with you if I needed it," Katie said. "And I will be excused and not have to sit the bench," Katie said as she sat down by Whitney. "He asked me if I preferred him to give the team the bracelets without me there. "

"Well, did you stay for the big announcement?" I asked her.

"Yep, and we all cried," she said.

I felt a deep appreciation for this kind gesture from Coach Fraker.

The following night was their first scrimmage. The season was about to start, and as usual, they had several scrimmages to see just how promising their team would be.

When the girls came running out to the gymnasium, I immediately noticed their bracelets. I looked at Coach Fraker and Coach Price, two young, good-looking men with so much style and charisma. There they also stood with the pink bracelets on. And the tears started flowing again. I decided that I had shed more tears in the last few weeks than I had in my entire life.

When ten teenage girls hear news and go home and tell one or possibly two parents, and those parents tell three to four friends, and the teens tell other teens, the news might as well be published. It just had not hit the local paper ... yet.

So my personal life, medical condition were new town gossip. Oh, I love my small town. And like any community, people care. Although gossip is not welcome many times, it is common. Concern is heartwarming.

12
The Lumpectomy

About two weeks later, David and I decided to consult the James Cancer Clinic, a nationally known cancer clinic in Columbus, Ohio. Many people I knew professionally and on a personal level had positive experiences there. I assumed they were probably the best, since their service was strictly treating cancer patients.

People travel from all over the United States to come to this clinic, and I felt fortunate that it is located one county away and only a half-hour drive from my home.

I found myself pushing David away. Subconsciously I wanted to show him I was OK alone, sick or not. I wanted my independence. He insisted on helping, doing extra for me, and showing me that he could change. He wanted to be totally involved and informed. He started barking orders to the kids, showing me he could discipline, and take the burden off me.

After getting my medical records from Dr. Schumer's staff and apologizing profusely to his staff that I was seeking a second opinion, David and I had an appointment with Doctor Number Two, a surgeon whose primary job was treating breast cancer patients.

Conveniently for me, my obstetrician-gynecologist's office was on the way to the James Cancer Clinic. I had made arrangements to pick up all my medical records to take with me for my appointment.

My attitude was poor toward Dr. Wagner, my ob/gyn since the cancer was found. I'd had a lump that would come and go in the spot where the cancer now was. We not only had a doctor-patient relationship, but we had become friends over the years. She had been my doctor for seventeen years and took care of me through my prenatal care while I was pregnant with Katie. Her son and Katie had gone to school together, and we had sat together at many school functions. She is also a neighbor to my sister. I'd always had faith in her.

I had routinely gone to her every year for the typical checkups, pap smears, and mammograms, and I was always conscientious of their importance. In 2002 and 2003, for the first time, my mammograms came back questionable. A recheck was done for two years on my left breast. A lump would come and go, always leaving my body about the time I was about to have my period. I always breathed a sigh of relief.

On the rechecks and mammogram comparisons, it was determined that I had fibrosis cyst.

"Try to avoid caffeine and you should be OK," Dr. Wagner advised me, after four mammograms in two years.

So there I was again in her office, knowing I'd never go back. The receptionist, a new, unfamiliar face to me, handed me my medical records. I combed the office for Dr. Wagner, wondering if she had been informed or had gotten any information about the biopsy that had been done on me. I hoped she would be concerned and care about me as an individual. I wondered if she felt she had overlooked me.

Dr. Wagner wasn't in sight. I felt angry as I held my records. "Tell Dr. Wagner I have breast cancer. I won't be back because I have lost faith in her," I said to the receptionist and turned, walking out.

As I walked out, David was sitting in the idling car, and I recall feeling so overwhelmed with sadness and apprehension, and I was cold. Snow was falling, and I did not see the beauty in it. It was the first snowy day of 2004. I hated snow, I hated the cold, and I hated winter. It seemed each winter hit my cold-blooded body harder and harder. My Raynaud's didn't like it either, leaving my toes and fingers always so cold.

My being sick in the winter was not my pick for the time of year. I wish I could have picked spring to have a lump. Spring is the promise time of year, when new flowers bloom, baby birds hatch, and there are warm, inviting blue skies. The Dairy Queen opens and I get my VW out of storage to go Buggin'!

I got into the car, closed the door, and started scanning my medical records as he backed out, heading for the clinic. I held records that had never been in my hands but were my property. I read rapidly, trying to learn everything I could about myself medically.

As I read each mammogram, I tried to comprehend the reports. I noticed the word "dense" on each reading.

"I wonder what this means when it says I have dense readings," I mumbled out loud as David slid along through the snow and traffic.

"I dunno," he said. "Maybe you can ask this new doctor when we get there."

"Oh, damn straight I will," I said with a negative attitude starting to boil in my head. "If I find out that this lump I have been messing with for two years was something that should have been looked at a little closer, I am going to be pissed off."

We pulled into the new office. The word *cancer* stood out on the building like a lit-up marquee sign to me. Never in any nightmare did I ever think I would be going to a cancer facility.

I immediately observed patients sitting in the waiting room. I wanted to see their heads, looking for wigs, and wondering if I would be able to tell a wig from a healthy head of real hair. I looked for signs of approaching death, and I looked for weakness in people, suffering people, now dependent on others to care for them. I wanted to see happy faces, no misery or pain among these faces that would now share a common problem with me. I tried to guess which ones had cancer and which ones was part of the support team.

My name was called, and we were ushered into a room.

Dr. Number Two seemed very professional and knowledgeable, but short, to the point, and cold.

He examined my breast and looked over the biopsy pathology report I had brought from Doctor Number One. He scanned over the mammograms from Dr. Wagner.

"Excuse me, sir, but could you tell me what dense means on all my mammograms?" I asked Dr. Number Two. "I notice that each one describes my results with this word."

"This means that you have thick tissue, and your breasts look very cloudy on a mammogram. Which means it is hard to get a good reading."

"Should I have had some other kind of reading, since I have had this one lump on and off for two and a half years?"

"Yes, someone should have ordered an ultrasound or an MRI, to get a proper diagnosis," he openly admitted to me.

I instantly became pissed off. "Well, that is great, just frickin' great," I told him. "I have always been faithful about having checkups. You mean this cancer may have been sitting here, stagnating in my breast, for two and a half years?" I asked him.

"Well, I can't say that. But, we will do our own mammogram today, and you will have an MRI and an ultrasound. We will also do a mammogram on your right breast, just to be sure it is OK," he warned me. "You will have a long day here, but we will have answers for you before you leave today," he assured me. "Our mammogram machines are state-of-the-art, and they will pick up what many other mammogram machines don't."

I was then left naked in a white terrycloth robe with James Cancer embroidered in pink on the chest. My slippers were paper, and I looked at David; he knew without asking. I was cold. I was pissed off at the world, and I was untrusting of doctors.

I was then put through the battery of tests: repeated mammograms, MRIs, ultrasounds; blood was drawn, and a chest X-ray was done. The entire ordeal lasted all day. I was eager to leave and still so afraid of what more I might find out about my health. My right breast was now a concern also.

David followed me from one room to the next, always positive and supportive for me.

In the last phase of the day, prior to being released to go home, I met with Dr. Number Two again. He came in carrying my verdict and numerous test results. I had two choices.

"You can have a mastectomy and then go through chemo, or we can do a lumpectomy with a sentinel node study while we have you in surgery, and I will then take tissue. The tissue will be examined and we will hope for a clear margin," he said as he hardly made eye contact with me. "It is important to be sure the cancer has not gone to your lymph nodes," he continued. "If we don't have to do a mastectomy, you will also have radiation after the chemo. The node study should have been done when you had the biopsy," he said.

Seems Dr. Good-Looking performed one job, but didn't do the whole job while he had me under anesthetic, and I was not educated enough to have known this.

"Most doctors do a needle biopsy and don't remove the entire mass until they get the results. I wonder why he took the whole thing out," Dr. Number Two asked as he thought about his question to me.

"Well, he said it didn't belong in me, and since I was having trouble with it for a couple of years, it would be best to just take the entire thing out," I told him. My mind wandered, and again I lacked confidence in hearing all these different opinions.

"Your cancer is an invasive ductal carcinoma," he advised me as he shuffled through my medical records.

"I have no clue what that means," I said. "What is it?" I looked at David and I was scared. Invasive sounded more serious than just a lump.

"Your cancer has spread around surrounding tissue in the left breast, and it not just in the breast cavity. It is also in the lining of the breast ducts."

As I sat and listened to his robotic voice, I began to cry. I knew he had said these same things to many women. His protocol was not different or special for Connie Curry. I was just an ordinary patient in his eyes.

"Well, if I was your wife, what would you do for her?" I asked.

Immediately, he said, "I would do a mastectomy on her to be sure to save her life, and then chemo, and assuming the nodes are clear, then suggest she have breast reconstruction, if she chooses."

"I don't want you to take my breast. Isn't it possible that you can get it all out of me with a lumpectomy?" I shifted in my seat. "And can't the chemo maybe kill all the bad cells?"

"It is possible," he said.

I wrapped the robe tightly around my waist for warmth as I swung my feet back and forth on the end of the examination table. David sat quietly, letting me make my own decision.

"Well, I am not ready to give up my breast. Let's try the lumpectomy," I decided. "You can take my hair, you can give me rat poison, but you are not taking my nipple or my nodes. Not yet," I warned him.

"Miss Curry, you need to change your attitude. We can do the lumpectomy and get chemo started, but down the road, you need to come to terms with a mastectomy," he said as he headed for the door.

"Jo, my nurse practitioner, will schedule your lumpectomy and go over what is expected for the next many months to come," he said, and out the door he went.

"Well, he talked about hacking off my tit like a foot doctor talks about taking out an ingrown toenail, didn't he?" I told David.

"Well, Connie, he wants to save your life, and if you have to have your breast taken off, it will be OK. You will still be beautiful."

"Beauty comes from within, David. If I don't feel beautiful within, I am not beautiful. And I know this *is* about my life. Who the hell loves life any more than I do? I am just not going to let a doctor cut me unless I know nothing else can be done."

"But ... but..."

"There is *no* but, David. How would you feel if some doctor walked in, flipped through a report, and said, 'Yep, we need to cut part of your dick off'?" I rambled on, raising my voice. "Would you feel like a man? Would you drop your head to defeat and say, 'Well, OK. Go ahead'?

"My God, I am willing to let them give me rat poison, do a lumpectomy, and steal my hair. I am not giving them anything else. Not yet!"

Ten days later, I was rolled into surgery, scared and untrusting. As the anesthesiologist approached me to make an introduction, I immediately barked orders: "Don't chip my teeth when you intubate me, and do not give me much anesthesia. Pay attention to me and don't be reading a magazine when I am under," I said with a chuckle.

I was serious, though. I recalled days long ago when I observed surgery in medic school. I remember the anesthesiologist reading a magazine as he sat beside the patient's head during surgery. I also recalled seeing intubations being difficult. I knew too much, and I dreaded that darn endotracheal tube, known as an ET tube, being put down my trachea.

I saw a patient go in for routine gall balder surgery. She was twenty-eight years old, a mother with two toddlers at home. She was wheeled out to ICU in a coma and brain-damaged from an irreversible reaction to an anti-nausea medicine.

I couldn't wait to know I was in recovery, done, and would maybe get news of a clear margin, with clean lymph nodes and my brain still intact.

My sister Cathy and David were with me in the pre-op, and would wait for me until the procedure was finished. I reminded both of them to ask many questions when the surgeon finished. I prayed that the cancer was not in my lymph nodes.

I remember getting medication through my IV and warning the nurse that I rarely take medicine and that I am very sensitive to medicines. "My blood pressure will drop easily. I am just warning you, OK?"

That was the last thing I remembered until I was in recovery. When I awoke, I remember that my hand was lying on my left breast, and I was crying. The tears were of happiness, thankfulness, and relief.

My breast was full and round and I continued feeling it, squeezing it a little, and then running my hand up to my nipple. I smiled. It appeared to not be deformed. I was elated. I rubbed my index finger across my nipple. I felt the sensation. I smiled inside.

As I started to move in the bed, I felt the pain in my left armpit. The sentinel node biopsy had been done, and my arm ached horribly.

The nurse approached me when she heard me groan. "Here is some medicine to help you with the discomfort," she said as she injected it into the IV.

In seconds, my monitor sounded and my blood pressure and heart rate plunged. I remember mumbling, "I told you I am sensitive to drugs," and my head started spinning.

After I finally stabilized, I was released to go home. David wheeled me out, and Cathy approached me, carrying a beautiful arrangement of flowers for me. Marcena, an old high school friend, had stopped by and left them. And … as always, dependable Margi had left work to come to check on me also. It felt great to see her, and although I talked like a drunk and staggered out of the wheelchair, I couldn't wait to get home.

"OK, so did you guys talk to the doctor? What did he say? Tell me everything he said … his exact words," I pleaded.

Cathy and David both started to talk. Margi listened tentatively. I had to sit down in the lobby. My head was spinning. I could tell my blood pressure was low. Wow, they send patients home quickly, but I was not going to argue or tell them how weak I felt.

Cathy placed the flowers on my lap. I ran the rose petals through my fingers and realized they were satin. "Marcena wanted to send real flowers, but the clinic won't allow them. It is against policy, so she made this arrangement," Cathy told me.

"Oh, Marcena—she was always so crafty. And homemade is special anyway. They are beautiful," I said. "Tell me … what did he say?" I asked again.

"Well, your lymph nodes were clear," David announced with a smile.

"Oh my God. I am so thankful. You are sure? He said that, right? They ARE clear?" I needed to be reassured again. This was my biggest fear after all I had read and been told about the stripping of nodes.

"He also said that he took tissue all around your breast, and he again mentioned how dense your breast is. He will send it off for testing, and we should know something in a few days," David said. "Right, Cathy?" he asked her, to be sure he had covered it all.

"That is what I understood," she said.

Cathy nodded, and just as she was about to say something, I stood up, looked at all of them, and said, "Look! You can't really tell because they put my breasts in this harness-like contraption, but ... I felt my boob, and I saw it. It is fine-looking. Whatever tissue he took, it didn't deform me too badly.

"Let's walk. C'mon, let's get the hell outta here," I said. "I need to call home, call Mom, Dad, and Katie. And guess what else, you guys? I have been thinking. Of course I have this scar from the biopsy and lumpectomy, but I think I will get a tattoo put over it."

They all looked at each other, heads shaking, grinning, and all three of them trying to get me up into the truck as if I was an imbecile. My legs were rubber.

"Don't you think a garland of flowers or daisies would look great across it? It is vertical like, so I think it would cover it perfect. What ya think, huh?"

I dialed Mom and Katie on my cell phone as we headed home. Katie immediately interrupted me when she heard my voice and knew I was among the living.

"Mom, my God ... the phone is ringing off the wall. Everyone is calling. I can't keep up with all of them," she said. "You are OK, right? What should I tell them?"

"Katie," I said as I turned the radio on for the first time in weeks. I loved music so much, but the lyrics would make me cry. I didn't need a motivator for tears, so I drove and rode in silence for weeks. I finally felt on top of the world. Surgery was over, my nodes were clear, and I didn't die in surgery. I had my breast!

"Just let the machine get the calls," I told Katie. "I'll call people back or send out a group e-mail when I get home, OK? And yes, I am OK. My nodes don't have cancer in them, and I am feeling good. Love ya. See you soon."

And that was the beginning of a huge surprise to me in learning what an enormous support team I had, and more was to come.

When I walked in the door, Amber, Allie, and Katie greeted me. Amber had brought me flowers, a nice surprise from a daughter who I hoped was learning how to give and not just take. Ryan, who had recently moved out, had come home to check on me too.

I was still feeling drunk from the Percocet they had given me, and the kids started laughing at my behavior and slurred speech.

I made up a song as I danced around the kitchen. "Mama has her boobies," I sang as I stuck my breasts out in celebration, and then I ran for the toilet and puked.

Allie followed me to the bathroom, rubbing my back as I hunched over the toilet, dry heaving and gagging. This little four-year-old was like a nurse maid to me, rubbing my back and saying, "It'll be OK, Grammy; you'll be OK."

Later, as the vomiting subsided, and Amber and Allie had gone home, I went on to bed with a cup of hot green tea, my new drink of the month. Two friends had brought me boxes of green tea, stating that it was a great remedy for breast cancer and had great healing additives in it. I didn't care for the taste, but the warmth of it was welcoming.

As I walked to my bedroom, carrying my hot tea, I looked at Katie as she watched me staggering to bed. "With a little green tea and a Percocet, Mama is a happy girl," I sang to Katie.

Katie threw her head back and laughed as I said my good night to all.

13
Attitude

My optimistic attitude and good mood about feeling like a bright future was a reach away ended quickly.

Four days after the lumpectomy, I had a follow-up appointment with the surgeon. Even though my breast hurt a lot, I walked in happy, and I left in tears. My medical condition had turned into the biggest roller coaster ride of contradictions.

I had e-mailed, called, and talked to many family and friends. From the news that Cathy and David had relayed to me, I proceeded telling everyone how wonderful everything had seemed. I was ready to take on the world and get chemo started, and my attitude was great.

Did I misunderstand Cathy and David? Did they not understand the surgeon? Did we all have selective, hopeful hearing? All I knew was that when I heard the pathology report, I was devastated.

Doctor Number Two said that the tissue he had removed was all positive cancer cells, meaning that a clear margin was not found. The frozen node that had been removed from under my arm was cancerous also.

The more he talked, looking down at the report, the more I cried. I couldn't believe it. I looked at David, and I immediately verbally charged like a bull. The doctor talked on, rapidly.

"You told me it all looked good. You told me he said it wasn't in my lymph nodes. You even said he thought the tissue looked healthy." I jumped up off the examination table. The surgeon looked irritated at me because I had interrupted his explanation of my fucked-up pathology report. I was livid!

Instantly, David started defending himself. "Cathy and I did not tell you that. We told you HE THOUGHT it looked good. You did not listen."

"Oh, I know what you guys told me. You said it was not in my nodes!"

The argument got uglier. "We attack those we are the closest to when we are upset," the nurse said. David and I glared at each other.

"You need chemo and a mastectomy, and I will probably have to remove about twenty of your lymph nodes," the doctor said.

"I might consider waiting to take the nodes, depending on how the chemo does, but we must do a mastectomy," he said.

"I'll start the chemo. I am not letting you take my breast off. Not yet."

David squirmed in his chair. "Connie, would you listen to him? This is about your life."

"I am listening. I am not having my breast taken off yet. I will start the damn chemo. It is not like I am ignoring treatment. The chemo can start killing the damn cancer cells.

"Can I get dressed now?" I asked, as I looked at the nurse.

The doctor did not even make eye contact with me. "Can you come in next Wednesday and I will check your breast again?" he said. "You have a lot of fluid on it. I will give you a prescription to fight the infection, and I'll check it again before we start chemo."

I made an appointment and I walked next door to meet my oncologist, a man I would learn to like, respect, and trust.

One week later, I walked in with fluid still remaining on my breast and a yeast infection caused by the antibiotic he had prescribed for me. I didn't know whether to hold my breast when I walked or scratch my crotch. So I did both!

The doctor got out a thirty-cc syringe and aspirated eighty cc of fluid off my breast. It hurt like hell as he sucked the infection out, but it was instant relief.

"Stay on the antibiotic, and by next week the infection should be gone and we can start chemo. Dr. Rhoades will see you and go over that with you. But I will recommend to him that you get eight treatments, starting next week. You can start the chemo before surgery, but I highly recommend a mastectomy sometime during your chemo treatments."

"But, wait," I said. "I called in a few days ago. I went off that medicine. It gave me a horrible yeast infection. The nurse told me to stop taking it. Weren't you the one who advised this?"

He picked up my file to read his cheat notes. "Let's double the strength, and I will write you a prescription for another medicine that will cure the yeast infection," he said.

"Double the strength!" I bellowed. "Obviously you don't know what a yeast infection feels like. This other medicine better cure it if you want me to take that crap."

He started out the door. He was fed up with me, and he hated being doubted. No wonder he doubled the strength. He wanted me to squirm all right, and maybe he liked the idea of this sassy woman suffering with an itchy-burning crotch.

"Hey! Thanks for taking the fluid off my breast. It feels better already," I told him, as he walked out.

"Double the strength," I mumbled as I jerked the robe off and starting putting my bra on. "I can't believe him."

The nurse who was still in the room with David and me looked at me with sympathy and said with a wink, "Men truly don't have a clue how bad yeast infections feel, do they?"

"Well, I am glad you understand," I told her with a smile.

"Connie, would you like to look at some pictures we have of women who have had reconstructive breasts? We have four plastic surgeons here that all do a great job. You will be surprised at how real they look," she proceeded to say. "I'd recommend these two," she said as she pointed at the brochure showing pictures of each plastic surgeon.

"But what about my nipple? Can I keep my nipple if I have a mastectomy?" I asked as I began to cry again. "I want my nipple. I don't want a dead, fake nipple. It'll be dead, won't it?"

"Yes, there won't be any feeling in it. They have to take your nipple, too. It is too risky to keep it, Connie."

As she continued reassuring me, she continued searching for the boob scrapbook. I saw boobs of all shapes and sizes in it.

"Wow, they do look good," I said. Just as I said this, I noticed a breast that was black. It was not a breast of a black woman, because the healthy breast was white.

"What is wrong with that breast?" I asked as I pointed at the dark, discolored boob.

"That is what radiation does sometimes," she explained. "She has been burned by the radiation. That picture was put there so women can be alerted. This doesn't happen to all, but if you get to keep your breast, it is likely you'll get 30–40 radiation on the localized area."

Then I noticed many breasts without nipples. I wondered why women would opt to go through the pain of reconstruction but not have a nipple put on their new breast.

I didn't ask. I had seen enough, and I wanted to go home ... my safe haven for the time being. My once hell-raising home seemed to start bringing me comfort as I left each appointment.

The ride home was quiet. I knew David wished for me to be more cooperative and to do as the doctors all wanted. But I always questioned and didn't like taking orders.

Why would I change at forty-eight? I'd witnessed too many mistakes in emergency rooms with doctors. I couldn't trust.

14

The Chemo Call From Governor Curry

Dr. Rhoades, my oncologist, and his staff were very friendly and made me feel like a human and not a number. However, I did not like the answers I got from Dr. Rhoades when I asked questions. Margi has always told me to not ask questions you don't want the answer to.

"Do you really think I need a mastectomy and my nodes removed? Do you agree with Dr. Number Two?"

"He is a great surgeon, and after looking at the kind of cancer you have, I do agree. We need to treat this hard and make sure you don't have a reoccurrence of cancer," Dr. Rhoades said.

"Your tumor that was removed by Dr. Schumer was almost two centimeters. Your cancer is invasive. It is a ductal carcinoma. It involves the margin, which is the tissue in the breast. We can't see how many tiny cancer cells there might be. All the tissue that was removed tested positive for cancer."

Again I asked, "Isn't it possible the chemo can kill all the cancer?"

"It is possible, but to be sure we both agree that a mastectomy and dissection of the lymph nodes is necessary ... just to be sure."

I looked at David, and gave him *that look*. When would I trust and stop doubting doctors?

I knew David thought I was chasing rainbows, looking for doctors to tell me what I wanted to hear. I kept thinking about all the doctors whom I had observed in emergency rooms, and medics whom I had seen overtreat. I did not want to be overtreated.

After a discussion and explanation about what to expect with chemo, my appointment was made for the following week, which was three days before Christmas.

I was obsessed with getting all my Christmas shopping, wrapping, and decorating of the house done prior to this mysterious day. I had no idea what to expect. I pictured myself hanging over a bucket or the toilet for days, vomiting, dehydrating, and feeling like I was dying a slow death. I had to prepare for the family. After all, we had Allie, who believed in Santa, and Santa had to come through. I had Baby Annabelle to find. Like the Cabbage Patch and Beanie Baby frenzy, I had this doll to find come hell or high water. And she was a hot item for 2004.

"Grammy, if I can have Baby Annabelle, I would never want anything else ever, EVER," she said as she watched the enticing commercial on television.

I immediately liked Dr. Rhoades and respected his self-assurance when he disagreed with Dr. Number Two, thinking I only needed four chemo treatments. I was happy to hear this. Four sounded doable. Eight sounded like a lifetime. And he sounded like a doctor not afraid to disagree with his colleague.

"Oh, you will lose your hair," his nurse told me. "Rarely does anyone not. The kind of chemo given for breast cancer will make your hair fall out. Remember that it will grow back. Many patients tell us their hair comes back prettier."

I sighed as she took the blood pressure cuff off my arm.

"Your hair will probably be thinning rapidly by your second chemo. Many just shave their heads because of the mess and hair coming out so fast. I am not trying to scare you, but you just need to know the facts," she said as she patted my arm. Her smile was genuine and kind.

Just like the perky breast that could be made, I was happy with my own hair and breasts. I didn't wish to be surprised with a new growth of mysterious hair after months of being bald.

I also knew the day would come after wearing hot, scratchy wigs and scarves that made me look like I was hiding a bald head, I'd probably be thrilled with any kind of real hair growth.

The Wednesday that David and I left to head south for my first chemo, my heart was heavy. I was scared. The weather was horrid again, with snow and such cold temperatures. I took my tote bag with my blanket-made-with-love from De.

All blood work was drawn, my vitals were taken, and I was seated to get the intravenous needle placed in my hand. I had been reading and talking to cancer vets. I knew that by the time all my chemo treatments were finished, my veins would be in poor shape. Starting my first IV was a piece of cake.

"You have pipelines," she said as she missed my vein. After starting many IVs in EMS, I wondered how the hell she could have missed that good shot!

The second attempt was made, successfully, and I was on my way for chemo.

A nurse came in and asked me if I had any questions or concerns prior to the chemo being started.

I immediately told her I had mixed feelings and lacked confidence in Doctor Number Two. I assured her I liked Dr. Rhoades, my oncologist.

"I have heard about Dr. Linda at St. Ann's Hospital. I have heard nothing but the best about her," I said, as I starting taking the tape off my IV.

"What are you doing," she asked.

"I think I already did things out of order. I let Dr. Number One take the mass out of me, and I wonder if he stirred up cancer cells. I went weeks without a node study when he should have done it then. I let my ob/gyn leave me with dense mammogram readings while a cancerous tumor was probably there for over two years." I continued pulling the tape off.

"Why are you taking that tape off?" she asked me.

"I am not comfortable doing this. I want to go to her and get the opinion of a female doctor. What if I start chemo and find out she won't take me as a patient after starting chemo?" I asked.

The nurse walked out and came back with Dr. Rhoades.

"I know Dr. Linda," he said. "We used to work together. She worked here several years ago. She is a fine surgeon. I think if you are not comfortable, you should wait and go ahead and talk to her. Christmas is three days away." I felt immediate relief. David probably felt immediate anger and assumed I'd lost my pea-picking mind.

"Go see her, and if you decide to have her take care of you, I can work with her also. Another week will not hurt you. Breast cancer is very slow-moving. We want you to be sure."

My IV was taken out, we walked out, and a new plan was about to begin.

I called family and many friends to let them know I didn't have my chemo as planned. Claire was the first one I called, since she had lined up a schedule of foods to be brought to our home. I certainly didn't want friends going out of their way to cook for me when I still felt good. Being independent was making this kind gesture from Claire difficult. I still did not feel or look sick. I planned on cooking and looked forward to it.

I felt good about waiting to do chemo later, even though I knew the inevitable would come. My procrastinating left me relieved, but was not the answer. I would have Christmas with no ill effects, and that brought me comfort. I knew I would have to get to the chemo, and soon.

I wondered if the doctor and his staff's tongues were wagging at my behavior and boldness in taking charge of my life. I might regret my decision later, or maybe I would find out I was right to take control.

As I later laughed as I told stories about pulling my IV, I joked in saying it was like being on death row and waiting for the governor to get the call to stop the lethal injection at the last minute. I just happened to have been the governor *and* the inmate, and I made the call!

Many of my family and friends supported me in my decision, and although I knew some might think I was risking my life, I knew most had faith in me. Or was I in denial? Was I playing Russian roulette and being selfish and careless? What in the hell did I know about cancer and treatments?

Don, my firefighter friend whom I had known for years, was one who spoke to me with much concern and felt I was being too bullheaded. "Don, you of all people know I do have some medical knowledge. Trust my judgment and decisions on this, would you?"

Don, always a big conversationalist, and one with a great sense of humor, said, "Connie, you can live without your boob; your boob can't live without you."

He shook his head at me, and I realized that his comment was made out of concern and was not to be taken lightly. He was truly worried.

"Oh, Don … simmer. I am going to be OK. You will be one of my pallbearers, but that is years from now. We are going to both grow old."

"God, Connie," he said, "can we change the subject?"

And that we did. Don and I have spent many evenings in deep conversations. He'd stop over to the EMS station many nights as he was leaving the firehouse. We talked about everything, from politics and family to sports, and told jokes. Don knows a little about a lot. I always asked his advice on how to fix something, or where to go to replace something. He was a man full of knowledge and was always there for me when I was in need of just about anything, and always fixing our cars when the jobs were too big for David.

Although it was an uncomfortable situation, I continued to be close to him and his wife when they went through an ugly divorce. I loved them both, and I told each of them I wanted to stay neutral during the heat of their ugly divorce: "I love both you guys. I don't want to hear bad stuff about either of you. This is between you guys. I know it takes two for a marriage to fail. Stay my friends, both of you."

And we did.

The following morning, before I had to leave for work, I found Dr. Linda's phone number. I was in luck. It was meant to happen. She had a cancellation the following day, and I was scheduled to see her.

I had some fancy, fast footwork to do, though. I had to get all my medical records and bring them in with me for my appointment. I got them!

Cathy, my sister, insisted on going with me and took off work. She was eager to go and see what this doctor was like. A co-worker friend of Cathy's was a patient of Dr. Linda's, and had already assured Cathy that she was happy I was consulting her. "She is just the best," she reassured Cathy.

And that she was. From the minute I met her, I knew instantly that she had compassion and understanding and was very knowledgeable. She was on a mission to help me, but would work conservatively yet aggressively.

Doctor Number Three would be my surgeon to the very end. What she said would go, and I would trust her no matter what I might have to face.

The first thing she told me that instantly was music to my ears was, "Connie, you absolutely, positively do NOT need your lymph nodes removed. The pathology report shows such a teeny cell of cancer that I can't even show you by drawing it on paper. The chemo will kill it, and the nodes will be fine."

I began to cry.

She immediately grabbed a Kleenex and handed it to me. "Oh, don't cry. It is OK. If I were you, I would worry more about dying of a heart attack when you are older or getting hit by a truck than breast cancer killing you."

"Oh, I am not crying because I am sad. I am crying because I am so happy you don't have to take my nodes. I am so happy I came to you."

"You are not out of the woods yet for this mastectomy. I wish I could tell you today that you won't have to have it. The James Clinic did not send all the reports that I need. They are awful to work with in getting patients' records. I want to get the rest of your pathology reports and study them, and we can talk again after I see them," she said as she touched my shoulder with kindness and sympathy for what I was going through.

"I am ordering an MRI for tomorrow if you aren't busy. We have the top state-of-the-art mammogram and MRI machines. I don't feel comfortable looking at the test results from either of the other doctors," she said.

Top state-of-the-art machines, I thought. *Here we go again.*

"But the James claimed they have the best mammogram machines," I immediately said to her.

"I went to medical school at OSU," she said. "I used to work at the James. Trust me, I know. Our machines are the very newest, most modern in the nation."

She examined me, looking closely at my lumpectomy scar, examining my breasts as she continued talking to me. I could tell Cathy was impressed also.

"I was supposed to start my chemo two days ago," I told her. "I didn't feel right, something just seemed wrong, so I walked out."

"Well, I am glad you didn't have it. The MRI would not have been an accurate reading if you had started it," she said with a reassuring smile. I could tell she liked my boldness. I wasn't so rude after all.

She proceeded on with her game plan. "We will get the chemo going. After you have had all your treatments, I can go back in and do another MRI. If the MRI shows improvement from the chemo, I can do another lumpectomy."

I was feeling very hopeful as she spoke.

"But, Connie ... you must know—if we can't get a clear margin, or if the MRI does not look good, I will have to do the mastectomy. I will try hard to save your breast."

"Oh, thank you so much. Thanks! By the way, do you know Dr. Rhoades, the oncologist?" I asked her. "He says he knows you."

"Of course, I know Chris. He is a great oncologist. I'll be glad to work with him, if he is who you want."

I left feeling hopeful and confident, knowing the holiday was around the corner, but I wouldn't mind starting chemo before Christmas. I would walk in and start with a good attitude. A doctor had rejuvenated me.

So I had my team at two different hospitals, I had my breast, I had my nipple and nodes for Christmas, and most of all, I had hope.

15

One Parade and Two Strangers

I was having a down day the Sunday before Christmas. I found Christmas a heavy burden, and it was very difficult to get into the spirit.

The week prior, I had a big fight, pouted, and threw a fit about the stress of trying to get everything up and ready in time for Christmas. I wondered why I cared, and if no one else noticed we had not trimmed a tree or decorated the house, why should I worry and try to do it?

I decided to lighten the load and not bake Christmas goodies. Katie and Allie did deserve a tree; even if Katie was rarely home since she had recently gotten her driver's license.

That particular Sunday, I took off in my car. Katie was preoccupied with being a teenager. She was always making plans and hanging out with her friends. David was watching football. Allie was with her dad. I was depressed.

As I entered town, I realized that it was the day of the Christmas parade. I had forgotten about it. I couldn't have cared less. But it was about to start and I was about to be blocked by traffic. I preferred to turn around. I didn't want to see happy people.

It was an unusually warm December day. The parade-watchers were on every street corner. It was going to be a huge success, no matter how big the parade was; people were out and in the spirit of the holiday.

It was easier to stop than to be trapped in the flow of traffic. A roadblock was put up by a police officer, as the parade was seconds from starting.

I put my car in park and pulled into a gas station. *Fine, I will suffer through this,* I thought. Bands played, and Christmas songs could be heard, courtesy of all kinds of contraptions that went by. The more Christmas music I heard, and the more people I watched who were so happy, the sadder I became. I was jealous because they were all in high spirits.

Growing up in Delaware, Ohio I always knew many people who participated in the parades. I'd always holler, cheer, and say hello to people I knew. They would see me and greet me.

Heck, I love participating in parades, too. Once I was a clown on a stick pony just so I could be in the All-Horse Parade. I didn't have a real horse, so I dug out an old Halloween costume and was a clown. I rode that silly stick pony through town. What fun that was. And I'm always in the Fourth of July parade with my VW Bug.

I had my sunglasses on and my hattitude, a name I gave my hats. I stood behind the crowd purposely with poor vision in viewing the parade. I did not want to see anyone I knew. I did not want to speak to anyone. The music could not be avoided. Christmas tunes played on. I wanted to plug my ears and cry.

I just wanted it to end and was mad at myself for stopping. I stood there like a fool, feeling sorry for myself.

I was starting to turn to get into my car and wait out the parade when I saw one of the local bands coming. I heard the song, but it wasn't the song that caught my attention.

It was a young high school boy playing a trumpet. I noticed how he struggled to keep in step with his band members. I looked down and I saw his deformed ankle and foot. His passion, loyalty to his band, and strength amazed me. My stare was in utmost respect.

As I watched him, tears welled up in my eyes. I watched him play and hobble. His foot was so deformed that his ankle lay sideways, almost touching the street as he walked. I wondered how he was able to walk, let alone march to keep up.

He was playing that trumpet, and he was staying in line, and he did not lag back. He did not miss a beat.

I thought what determination, spirit, and strength he had. I finished watching the parade and my spirit had been lifted. He was my wake-up call and he didn't even know it, as he marched upward and on.

I realized that if this young boy could be so brave, I could too. I would take one step at a time, just like he had done every day of his life.

16
Hope And Hair

After weeks of anticipation of having rat poison titrated slowly into my veins by intravenous therapy, the day came. My excuses, delays, tests, and changing game plan in the middle of the third inning came to an end.

My new surgeon had given me thumbs up (or thumbs down, depending on how one looks at this) to keep my tentative schedule and start rat poison. As I write and slowly start feeling positive, I hope I will be able to refer to it as chemo, or chemo cocktail, and smile.

So approximately seven weeks after one invasive biopsy surgery with the entire tumor from hell removed, and after one lumpectomy with a sentinel lymph node study done, preparation for this war on my life was about to begin. Throw in two MRIs, three mammograms, numerous blood draws, urine specimens, weight checks, and aspirations of fluid off my left breast, and I am still holding on for dear life. After one oncologist, three surgeons, one social worker who was sure she could turn my attitude around, and more nurses than you can shake a needle at, the time arrived.

I arrived early to stop at the boutique that adjoined the chemo facility. My wig was in and ready for pickup. I have to admit that I was excited to see it. Hopefully, the wig would be my salvation to enter the public arena once again when my hair rudely left me for many months to come.

My thought was with Doctor Number Two as I entered the wig shop. "You can take my hair; you are not taking my lymph nodes or my breast."

"My body is like a forest of trees," I tried to explain to Katie when she watched my boldness and listened to my outspokenness to the doctors. "One tree has a disease in it. The disease might kill the tree. The tree needs to be cut down to prevent the disease from spreading to the forest. Doctor Number Two wants to destroy the entire forest without giving the trees a chance to survive. Just a case of how doctors think when they treat. If it is not broke, don't fix it," I told Katie. "Have faith in me. I have some medical knowledge; I have seen so much in my years working in EMS and with doctors and nurses. I will NOT be over treated. Doctor Number Three is willing to try chemo first and then do another MRI and possible lumpectomy to see if the chemo is killing the cancer cells. She understands how a woman feels," I continued telling her. "If she cannot get a clear margin, then I will have the mastectomy, Katie."

I wanted Katie on my team. I wanted her to have hope, and know my judgment and decisions were rational and not ridiculous. Most importantly, I wanted her to know it was not all about selfishness and my vanity. David supported me ... finally.

I was concerned about secondary problems that can occur with lymph-node dissections. I wanted my immune system intact. Lymph nodes fight infection, and I did not want to risk having a handicapped arm. I did not want to deal with lymphedema, a medical condition caused by the dissection. Doctor Number Three had told me with much confidence that it would be safe to keep my nodes.

Hallelujah, was my thought. I also knew I would be in a lot less pain, and I could recover and continue to work much more easily. I needed to lift the CPM machines for my job, and I did not want to be slowed down.

I had read much positive information about bust reconstruction. I also had talked with many breast cancer patients who had reconstructions from hell. But I was sure things had improved with cosmetic surgery.

I was also aware that the side-effect precautions that are on all prescription drug labels must have those warnings to inform patients. I understand that it is just a small percentage of patients who have negative side effects from some medicines. And doesn't every bottle have a warning about nausea, vomiting, and diarrhea? Amazing! For the first time, I just might have bowels that move. Yeehaw!

And like the problems that can arise, or secondary illnesses from surgeries, I am sure that many of these problems would not happen to me. I'd been very healthy. I do recall, though, that one in ten is cancer and how the odds beat me. But life and good health were always on my side until this bump in the road.

I wanted the kids and everyone who loved me to know that I will not (and they know me well enough to know this) lie down to doctors and let them do as they please without questions, disagreements, and some mistrust and lack of confidence. Like teachers, accountants, housewives, dads, and mailmen ... there are good and there are bad. There are people who love their jobs and want the very best job done because of pride and concern. They want to make a difference, and they like helping people. And then there are those who are burned out, tired, overworked, need the income, or maybe just think they are good at their job, but are not. Many like to follow a safe, unchangeable protocol. They are comfortable with it and won't take risks or try something new, even though each patient's case is different, and each patient's medical history is different, too.

And yes, those doctors are human, like all of us. We all are capable of errors. We all make mistakes from time to time.

I just did not want my forest destroyed because of error. I wanted sunshine again someday, and I wanted shade sprinkled with hope of a once-again-healthy life. I wanted my forest to have a second chance.

I waited in line at the boutique and noticed a gentleman standing and waiting patiently as he held a woman's purse. I guessed he was waiting for his wife. He looked about fifty-five, a gentle-looking man with obvious support for his wife.

"You don't need a wig; you have a nice head of hair," I said to him.

"It's my wife. She just had her second round of chemo, and she shaved her head last night. She already got her wig, but is shopping for some new scarves," he replied with a grin as he rubbed his hair.

"I will be losing my hair soon," I told him. "I find this difficult to think about. But my new wig is in, and I am eager to see it," I told him.

Then the questions began from both of us as we stood talking. We cancer victims compare notes, stories, support, and immediate compassion for each other.

His wife had been diagnosed with a rare cancer—sarcoma cancer, a rare form that usually attacks the major organs. For some reason, it chose to attack her breast. I am sure it was better that it hit her breast and not a major organ. I don't know but that is the bright side to cancer.

She opted to take chemo, not knowing or being given any promise or advice from her doctor that it would kill the cancer. Few people in the United States have this form, and it appeared she was about to become a guinea pig in hopes of helping find a cure and saving her life.

She had a mastectomy weeks prior, and he said her attitude was good. The chemo had not made her feel too bad. She was productive and optimistic.

"I wish her the best," I said, as my turn came to be waited on by the boutique salesman. I noticed a box lying on the counter. I read the word "nipple." I opened it. I'll be damned! It was a perfectly round, plastic nipple. I did not ask, and I did not want to think about needing a plastic nipple. But it was cute.

"Ya know," I said to the girl at the counter, as I placed the nipple back into the box, "I am sooo selfish. I want my lymph nodes, I want my breast, I want my nipple, and I made a promise I would let them have my hair. I now want my hair, too. The closer it gets to falling out, shedding like a dog, the more frightened I become.

I am so scared of chemo being put into me. I think I might die of fright before I die of cancer."

She smiled with understanding.

"Wait until you try on this wig, now that we got your color in. You are going to love it," she said. "And you can do all of this. It is just tougher than you have had to deal with in life. Many women do it, and you too can survive, and you will. The chemo is never as bad as you think."

As she said this, I began to cry. A woman came up behind me, and she looked happy and healthy, her skin full of vibrant color. Her hair was beautiful. It was the sarcoma woman. She hugged me, and I wept.

"Let me tell you about a friend of mine," she said. "She was in a horrible car wreck. Her car caught fire, and both her hands were burned off. They could not save her arms. Her face was so badly burned; all that was left of her own skin was about the size of a quarter. Her hair was burned, her scalp damaged badly. We collected money for her to get a wig. She had very little money. She has gone through so many surgeries to graft skin onto her," she said as she touched my arm. "So you and I have it tough right now, but think of my friend who has so much fight to come back."

My sarcoma friend paused. "I already know," I said. "If she can do this, I can too. There is always someone out there in far worse shape than me. I must remember this."

"And look," she said. "I even have a fake scalp on my new wig. Doesn't it look real? Yours will be pretty, too."

I hugged my new friend, and I touched her hair. It felt so real. I hoped we would bump into each other soon for our chemo cocktail. And I didn't even know her name.

I walked in for my chemo. They waited, looking at me for a sign of good attitude. They remembered me from the week before, when I had pulled my IV out and left the scene.

My walk was faster, my heart was lighter. "I'm ready," I said as I smiled.

They smiled back.

17
Rat Poison With A Cure

My CBC (complete blood count) looked good, and I appeared healthy except for this glitch of cancer. With a good WBC (white blood count), HGB, platelet count, mean cell volume (I bet they thought my mean cell volume would be high, since I am so bold and outspoken), I was a prime candidate for feeling better than many who have health issues to begin with. It was guaranteed that my white blood count would go down when the chemo started going though my system, but I at least had a good start with having all my counts at the normal levels.

My IV was started, and three pills were taken orally to give me a jump-start on the nausea that is so prevalent with the three chemo drugs that would be put into me intravenously. The brand-name drugs that were given to me and also sent home to be filled at the pharmacy were Decadron, Reglan, and Ativan.

And guess what? All three have possible side effects of constipation, diarrhea, and possible nausea. Of course, I am smart enough to know I wouldn't have constipation AND diarrhea. With me, I knew it would be constipation. And no drinking of alcohol. Good-bye beer burps; hello Metamucil but that would be easy since I drink very little. Give me diet coke.

One less serious side effect to Reglan is trouble with sex. I wondered how and wished they would be more specific about this problem. Trouble because I am on the toilet with diarrhea or too hyper from the steroid that is a stimulant, or because my attention span flies from here to over yonder? I might have convulsions from Decadron. This all sounded alarming to me.

Irregular periods may start while taking Decadron. And how would I know this? I am not even sure if I am in pre-menopause or menopause. I am sure I am not in post-menopause. I have been irregular for about a year. So this side effect did not concern me, but simply confused me.

After a half hour waiting for the anti-nausea pills to take effect, it was time to start the big boys: Adriamycin, Zofran, and Cytoxan. The medicine was slowly titrated into my veins while the nurse watched for signs of allergic reactions.

Adriamycin was the first to be put into my arm. "This is the red one, the one that will make your hair fall out," the nurse told me.

"Oh! So this is the bastard one, huh? The creep of all the creeps," I said.

"Yep, this is the bastard," she said. "Your hair will begin thinning out by next week, and when we see you in three weeks, your hair will be very thin, or you might have already shaved your head. You have a very pretty face; you will look just fine," she said as she looked at David. (Maybe she was warning him to not be scared of a bald woman in bed with him.)

"You need to drink lots of water to hydrate your body, and to flush this red medicine out," she warned me. "You will pee red for a while because of it."

"Well, I have decided one thing," I started to say when two more nurses walked in.

It was the nurses from the Doctor Number Two side of the clinic. They had heard that I had switched to Doctor Number Three, and they came over to visit me briefly. I remembered them. It appeared I had found a fan club. They were not upset and were very understanding about me leaving their boss.

They came over for some laughs and to check out my trendy outfit. I asked them if they were truly coming over to see my clothes, and me, or just maybe stopping in to see if my head was bald yet.

"Anyway, as I was telling Dora here, who is feeding my veins the bastard that will make my hair fall out, I have come up with a plan. Do you want to hear it?" I asked Linda and Amy, my ex-nurses from Doctor Number Two.

"I have decided that I am going to find some big, pointed buttons to stick in my bra for the twins, who are not identical, as you know, thanks to Doc Number Two and Doc Number One, who have already butchered them. Men's eyes will never leave my chest when they see these biiiiggg nipples. They will never make their way up to see my bald head. You know how men are!" The nurses just stood and shook their heads, grinning.

I continued, probably prattling ... a little nervous because of the chemicals that were going into my vein. "I notice the way my friends look down at my chest, anyway. They are always curious if I am minus one breast now."

"Gosh, we are going to miss seeing you next door. When do you come back for your next treatment? We'll stop over and check out your new *do,*" said Amy.

"Oh, and one more thing," I told them as they headed out the door laughing, "That pharmacist came over to meet me, explaining about all these drugs that I am now taking. He wondered if I had any questions. I told him that so many friends had told me that smoking pot was the best remedy for fighting this nausea that I might get. Can you believe he would not give me the thumbs up to use it?" I announced. "I mean, heck, I would use it medicinally, and I wouldn't abuse it," I said with a snicker.

"Do it; just do it," Linda said very discreetly. "It does work, and it does help."

Wow, I thought. *Mom would kill me.*

18
The Unforgotten Soldiers

I think about cancer frequently since my diagnoses. I recall all the wonderful people who have died from it. They touched my life and I miss them. We all have suffered losses of someone close to us ... many victims of cancer.

It amazes me how they can do organ transplants and eye surgeries to prevent blindness, and give fertility drugs to women who can't conceive a child to make this miracle happen. Hearts are transplanted, severed limbs are surgically replaced, and blood flow is rejuvenated.

We know cancer treatments have come far. People are cured today who never would have survived it twenty years ago. However, there is still much work to be done to save people diagnosed with cancer.

We all have known someone who couldn't beat it. I think of Tom, a gentle, kind friend of my family. I will always respect Tom, who chose quality of life when he was diagnosed with liver cancer. Chemo would not cure him but would only prolong his agony. He made a list of things he wanted to do, people he wanted to see again, and places he needed to visit, and he opted to not take chemo. He was given six months to live. He lived nine months and checked off most on his list before his passing.

There was Mike Anderson, known as Good Ole Pud to everyone who was blessed to know him. Unlike Tom, he fought to the bitter end. His cancer, a rare form in the chest wall, was inoperable. Many rounds of chemo would not shrink the tumor. I remember his sadness when the doctor told him the tumor had not shrunk. He picked his head up, lifted his drive to fight on, and held on for many months.

He was my high school buddy, and he touched the lives of countless friends. Pud, the class clown, was always pickin' on the girls and putting other kids up to foolishness. I will never walk by a yo-yo or pick one up and not think of Pud. During lunch break in high school, he taught me every possible trick that could be conquered with a yo-yo. I can still walk the dog, go around the world, and rock the baby with something as simple as a yo-yo. And quite impressive I am to Allie. There will never be another Pud. He was unique. He brought laughter and love by the boatloads.

There was Dan, my brother-in-law, who fought to the very end and left behind two grade-school children and a grieving wife. Oh how he suffered. I remember when I first found out I had cancer. My mind drifted back to Dan on a Thanksgiving several years ago. We all knew it would be his last holiday. The radiation had burned him badly. He was thin, sick, and in so much pain. His desire to eat was gone. I remember him sitting at the table of my in-laws, holding his chin up with his hand, his eyes shut, trying to find comfort. His skin was red and brittle-looking. No type of food appealed to him. He was too weak to make conversation. His laughter and humor had always been welcome. His fight to live was gone.

Dan died just weeks after Thanksgiving. His parents buried their second young adult child, both victims of cancer.

Wonderful Pam left behind a daughter in high school and a dedicated husband who is now trying to play a double role to Whitney, just a child of seventeen. Rarely a day goes by when I don't think of my friend Pam. I call Whitney just to check in, wondering if she needs any female-motherly advice.

So when we hear the word *cancer,* we panic. Some just don't have the chance to live into their golden years. We feel cheated because some of our family and friends must leave us too soon.

Children are left without a mom or dad. Parents outlive a child who is struck with cancer.

When will there be a cure? We eat, breathe, and walk in too much crap. Our environment is destroying mankind, and cancer remains a mystery.

Money is donated to help find the answers to this horrid disease. We march, we walk, and we give money in hopes a cure is found. We honor those we lost. We live with hope that this war will be resolved. Cancer research has come far, and many survive today who would not have years ago. Someday, maybe it won't be a death sentence for anyone.

19

Pride

For some odd reason, I have always felt that illness is a sign of weakness. I almost felt ashamed that I had become sick. I was letting myself down, as well as my family. I felt guilty and hated causing a disruption.

I grew up in a proud, hard-working, middle-class family. We were taught how to be independent and responsible and to not expect a handout in life. We worked for everything we achieved. Dad worked constantly; sometimes two jobs. I recall Friday nights when he would actually lie down on the couch and rest after a long week of hard work. It was rare to see Dad or Mom resting. Bills, dirty laundry, animals and kids to feed, clothes and shoes to buy marched on—never ending.

There was a Friday night ritual that happened for years. Mom, Dad, and we four kids would load into the car. Wayne, being the only boy, always sat up front between Mom and Dad. He was the skinniest, so I suppose that is why the front seat was appropriate for him.

Cathy, Tina, and I rode in the back. Dad always had a two-door car, and I remember the doors being very heavy as I climbed into the back. Tina, the youngest, always had to ride in the middle. Cathy and I were privileged to have both window seats, with me always riding directly behind Dad, who always, always drove. Dad would smoke Camels with his window cracked, and many times the ashes would come back and hit me in the eyes. I would scream, and Mom would scold Dad. She never liked his bad habit, and like the no-seatbelt rule, in the sixties, cigarettes were not looked upon as vulgar or unhealthy, and the surgeon general had not yet put any warnings on the packs. When Dad would cough, or have sputum in his throat, I recall many times Mom warning him, "Donnie, some day they are going to find out that cigarettes are not good for you. There is no way those things can be good."

Every Friday as we headed to town, Cathy, Wayne, Tina, and I would have our allowance in hand. Dad would drive around the block for what seemed like hours, looking for a decent place to parallel park. We couldn't wait to go in the McClellans Dime Store and then on down the street to the music store. The top twenty-five records were always posted above the file full of forty-fives. We made it a mission to try to collect as many records as we could.

We loved our record player, and we loved our rock-and-roll, even before we were teens. We would get fifty cents per week, and even in the sixties, inflation occurred, and our allowance was later raised to a dollar per week. No matter how poor Mom and Dad were, they always gave us our allowance.

The dime store had the biggest selection of any store in town. They also had a glass window with various candies, and warm peanuts under a light. The light gave off such an appealing, shiny look to the peanuts and warmed them just enough to bring the aroma throughout the store. Chocolate-covered peanuts were the hit with me. For fifty cents, I could get a small bag of those delicious chocolates. If I managed my money properly from week to week, I could return home with peanuts and a new forty-five record. I was thrilled.

We would all discuss which ones to buy so we didn't duplicate our collection. We would then share them, playing records on the little turntable for hours. We loved it when Mom and Dad were outside, or would take a quick trip to town. The volume was cranked up to the max. We felt so cool! And like clothes, we shared our forty-fives and our simple, inexpensive record player. Once in a while, a fight would break out and one of us would lift the needle while the song was playing, threatening to skid it across the forty-five to ruin it.

Wayne bought models. He bought models, models, and more models. His passion for cars came early. He also learned at a young age how to manage his money. He would go weeks during our Friday ritual never buying anything. He would go into his room and count his money over and over.

Wayne was also trustworthy with his money. Tina, Cathy, and I would need fast cash, and he would always float us a loan. There were rules. If we borrowed a quarter, we had to pay him back an extra nickel. We also signed an I.O.U.

Today, he is still ambitious, and his love for cars continues. He knows everything mechanically about cars and owns a reputable, prosperous auto-repair business.

When we returned home with our loot, Dad would lie down on the couch. The couch was his domain on Friday nights. Mom would open the potato chips, and we were permitted a special drink once a week to go with our chips: Pepsi! Pepsi in a bottle was opened and divided in glasses for the four of us. Dad got a full bottle *AND* the couch *AND* his choice of what we watched on TV.

As we became teens, forty-fives started to become obsolete, and as our allowance accumulated, we girls set our sights on the clothing stores for style and started saving our money for music albums, perfumes, fingernail polish, and makeup.

I rarely saw my parents drink alcohol, and many nights our parents had company, playing cards. Our coffeepot was always on for an abundance of unexpected, welcomed friends. Our home was the teen hangout, and every friend we four kids had found my parents to be the coolest of cool.

Dad managed to kick the smoking habit years ago, and Mom and Dad started buying four-door cars—used cars, of course. With four kids, and dentist bills that never stopped, the luxury of purchasing a brand-new car would not come until years later.

20
Strength

My tough mornings continued on through my chemo treatments. It seemed that my ritual of getting up, brewing my coffee, and starting a load of laundry had additional chores added. Taking medicine, a new experience for me because of years of being healthy, was added to my list.

My other morning ritual was assisting Katie out the door for school. If I got up without crying, it was unusual. I still wonder why my mornings were the toughest and I was the most emotional. Poor Katie had to endure my tears. Being a teenager with schoolwork, sports gear, and being punctual out the door was enough for a child. She was dealing with a weak mother, and I was ashamed.

I fought each morning to get up and get moving. One day she was walking out the door as I forced myself out of bed. She looked at me inquisitively, wondering why I was crying again.

"Mom, why? Not again," she ordered me.

"Katie, don't yell at me. Stop being mouthy to me. Mornings are hard. I can't help it. I am sorry," I growled to her. "This is not always about you. I am having a tough time. And furthermore, I am crying today because I didn't get up to see you off, and now you have to go."

"Mom, but I do have to go … now," she said, and *slam* went the door.

I sat down, hung my head, and cried. The phone rang. It was Katie on her cell phone.

"Mom, I am sorry. And it is OK if you don't get up with me. I just had to go. I love you. But you do need to think positive from now on."

Depending on my work schedule, and where my destination would be for applying CPM units to patients at the many hospitals, I always found time to check my e-mails before work.

Then, invariably the tears would begin again. No matter the day, I was always greeted with inspirational, thinking-of-you messages from my friends and family via e-mail. Their thoughts of me were heartwarming, but yet emotional for me.

Many sent me the online e-cards, and the music and the kind words as I scrolled to read brought me to sobs at times. But somehow they helped me feel stronger, erased the tears, and gave me comfort to move on to beat this unknown future. Would I grow old and see my grandchildren grow up? Allie continued to need me and love me. Katie was my shining star. Amber needed to be the adult I knew she was capable of being. Ryan was so smart. I wanted to see him apply himself and become a successful man. He was ever so handsome.

The thought of keeping my breast worried me so. That thought never left me. My arm continued to hurt from the four-node dissection that was done. I worried and prayed big thanks for keeping my many other lymph nodes. I began ball-squeezing exercises to strengthen my arm.

Amazing get-well wishes arrived in the mail daily. Flowers and gifts came. The surprises never stopped. Friends dropped me notes and called me. A food chain was set up, thanks to my dear friend, Claire. I tried desperately to always write thank-you notes and to reply back to each friend on e-mail. I worked to make each a personal note and not turn them into group e-mails. (I did do this to give updates on my health and doctor information.)

My dear, loyal friends flourished from one continent to another: Godi in Germany, Shell, my Aussie mate, in Australia, Mackie and Mike in South Carolina, Tom and Rudy in Chicago, Carolyn in California, Lois in New York, Patti in Georgia, Ben in Texas,

Derold, my publisher, in Georgia, and Jess in Jamaica. The list goes on—all my Ohio friends, and even Nam, my Vietnamese friend, who now is a citizen living in Colorado.

I remember when we first hooked into the Internet. I did the responsible thing and put parental blocks on the computer to protect the three kids. Somehow, Katie had posted something somewhere on the Net about loving old coins. Her grandpa, who has collected coins for years, must have triggered this interest with her.

I noticed that she was communicating on the Net with a man who collected coins. I was leery and worried, and I began to watch this unknown, mysterious friendship evolve.

Nam, a kind, innocent man with a heart of gold, started mailing coins to Katie from Colorado. He and his fiancée and family had lived the typical deprived, dictated life in Vietnam. Nam, like many, had left his country to better his life and to protect what remained of his family. He was a lonely man, waiting for the arrival of his fiancée. The paperwork to get her to the States took months.

Today, five years later, Yen is here with him, and they have their first child and live a good life in our country. The coins still come periodically in the mail for Katie, and Nam and I share pictures of Justin, his son, and never lose touch. Their wedding pictures were shared over the Net with my family, and I continue to watch Justin grow before my eyes with the touch of a downloaded picture. Nam cried when I sent him the coverage of Katie making the news here with her football success. Computers! How easy and convenient.

We all talk of meeting someday. Our voices have been heard on the phone. Nam, who writes and speaks great English, is a true friend. "Connie, slow down, slow down. Talk too fast," he tells me when he calls us. And of course, I send Justin anything I can find at stores that have Volkswagens on them. His infant Bug socks came from me, and I smiled as I dropped them in the mail.

I met someone on the Net and loved the writer's on line group. Would I leave home for a man I had never made eye contact with? Did I go into chat rooms, cyber all night with strange men? Did I gamble on the Net? My poor mom was convinced I was up to no good on the Net. She had watched too many talk shows. I tried to convince her that the Internet was full of wonderful resources. My writing career had opened new doors for me on the Internet.

I met Patti in a chat room. Patti, my Southern belle friend whom I adore to this day, would always be there for me no matter the miles. Curiosity had gotten me when I first signed on to the Internet. News Paradigms was the name of this room. We called it NP. It was a blast. And as the novelty of chat rooms wore off, I continued special relationships with many people. Innocent fun, interesting conversations, and special friendships developed. I hold tight to all of them, five years later.

Patti, from Woodstock, Georgia, a registered nurse and a mom to three children about the ages of my children, became my best friend in NP. We talked on the phone regularly and sent each other special-occasion cards and just-for-the-heck-of-it cards.

On Christmas of 2001, I opened my Christmas present. Inside was a round-trip ticket to Atlanta, Georgia. David and Patti had planned my surprise trip. I would fly out immediately after Christmas to hug my friend whom I had never made eye contact with. I cried tears of joy.

Weekly, I receive cards, magazine clippings, pictures, and special notes from her. "I'm going to get in that damn book or else," she would write. "Just because I am far away, I want to be in the book."

As I read this recently on a note from her, I had to laugh. She was full of humor.

The friendships I have built over a forty-eight-year span are amazing to me. My love of people paid of in high school and I value each friend I have ever made.

To this day, Mom remembers heartwarming memories and how I stood up for kids who were different in looks or personalities. I always worked hard to give them comfort and let them know they had a friend in me. I was quite athletic, and Vickie, a girl who was my stiffest competition in gym class through junior high, was also my friend. The gym teacher would purposely split her and me up for dodge ball. We were the captains. I recall always picking the less fortunate, not caring if it weakened our team. I remember seeing many breathe a sigh of relief because they were not the last one picked.

Boys chased me and took turns having me for a girlfriend in those early, innocent grade- school days. Life was good, my memories of school were wonderful, and I loved making new friends and keeping them for always. Summer days, putting Sun-In on my hair at the public swimming pool, and even hanging out with my sisters and brother as we all began to drive, date, and share friends are also warm memories.

I was the tomboy who loved being with my brother and hanging tough with him in all the summer activities we did. The neighborhood boys would organize various ball games from football to dodge ball, baseball, or basketball. It didn't matter—we played for hours until sweat bubbles formed, and we would be exhausted. Then we'd jump on our bikes and head home, crossing the big bridge over the Scioto River and sometimes stopping to wade in the river before going home.

Scioto River! What memories. I recall the day in about 1968 when the bridge was rebuilt. We felt imprisoned. We could not reach the other side to get to our friends.

Wayne and I would ride our bikes to where the bridge once was, and watch the process as it was being rebuilt. We'd sit on the other side, dangling on huge steel beams, looking across and down to the deep river. We'd wait and watch for our neighborhood friends to come riding by, in hopes they didn't forget us. Sure enough, they would park their bikes and sit on the beams across the way as we threw stones and talked from one side to the other.

We worked hard that summer to socialize and keep in touch with our friends.

I think that was the same summer that Dad helped to decrease our boredom and improvise cheap entertainment. After all, we had only each other until the bridge was completed.

My dad grew up a poor boy. Toys bought from a store were rare. Entertainment was plentiful for these seven siblings, growing up on a farm. But being poor has advantages. They learned to appreciate and respect personal items and let the imagination fly.

In the case of these poor, happy siblings, their minds expanded and they became masters with their hands and minds. Nothing was thrown away until numerous repairs had been made and it was impossible to fix it again.

Their knives whittled. Their mechanical skills and the *jimmy-rig* kept automobiles running. A simple thing like a button could keep them out of trouble and busy, playing. Hide the button was the name of this simple game. The button was also placed on a shoestring, and with the right touch and talent, you could spin it like a top.

They made little wooden boats with their knives. They could float and race and were perfect for the Scioto River, our same river of fun. Winter brought skating without skates, and summer was for wading, swimming, and fishing.

The kites were the best original invention these siblings made. They soared in the sky for hours and went up as easily as a summer breeze could carry them. The entire kite was made from recycled items in the house. Rags, newspaper, and string that were collected and knotted to extend for miles were used to produce a kite. Dad stole Grandma's curtain rods for framing the kite. After numerous scoldings, he found sticks from trees for framing the kites.

Horses were a luxury, so they were never given the privilege of having one. They rode the pigs, cows, and even the mean old goat named Billy. He was mean as a snake because these boys tried to turn him into a horse.

As corn-picking season approached, Dad picked corn by hand as he searched for mice to capture. He'd take the mice home, terrorize Grandma with them, and produce a new toy.

With a small matchbox, string, and scrap material he snitched from his mom's stash for quilts, he made a harness and hitched it to his new pet mouse.

All these creative toys and entertainment were handed down to my siblings and me. Dad continues to make the best kites, and we were privileged to grow up on the same river with those same homemade toys.

Although we were not nearly so poor and were privileged to have store-bought toys, we were always fascinated with his treasures.

The game he taught us was the purse trick. We gave it this official name and just to mention playing the purse trick would excite us and keep us entertained for hours that summer.

All we needed was an old purse, string, and nerves of steel. The little bridge south of the big bridge served as our hideout. Dad gave us the instructions, and off to the bridge we ran, purse and string in hand. It was to our advantage to have Dad on the roof on this particular day. After all, we were inexperienced and amateurs.

Dad can whistle louder than anyone I know. It used to irritate me because I could never whistle like him. I would try placing my tongue everywhere possible around, over, and between my teeth, and I could never whistle.

As he hammered away on the new shingles, he would watch for cars to come up over the hill. He would produce his famous whistle, and we would prepare for the battle of the purse. We soon had down to a science how many seconds we had to prepare when he whistled.

There are rules, goals, and a winner in this game. The winners would be us. The goal was to not be caught or piss our pants. The rule was to convince and trick these automobile drivers into thinking they were the winners. In addition, of course the ultimate best part was making people think their minds were playing tricks on them.

Let the game begin! We four siblings tied the purse to a string. Dad would whistle when he saw a car coming down the hill north of us, and we would throw the purse out just the right distance. We would scamper rapidly under the bridge to hide as if we were turtles hiding in our shells.

We would listen, ever straining our ears, and be as quiet as mice (Mom would have been shocked at the silence of her four children). We would hear the car drive over the bridge and listen for brakes. That was the fun part that brought the adrenaline rush. When we heard brakes, we knew we had found a sucker.

As the car was backing up, we silly, ornery children were pulling the purse in. It is amazing how a person backing up a car loses his sense of direction and visibility. With a slight, slow tug on the string, the purse followed us down the ravine and into the tunnel.

The amazement was in realizing that the drivers concentrated more on their skills of backing up and would not see the purse vanish.

It was hilarious when we would hear them backing up. The whine of reverse seemed to go forever. We were sure they had lost their *plum minds*. They would back up and back up, and we would think they might back up all the way back to town.

The sounds and listening and fears were such excitement. We would listen and hide. We would be so silent that moisture dripping off the tunnel was audible as it dripped near our heads. Cars would back up, go forward, and back up again. Some people got out of their cars and walked. I remember many walking back and forth, kicking the gravel or sliding their shoe over the grass along the ditch. We could hear their voices and count their steps. Some would be so discouraged, and their bubble would burst because their possible fortune was a figment of their imagination (or so they thought).

"Now, Tom, I know I saw a purse! It was about right here!"

"I KNOW I saw a purse!"

"It was black and about this big."

"We have to find it! It might be loaded with money."

"Margaret, get in the car. There is not a damn purse. You weren't seeing ANYTHING."

"Listen, do you hear something?" we'd hear a victim ask. We would hold our breath, trying to keep our laughter quiet.

These were a few of the many comments we could hear as we sat in the tunnel, under the bridge. Tina always had to tinkle. She was the baby, and the excitement would overwhelm her. Wayne was the brave brother who would keep us in tow as we were about to be busted. We expected him to protect the three of us!

Cathy always behaved and kept her composure, but we feared that her allergies would surface and she would get one of her many summer sneezing spells. I would whisper silly things to try to get Tina to pee and to make Wayne mad at Cathy for getting us caught by the purse-seekers. He never got mad at Cathy—ever!

The reality of it, though, was that we all almost peed down our legs, and our hearts raced. We would silently crawl further away into the tunnel as the feet and voices got closer. Sometimes from fear of a masculine, strong voice overhead, we would slither all the way across the road, through the tunnel on the other side.

"Shhhhh!" We all in unison would look at one another and say, "Shhhh, shhhh!" The more we tried to be quiet, the more we would hold our mouths to prevent our giggles. Our faces grew red; our stomachs were ever so tight in fear of breathing loudly. We prayed for them to walk away.

Once we heard a man tell someone who was with him, "C'mon, let's go. It's those bratty kids who live up on the hill."

We fooled the majority of our victims. We no longer needed Dad on the roof after we learned the purse trick and became experienced.

We would shake up our summer days and add some color. We could not wait for Mom to buy a new purse so we would get her old one for our victims.

Sometimes we would stuff the purse with newspapers to give it a rich look.

There were times when we were playing and Dad would drive by us, heading home from work. We knew it was Dad because he would see the purse and honk. Then we knew it was chow time.

We are all grown now and with children of our own. YES! They love to go "out home," and of course they do not play Monopoly at Grandma and Grandpa's. They prefer Grandpa's kites and love this simple game, too.

The same bridge and tunnel are there, and the purse is a little more stylish now as we approach the third generation. However, a sucker is still a sucker!

I truly would love to know why some of the losers would get angry. They would swear, kick gravel, and slam their car doors. It was not their lost money or purse, anyway.

We did survive that summer without the big bridge, having just the little bridge and a funny dad to give us fond memories. And what we lacked in money and fancy material things, Mom and Dad made up in hugs, kisses, and even old hand-me-down purses.

21
True Friends And Allie

I started hanging my get-well cards on the kitchen walls, over the fireplace mantel, and on other walls. I began to run out of room, but they were very important for me to see. The responses warmed me and began healing me mentally for my tough task at hand in my treatments to come. I had so *many* who loved me, and I needed to fight hard.

The telephone rang constantly. I will never forget some of my funny phone conversations. At times, I was overwhelmed. When I had an appointment, and would arrive home, the answering machine would beep, beep, and beep with message after message. I began writing names down to return calls. My worries were their worries, and they deserved eased minds also.

Frank called. Frank, my friend and neighbor since first grade. We rode the same bus and changed schools as the elementary consolidated, moving us to another school for second grade. We graduated high school together and were in many classes together. He was so damn smart—book smart—and he loved science class. I hated it. He challenged Mr. Sheets, our science teacher. Frank harassed him behind his back and never got caught.

Ya know, they say that gay friends make the best friends. Frank was mine, and to this day he is important to me. Shoot, I think I knew he was gay before he knew he was. I didn't care. He was kind, funny, and a loyal, true-blue buddy.

Over the years, Frank and I had many serious conversations. He confessed to me one night that he was gay.

"Nooooo," I said. "No damn way," I said as I roared with laughter. "Do you honestly think I didn't know, or I care? I love you. Who the hell cares?"

After that confession, he opened up to me about his personal life, and like anyone, he wanted a companion. I gave him advice, listened to his heartaches, and thought positive for him when he was in a new relationship.

He would whisper in my ear as he kissed my cheek, "If I wasn't gay, I would ask you out, you hot thing, you."

"Well, I am married; love ya, but no, no," I would say as we laughed more.

And of course, Frank or any of my numerous male friends never threatened David. Heterosexual or gay, my life was full of many male companions.

As we talked on the phone that night, and I heard the concern in his voice about my breast cancer, I rambled on. I was in the upbeat mood; he was sad for me. Our roles reversed. I found myself comforting him and reassuring him that I would be OK.

"I've been thinking about this, Connie. I have a nipple. I don't need it. If I could donate it to you, I would."

"Frank," I said with a big, exaggerated whine. "I don't want a hairy nipple. I have enough shit to shave."

"But, Connie ... maybe they can give you some hormone stuff, maybe keep the hair from growing," he said with a chuckle.

"Knowing my luck, I would take that hormonal crap, and I would grow a dick," I forewarned him.

"Honey, if you grow a dick, you are going out with me," he said. We laughed, and I laughed until I cried, holding my full bladder.

"Shit, Frank, I just pissed my pants."

My cousin Karen called. She had bumped into my mom at the bank. Mom was worried about me. My brother's life had spiraled downhill also. His marriage of twenty-seven years had finally collapsed. Amen to that, but the divorce would turn out to be an ugly, expensive battle for him. He did not deserve such manipulations and evilness. He'd given her and his three daughters everything and was a wonderful father. The girls were being poisoned with lies, and it affected the entire family. Wayne was devastated.

And as always, my sixth sense had kicked in. I knew twenty-seven years ago that he had married the wrong woman. When the marriage started crumbling, we realized that it had ripped him of self-esteem, and he truly lived with mental abuse like no other I have known. His spirit was broken.

He confided in me and it brought us closer than I ever knew could be possible, because of the strong bond we had always had. My brother is a man any woman would be thrilled to have as a partner. A hard working man, he had built a lot financially, money made alone from turning wrenches and from a need to find happiness somewhere, he worked long hours to feel useful and needed.

And as Wayne said to me one night on the phone, as we talked almost daily, "Connie, I can rebuild, I can get through this. I can do this. I have my health. You can rebuild, too."

Karen had called me because she had a mastectomy just a year prior to my diagnosis. We compared notes, and I had numerous questions for this soldier of the breast cancer war.

"OK, Karen, tell me everything you can. If I have to have my breast taken off, how do they reconstruct? I have numerous pamphlets that the doctor gave me, but ..."

I walked over to empty the cat litter box as I cradled the phone on my shoulder.

"I am a better, stronger person from this, Connie. You can be too," she said as she reassured me.

"Do you have a nipple? I don't want to lose my nipple. I know this sounds crazy, but I like my nipples. They are sensitive; they like sex. I fear losing it, Karen."

"Well, it is true. They will make you a nipple and it won't have sensation," she said.

"What is your nipple made of, Karen? Can I see it? You show me, and I will show you my lumpectomy. Shit, we grew up together on the Scioto River. It is not like we can't compare."

"Connie, I would show you, but mine sprung a leak. I'm going in January to get it fixed," she said seriously, but with so much humor in her voice. "I will show you when it is repaired. Jamie loves it. She said it is beautiful and was impressed when I first got the reconstruction."

"Amazing, I just can't fathom how these plastic surgeons can work such wonders," I replied.

"In answer to your question, they took skin from under my arm and made me a nipple."

"Skin under your arm," I asked loudly. "What the hell, don't tell me you have to shave your nipple? I just had this conversation with Frank, our old high school friend, who offered to donate me his."

"Oh, you goofball," she said. "They don't take the skin that high up under your arm."

"Ok, this sounds dumb. But do they offer you a choice. Hard nipple or soft nipple?"

"Well, they didn't ask me my choice, but mine is hard," Karen said.

"Whew, good," I said. "I am so damn cold all the time, so my nipple should be made to look hard to match the other. I also am still such a horny wench, and if it can't feel hard from arousal, at least it can pretend it is."

"You will never change, Connie. You crack me up."

These special people in my life don't change much either and are loyal.

My friends and family all want to help. "Call me anytime, if you need anything." I used to think people said this just because they didn't know what else to say. "Call me anytime, day or night, if you can't sleep. I will talk to you; just call, Connie." I thought they just felt sorry for me.

"I am a phone call away."

"You have done so much for so many; it is your turn now. Call me."

"I am two doors down. You are the best in a neighbor."

So I thought about all these zillion offers made to me. I called Marcy, two doors down. She had e-mailed me, offering to help however she could. Her words: "And I will do anything, absolutely anything."

After we talked awhile about my illness—and yes, it seems this is the hot topic of conversation, no matter how one tries to steer away from it—I just blurted it out. "Marcy, remember at the block party last summer when we were comparing notes about all the work you had done on your rooms? All that wallpapering, sponge painting, and stripping of those old floors?"

"Connie, I am not stripping that wallpaper off your living room," she said as I visualized her throwing her head up with her hearty laugh.

"Shit-fiddle-de-damn," I said. And we just laughed and laughed. I don't even know how to sneak in a little manipulation. I know if I had hung out more with my ex-sister-in-law, I might have learned this trait.

Then there's my sister, Tina. She is the master of a clean house. I don't want to use that phrase, *Her floors are so clean, you could eat off of them.* But it is true, so true.

And what is really nuts about this is that she tackles housework like a woman tackles a sale at a mall. She loves it! She parties with it. She is like the Energizer Bunny. She rarely comes up for a breath, except to bend back over to rinse out her cleaning rag and to make eye contact briefly as she talks and cleans, talks and cleans.

I know that in my months of treatment, I could have had my house spring-cleaned, each room, in the winter, spring, and summer. She offered and I declined.

Silly me! Why didn't I take advantage of her? She loves this stuff, and it would have all been done from her heart. A labor of love!

Tammy offered to give me a foot massage and paint my toenails. She had gone to manicure school and loved my toes and me. She just hated manicure work, but still had all the loot to do manicures and pedicures.

Shirley, my high school friend, brought us lasagna. Shirley, the master of lasagna, had taught me years ago how to make homemade lasagna and how to ride a unicycle. Marcia brought us a roast.

De, my hairstylist friend, loves to cut hair and works in a very nice, upscale hair salon. She wanted to cut my hair whenever I wanted to shorten it in preparation for my hair loss. She wanted to fix it however I wanted. Dye it, shape it, layer it, weave it, and FREE!

I was her guinea pig while she was in hair school a couple of years ago. I would make appointments and go up to her cosmetology school when she was in clinical learning how to cut hair. Boy, what a brave girl I was. I think I was her first pedicure, manicure, haircut, hair dye, and makeup application.

"I'm putting my life in your hands, De. You know how a woman loves her hair. Don't fuck it up," I'd say, as she was putting the big apron on me. The students next to us at the other school chairs would just look at us and laugh.

"This is Connie, a good friend, the crazy one I told you all about," she would say.

"Mess my hair up, De, and I am going to drop the dime to all these girls about you and what you did that time when we were…"

"Shut up, Connie."

So I walked out of hairstylist school always looking chic and being frugal, pleased with a new free *do* that looked sensational.

About two weekends after I had come to terms with having cancer, I was having one of my many low days. De had dropped me many pick-me-up notes in the snail mail. She didn't want to call me. She feared bothering me and assumed I was bogged down with phone calls. I was, and I was so tired of talking about it. De was originally a dear friend to my sister Cathy, and through Cathy, the three of us had formed a mutual close friendship that has lasted for about fifteen years. Cathy had talked a lot to De, and De was just a mess. She worried so about me.

I picked up the phone to call her. I gave her all the updated information about my diagnosis and how I felt. She became silent on the phone. I heard her trying to talk. De wanted to be brave, strong, and optimistic, because that is De's nature.

"Connie, your boob is just your boob. Do you know how many of us can't live without you? It is about you. We all love you soooo very much. I am so worried because I know how you feel about your looks. You have so many other beautiful traits, and so much more to offer. We need you around."

"I know, De. And I need you guys, too." And we cried that quiet Sunday afternoon on the phone without many more words spoken. I listened to her blow her nose, and she heard me blow mine too. Time seemed to stand still as we cried into the phone.

"De?"

"Yeah?" she replied.

"You know how you always want to change my hairstyle? Remember how mad I would get toward you because you insisted I go short? You were always pissing me off, wanting me to go darker, cut this, do that."

We laughed, recalling all these suggestions she had made in the past. I stood firm and would never let her do with me as she pleased.

I remember the day she had finished school and was an official hairstylist. She was excited about her new job and building up her clientele.

"Now, De ... let me give you some advice," I said. She looked at me and rolled those big hazel eyes. I heard her sigh. De, knowing my outspokenness, knows that when I voice an opinion, it is constructive, bold, and maybe not even something she wished to hear. She would listen, though. She knew.

"When you start getting clients, you need to learn to cut their hair how they want. NOT how you want. You only suggest a new hairstyle IF they ask for it. You tend to be a little bossy. They want their look, and not yours. Those little old ladies with the blue cast hair who have worn this hairstyle for fifty years will not want a new De look."

"Anything else?" she asked.

"Yeah. Talk to those little old people. Make them feel special. They are special and even when we are all old, blue haired women, our hair makes us feel pretty. Make them pretty, De. You are going to be good at this."

I couldn't wait for our annual summer weekend of fun at Put-in-Bay, a party island up north of us. We were always ready to party like rock stars.

After we stopped crying that day on the phone, I said, "I was wondering if you want to cut my hair, De. I decided that maybe if I cut it short, the transition won't be so emotionally upsetting to me when my hair starts falling out."

"But, Connie, how do you know it will fall out? Maybe it won't. Why not wait awhile and see?"

"De! Listen to yourself. For two years, you have wanted me to go short. It is going to fall out. With the kind of chemo they give to breast cancer patients, it will! You have told me over and over how good I will look with short hair. Let's do it; let's rumble, Mama! Don't let me change my mind."

And it was that very Sunday when she dropped everything for me and we met at the shop. She unlocked the door and turned the heat up; on came the music, and great conversation and laughs began as the hair started hittin' the floor.

We had even called Cathy, who also dropped everything so she could come to the hair party and witness my hair being transformed from an I-think-I-am-a-beauty-queen to a my-God-what-in-the-hell-was-I-thinking look.

And it was a fabulous new look. And free, just like our free-spirited, wonderful friendship. Over the next month, as I got to hold on to this new hairdo, I wondered if people were truly sincere. I think they were. I would humbly smile, thank people for all their compliments on my new look, and wonder if they were saying positive things because I was sick. My favorite comment was, "Connie, I swear. You look ten years younger. That cut is soooo cute." I heard this over and over. I hoped it was true.

I believed them, hook, line, and sinker. I was feeling younger with new sassy hair cut. Of course, I had to make comments back. I almost always get in the last word, and they all know this.

"Well, enjoy it now. Give me about three weeks, and then tell me how young I look. Enjoy it now, baby."

Friends offered to come over and get the cobwebs off the cathedral ceilings. Some offered to go to the grocery store for me.

The basketball team wanted to scratch my name off the list on my supply day to provide food for the basketball team's away games. People wanted to assist me in walking, or climbing the steps at the gymnasium. Now this part was driving me a little insane. I had always been so physically fit, limber, and active.

Gifts were placed in my hands everywhere I went. A special quilt was made for me by De. The blanket material screamed my name, according to De. Tie-dyed, with numerous colors splattered throughout the material.

Chemo lab was cold. They kept the temperature down to prevent germs from flying. Our immune system was down, and the chemo patients froze, but the importance was those darn germs and killing them.

I, being so cold-blooded, learned to take along my travel bag, compliments of Cocoa Beach, Florida, which was literally a warm memory. I would take my De blankie with me and wrap up for my IV cocktail. De made a corner pocket in it and tucked a cross in it that was given to her by her mother, who had traveled to Bethlehem years before to get it, and De wanted me to have it. Today it still rests in my tie-dyed blanket pocket for security, faith, and hope.

One night, I sat down at Katie's basketball game. As I had walked to my seat, I could feel eyes on me. A basketball mom came over to me and handed me a wrapped gift. At the same time, my sister Tina handed me cinnamon licorice.

I had told Tina I could never find cinnamon licorice. She was on a mission and found it just for me. It was an offering out of love.

I opened the gift from the mom, who by the way has a boob job and is a sensational, "built like a brick shithouse" woman in her forties. "I saw this in the Avon book and thought of you," she said as I opened it. The game was about to begin. The girls were in a huddle with the coach, directly in front of me.

I saw Katie glance up as I was opening the gift. I am sure she was thinking, *My God, she is crying again. Now why.* Her coach was talking to the team, a last-minute chant of encouragement. She watched me break down and cry as I looked at the gift. It was the breast cancer Christmas ornament for 2004 with the beautiful pink bow on the front. My hope, my ornament, and my new friend had made me cry welcome, healthy tears. As I hugged her, I heard the referee's whistle.

Katie had gotten the tip ball, and the game began as I chewed my licorice and held my gift box on my lap.

I know people look and stare for various reasons. They care, they are curious, and they wonder about my hair. I rag on about this hair thing so much. I worried for days and weeks prior. I watched my hair start to die on week two after my first chemo. I caught myself pulling on it to examine my hand for hair loss. It was still snug to the roots. But it was dying. It was lifeless, and no matter how much hair gel, conditioner, and attention I gave it, it would droop. The texture changed. My soft hair had plunged to defeat. My heart ached, and when I touched it, the sensation on my fingertips saddened me.

Then my once-strong immune system that had hauled in every kind of germ via emergency squad took a downward plunge. Amber and Allie stopped over for a visit. The little knock-knock of Allie's little fist on the door, "It's me, Grammy, Papa!" is a happy welcome that always sends laughter through the house.

Amber had a cold and I figured I'd catch it.

The sores I heard about from a cancer survivor began to form in my mouth. She told me that the chemo might bring me these nasty souvenirs. And then my veins started swelling and discoloring, and they hurt.

Allie saw my wig, awaiting use. "Grammy, what is THIS?" She lifted it out of the bag. I had protected her, put off telling this four-year-old that Grammy was sick and that my appearance might change. It was time.

"Allie," I said as I held my hand out to put the wig on and show her that I would still be Grammy. "Grammy has to take a special medicine. I am a little sick." She looked at me with immediate concern. "But, I will be all right. It's just that this medicine will make my hair fall out. It will grow back, though, and the medicine will help Grammy."

She ran to my arms with an immediate release of tears. "Grammy, oh Grammy, does this mean you won't be my grammy?

Will you be a boy?" She wrung her hands together in a worrisome manner.

"Allie honey, noooooo. I will always be your grammy. I might look a little different, but I will never be a boy. I will be the same ole Grammy. Papa is bald because he wants to be, and he IS a boy. You see him shave his head." She nodded yes. "I will let my hair grow back when it wants to grow. I will be OK ... OK?"

"But, Grammy, when will it fall down?" I grinned at her use of the word *down* instead of *out.*

"Grammy," she said as she started to cry again. Just as I thought our conversation had reassured her, this innocent child's mind traveled more. "I take vitamins at my mommy's house. Will my hair fall down? Will I have to get a wig?"

I picked her up, hugged her tight, kissed her cheek, smelled her beautiful soft, always-so-good-smelling skin, and said, "Allie, you take those vitamins. Your hair will not fall out."

She ran off to play ... reassured.

22
The Flasher With A Cause

"Connie, this is NOT about your vanity," my sister Cathy said one day as she grabbed the door knob, walking out as she slammed the door. She was in tears. She had had enough of my mood swings and my let's-feel-sorry-for-Connie days.

She was right; I was wrong. But my personal hygiene and too much vanity had been with me for years. My attempts as I grew older each year made my efforts of personal maintenance a tough assignment for a woman who was not enjoying the aging process.

I never left the house without makeup. Occasionally, I would run down to the convenience store without makeup, for an important item. But I never went in without sunglasses on to hide my bags. I rarely walked to the mailbox without makeup on. My nails were always polished and my hair clean and my outfits matched. And I never EVER went without a bra, except when having sex.

As a teen, I noticed girls going braless. I found it gross and a true displeasure as they bounced. And I also recalled information from my ob/gyn: "Connie, if you don't want to sag, never go without a bra. Now that you are pregnant, wear a bra, day and night."

And so ... I did. I found bras comforting. My boobs didn't stick together on those sticky summer nights before we could afford central air-conditioning. And I stayed perky. I was proud, and I flaunted my nice set. I had great cleavage, and I loved to dress with sexuality. I did not dress trashy. OK, maybe once. Put-in-Bay Island, Ohio, vacation homes of the party hound dogs, was appropriate for any dress attire. There were no rules.

Most people like to be looked at in a pleasurable way. Some may not admit it. I confess! I have enjoyed men whistling as I walk by, and I love the toot of a semi as it passes me on the interstate. If a woman shows cleavage, the man rarely notices much more about her attire. He has trouble making eye contact, and his eyes invariably drop down to her chest. And what is it about blonde hair? I have dyed my hair brown and was born blonde. With age, I am no longer blonde. Men respond more often when I am blonde. I don't NEED their attention. I just enjoy observing their behavior.

My family would be mortified if they ever knew what I did once on a long, boring trip out of town. I was traveling alone. Katie had left ahead of me with her travel softball team. David was working and was unable to go to the softball tournament.

I was driving for miles up an interstate—70 West. I remember that it was a hot, humid summer morning. Two men in a construction-type pickup truck were toying with me. Their truck looked old and overused, and rattled as they drove up the highway. The truck was loaded down with various tools and equipment.

They would zip in and out of lanes to follow me. I would speed up, and they would follow suit. I'd slow down; they would creep up beside me, waiting for me to notice them. My peripheral vision was good, and I would see them driving beside me. I looked over, smiled, and threw it up to third gear, zooming ahead. (I will never drive an automatic. Sifting gears is just too much fun.)

The play became a little more aggressive. Not dangerous, but they flirted more as they winked, honked, and motioned me to pull over. My mama and daddio did not raise a heathen or a stupid girl. I was not pulling over.

The next dare was more than I could ignore. The one guy flipped his T-shirt up and showed me his breast. His eyes said, "C'mon. I showed you mine. You show me yours."

He pointed and hollered.

Without even one second of hesitation, I lifted my tank top. In one upward jerk, I had pulled my bra and tank top up, flashing my left breast as they rode beside me in the pass-and-get-the-hell-over lane.

As my top was heading back down to cover me, I saw my exit. I hit that exit without a moment's notice. As I looked over my left shoulder, I saw that their heads were tipped back and they were laughing and honking as far as I could hear.

My first thought was, *I am a wicked wench. My mother would be ashamed. David would kill me and leave me to rot in hell if he knew.*

And as quickly as those thoughts left me, I smiled. I gave two hard-working guys heading to work something to smile and talk about on that hot, humid day. And I also realized that I had put too many EKG patches on chests while hooking patients up to monitors. I have seen so many nude bodies over the years that it caused my comfort level with the human body to be very comfortable.

In my breast cancer episode, as doctors probed, touched, cut, and checked my breast, I thought of that left-breast flash. My conscience wondered if God was punishing me for my temporary act of sleaziness.

God made me high-spirited. Mom taught me to not be ashamed of my body.

At forty-eight, I felt much younger. I always liked to boast to the kids that I could still do the splits. When Katie was younger, she would come home with friends, pop in the door, and many times introduce me to a new friend. "And my mom is old, and she can still do the splits. Show 'em, Mom. Just show them," she'd say as she pointed for me to hit the floor.

Everyone wanted to take me to lunch, take me to a movie, go have a drink, or invite me over for dinner. My social calendar was filling up, and it was helping me to deal with life, family, and friends. Amazing.

23
Christmas Survivor-buff Style

I knew Christmas might be tough. My brother Wayne and I were going through major changes in our lives. Our family was worried and prayed for us daily.

Wayne's vicious ex-wife worked harder to turn the three kids against Wayne than she had ever worked on their marriage. We only hoped that someday they would remember and recall the warm memories with their dad, and realize that the divorce didn't have to be so traumatizing.

My parents had suffered also. They had lost three granddaughters, to whom they had always given their unconditional love. It was painful, but they could only hope, as Wayne did, that time and maturing would help the girls to see the truth and come back to all of us. It would take therapy for the damage that had been done to help these girls.

Wayne walked in on Christmas Eve at our parents' home, alone for the first time in twenty-seven years. It was a tough holiday for him, and he missed his children horribly. His mood was hard to read because of the years when he had been so private and always choosing to try to solve his own problems. We knew ... he was feeling empty.

His divorce has cost him a fortune. The dissolved marriage had cost him more than the value of the money and starting over. His spirit and hope for a peaceful future felt heavy-hearted. For all the sacrificed years of unhappiness and reasons for staying in such an abusive marriage, he wished for peace of mind and a happy new chapter. We all did.

Allie, being only four, must have sensed emptiness in her great uncle Wayne. Was that possible? She climbed up onto his lap. I saw his welcome smile as he helped her up to his lap. With his kind heart and giving nature, all his nieces and nephews love him. Then Bryce, his other nephew, climbed up to his other knee.

The typical, traditional meal was eaten with many laughs and good conversations everywhere. We mingled as usual, with everyone always telling a story, chairs shuffling, fresh coffee poured, and the little ones wanting to know, "When can we open our presents?"

The rules had changed for our gift exchanging. There was to be no excessive gift buying. *Yahoo,* was my thought. I am not a shopper, and Christmas has never been my favorite holiday. I find it to be a command performance, and costly to the point of causing financial burdens. There truly is a reason for the season, and it is not about excessive spending. Thanksgiving is my favorite. Good cooking, family, and inexpensive fun.

Wayne's happiness and my good health were what he and I wished for. We held each other up, giving each other support so many times through our temporary turmoil. These were the gifts Wayne and I wished for that no money could buy. They could be wrapped in hope without a dime spent.

Dad's health was always a worry for all of us. Good health for him and Mom to be with us for years to come is worth more than gifts. Money couldn't buy this either.

But with all the family love and silliness we all share, we knew we could kick in another memorable, fun holiday for a family minus three granddaughters.

We decided that each would bring a gift, and we would each choose a number as the presents were all stacked, separated by genders. Shelley, my niece, was in charge, and the rules were being announced.

"But what about Jeb and Lisa? Who has their numbers, since they had to leave to go to their in-laws'?" someone asked.

With her hand up in authority, Shell said, "Hey, too bad, they get whatever is left over on the table. They left!"

The advantage was to get the higher number. The numbers were called out in order. The first person had the disadvantage. If she or he got a really wonderful gift, chances are that it would be stolen by another family member. That next person could opt to go take an unopened mystery gift or steal the gift that was opened.

Of course, we all brought gifts for the little ones; after all it is about the birth of Christ, and a holiday for children. Besides, who would want to snatch a gift out of a child's hand to make them cry? The tree would fall as a fight broke out with kids rolling on the floor, holding on to gifts for dear life as they screamed and cried, parents defending or maybe trying to rip it out of their little hands. Call that worse than the Christmas vacation movie.

Cathy had number one to draw. Not great. She had to hope that she chose a great gift and, if she did, she had the worry of someone stealing it. We could hide the gifts in hopes that when someone else's number was drawn; they'd be distracted and not steal the good gift.

Some of the family spent much time thinking as they shopped for this gift exchange. Many purposely brought gifts they knew many would want. The incentive to watch grown adults fight over, negotiate, or plot for a tradeoff was fun. Lottery tickets, Cleveland Browns apparel, or Ohio State shirts were popular. We wondered if they would be ripped as people snatched them as the prior owner rebelled, holding tightly and yelling.

The little ones seemed to have reversed roles, playing like mature adults, quietly and happily, with their new toys.

Hiding is cheating, but one had to do whatever it took to keep the perfect gift. If someone opened a new one and hated it, chances are that others might hate it too. That person would be stuck with it. Then they would become the high-pressure salesman, trying to convince the new number-picker to take their worthless gift.

My number was called relatively early. I had not seen any opened gifts that appealed to me. I walked over to the stash of beautiful wrapped gifts, and I took one.

I carried on about how beautifully wrapped it was. "Oh, I wonder what is in this. I am so excited. It is heavy," I said as I proceeded to tear it open. All the vultures were glued to me to see if it was one worth having a boxing match over. Then, if it was stolen, I would proceed to act like a pouting child and have to steal from someone else or go get another wrapped one. "Look at this beautiful wrap job," I said as I ripped into it.

"Mom, you brought that gift. You shopped for it, you wrapped it, and you picked your own gift," Katie said as she let the cat out of the bag.

Inside was a beautiful, heavy blue blanket. I am always so cold-blooded, and I loved this big plush, practical item. It was on sale, too, and well-made. I had also put some wonderful Victoria's Secret body lotion in it, and of course it was my favorite scent.

I rambled on about how great the blanket would be to take to chemo lab. "No one has the heart to steal this from me, do they? Ya know … I am sick." I stuck my lip out, as I sounded so dramatic.

"Hey, that is cheating," someone said. "You can't take your own gift that you brought."

"Ya know, we are tired of hearing that line about you being sick. Hey, hey you guys," Cathy said with her hands up trying to be heard over the entire ruckus. "Connie called Mom before we all came out, wondering what food she should bring," Cathy announced. "She whined, and Mom told her, 'OH, Connie … we have plenty, don't worry about it.'"

It was so damn fun to use the sick story on them, and I knew no one would have the heart to steal my heavy new blanket.

Dad decided to put his hearing aids in. He feared not hearing his number or hearing about what gifts the guys were getting from afar. He cleaned his glasses as he walked by to examine all the gifts that he might be the new owner of.

His hearing aids were squealing so loudly that everyone could hear the squeal but him. Amazing! They were in HIS ears, yet everyone heard it but him.

"Donnie, your hearing aids are whistling," Mom said as she punched his arm.

"Oh shit, they are not. I don't hear whispering," he said. We all laughed.

"Dad, I said whistling, NOT WHISPERING," Mom repeated to him.

Poor Dad. After too many years of abusing his ears with his hobby of trapshooting, his hearing was horrible. We do often wonder if he has selective hearing at times, though.

Dad is cold-blooded like me. One night, Dad grumbled about the cold.

Mom said, "Oh, Donnie ... think warm thoughts."

"I do have on warm socks," he yelled back.

The night wore on and slowly ran down. The kids were all anxious to get home to wait for Santa. It was a typical cold winter night with six inches of snow and flurries continuing. The temperature was the usual biting Ohio cold. The moon was full and the skies quiet.

We talked to the kids about the silence and told them to listen for Santa and the sleigh, maybe hearing the bells as he was soaring through the sky en route.

We all hugged Mom and Dad, thanking them for the wonderful-as-usual holiday.

As we headed home, Allie and Amber decided to spend the night. I was thrilled. Amber had packed and hidden the Santa gifts for Allie in her car. With the roads being so hazardous, Ryan decided to spend the night also. His new apartment that he had recently moved into was an hour away.

The children would be all home for Christmas morning, and I was excited. The magic and anticipation of Allie preparing for bed brought me so much happiness.

I helped her lay carrots out for the reindeer, and a muffin with milk for Santa. She was bursting with excitement.

"I want to sleep with Aunt Katie," she said.

"Great," Katie said as she rolled her eyes, knowing how Allie thrashed all over the bed.

Amber, the procrastinator of all time, immediately went to her car to get the gifts for Allie so she could wrap them.

I, being the Virgo who always had things done early, watched, listened, and worried that Allie might get up wanting to play musical beds, or needing a drink.

There was Amber on the living room floor, gifts scattered here and there, cutting paper, sizing gifts into boxes, and taping.

Amber, being a single working mom, had made me proud. She had managed her limited finances and put a lot of thought and time into buying the perfect gifts for Allie.

Baby Annabelle would be the last gift Allie opened to not take from the special efforts of Amber.

Aunt Tina, the thoughtful, thrifty shopper, had found a beautiful child's desk for Allie, and given it to Amber to use as a Santa gift. It was perfect, and Tina, as always, wanted no credit for the purchase and wanted to help add a gift to help Amber.

Tina and Jared had chosen to not have children. I often wished they had because of their love and patience with children. The kids loved to go to their farm.

I found myself so excited to have the pitter-patter of a child squealing though the house when she knew the long wait for Santa had come.

My evening had been tough, since the first chemo. As the evening got later, I was sicker. But like many cancer soldiers, I toughened up for the kids.

As David and I retired to bed, he handed me a beautifully decorated gift box. "Open it," he said as he slid it across the bed.

I tore into it and spread open the tissue paper. A beautiful red negligee trimmed in black lay in the box. I held it up. "Oh, it is beautiful. Thank you." I picked the thong up horizontally and laughed. "You don't honestly think I can get my fat ass in these, do you? If I do get them on, they'll be stuck for life."

We laughed and covered our mouths to muffle the noise in the quiet house. "Yes, it will fit. I want you to put it on."

It had been weeks, and although I felt tired and weak, I put the beautiful silk on, and with it against my skin, I felt beautiful. My breasts looked inviting as they peeked out of the low v-neck cut. He laid me down on the bed and lavished me with kisses and overdue passion. And like always, our sex was good … very satisfying.

David's romantic gesture had done the trick. It had livened me up as he tried to kiss all the hurt, worries, and pain away.

Christmas morning came, and the entire house was awakened as sleepy-eyed Allie came bouncing up the stairs. "I love him. Santa is my very, very best friend," she said as she ran to see all the brightly wrapped gifts. She grabbed her stocking off the chimney and began eating chocolate for breakfast.

"Oh, Allie! Look at this mess Santa's deer made last night when they came in," I said as I pointed down to the floor. I had literally scraped carrot skin off the carrot to give it the look of Dasher sliding his teeth through it as he dropped some on the floor. She was fascinated with the carrot mess.

She was so excited when she saw the partially empty glass of milk that Santa must have drunk in a hurry as he worked.

It was a wonderful Christmas. Each one opened gifts individually, watching the others open their gifts. Allie was the hit of the morning. And the thrill of getting Baby Annabelle was worth all the shopping it took to find her. I remembered those words over and over, "Grammy, if I could get Baby Annabelle, that is all I want."

When it was my turn, I became very emotional. The cancer and the chemo, along with the steroids I had been prescribed, had turned my heart to mush.

David had obviously put much thought into shopping for me. When I opened the beautiful, leather-bound journal, I held it in my hand as I smelled the leather and slid it down my face, rubbing the smooth leather. I flipped through it, smelling the clean, blank pages. "I always said I wanted to write a book before I die. I am not going to die, but I am going to write a book," I said as I choked on my words. "I was sick during the night. I wanted to get out of bed and try to write. It is therapeutic for me, but I didn't have the strength. It felt so awful not being able to be productive, and I kept thinking, if I can only write, it will soothe me." I sobbed as I told the kids how I'd felt during the night. "I couldn't get up. It scared me. But I am OK now," I said as I continued rubbing the beautiful leather on my new journal.

Amber and Katie cried with me. But they were happy, reassuring tears as David handed me another gift.

Gifts were handed to me one after the other. David and the kids had put a lot of effort into the gift they had chosen for me. And no candles! (That is another story.)

I then opened an electric blanket. I knew this was perfect for me. When I opened the next gifts, I dropped my head, and the tears would not stop flowing. I was holding two *Survivor* buffs. The show has always been a big hit in our family, and I had said for many years that I wanted a *Survivor* buff. David and Katie had gone to the *Survivor* Web page and ordered these oh-so-practical and waiting-to-be-used buffs for me. I was not looking forward to my hair falling out, but I knew I would be chic. A *Survivor* buff symbolized what I was determined to be. I would alternate each buff on my head, and I would pull strength into me with that one strong word atop my head ... survivor.

Allie climbed up on my lap with her new Barbie high heels on, with the shoulder purse draped over her arm, along with her toy cell phone, and with Baby Annabelle in the other hand. I knew this child would grow up too fast. And she was all girl.

24

It Is Her Glory

But if any woman has long hair, it is glory to her. My sister read this to me out of the Bible, Corinthians, chapter 11, verse 15. Tina recited it, sympathizing with my emotional worries about losing my hair. It was true. We women feel glorified with pretty hair.

Christmas was over. Decorations were put away, there were charge cards to pay, and my hair was thinning.

Shelley, my niece, had told me about a hair product called Bed Head after she saw my new short haircut.

"Aunt Connie, you should get Bed Head," she suggested after seeing my new short "do." "This girl I work with uses it, and it makes your hair spike up really cool."

"Bed Head? What a crazy name," I said. "OK, I'll look for it."

I needed a stronger hair gel to get my hair to spike out the way I was wearing the new short style De had cut. It had grown, and the top was a little too long. I put off getting it cut. "Isn't that like paying to put a new roof on a house when you know the storm is going to blow the house down?" I said to many of my friends.

Each day since my very first chemo, I would feel my hair and tug on it, looking for signs of it falling out. When I bathed, I would check the drain as the water washed away, always looking for clumps of hair.

I knew I still had a few weeks to enjoy it, but I was obsessed with worry and hoping hair wouldn't be in my hands as I continued tugging it. My treatments were three weeks apart. The nurse had forewarned me that it would start thinning out a week prior to my second treatment.

On week two after my chemo, like clockwork, it began, just like the nurse had told me. For some silly reason, I started thinking I might be different, and an unusual case. I actually thought I would be one of the lucky ones who would not suffer hair loss. I should have known better. I noticed I didn't need to shave my legs as often. My unwanted chin hairs were gone.

People would tell me that they had friends or relatives who didn't lose hair from cancer treatments. I knew those chemo patients were probably being treated with different kinds of chemo. Adriamycin, the hair-thief-heartless-bastard-chemo, was pumped through my veins, and its reputation was brutal.

January 4, 2005, was a day that stands out in my mind as much as the day I was told I had breast cancer. The warnings I had heard from other cancer survivors were true.

"The toughest thing to deal with is when your hair falls out."

That Tuesday, on the fourth, I was preparing for work. I got up feeling good and eager to take on a new day. I had just bought the Bed Head product. I even mumbled to myself as I stood in the drugstore the day before, thinking how expensive it was. *Why am I wasting my money on this when I know my hair is leaving me any day?*

I dressed for work and poured another cup of coffee. I sang with the radio, as Brooks and Dunn were playing.

I walked into the bathroom; I combed my hair and put the Bed Head in my hands to spread across my hair. I rubbed it in, spiking parts of my hair to give areas the defined look. It looked great. I looked chic.

I took my hands down to the water running out of the faucet to wash the goop off, and that was when reality hit me in the gut. I was molting like a duck.

My hands were covered with hair. The sticky Bed Head stuck to my hands, and they were covered with my hair like glue. I felt like someone throwing their hands in panic trying to remove cobwebs. I immediately looked up in the mirror and rubbed my hands together vigorously under the faucet, trying to get rid of the hair on my hands. I started crying.

But it was obvious. I was now shedding, and my days were limited. As I cried, I looked at my wig, sitting on the shelf.

I hoped I would look as good in it as the pretty mannequin face that it sat upon. I wondered if I would have eyebrows and my long eyelashes that everyone had told me were so pretty. If I lost them, would they grow long again? I had never used eyebrow makeup. I might have to learn how to paint eyebrows on without even having eyebrows to work with.

Each day, more hair fell out. I was afraid to wash it as I combed it gently. I looked at my shoulders like one who suffers with dandruff. I would swipe hair off my shoulders. I used the lint brush to clean up the messes on my clothes.

My bed pillow was full of hair. I didn't know one head could have so much hair. MY HEAD HURT. I knew this was not my imagination. My scalp hurt even to lie down on my pillow. It must have been my hair follicles, rejecting my hair. The ache was like a bad toothache. I wanted to rub my head to soothe the pain, but I feared more hair falling out.

The time was coming to buzz my head. Each morning I would get up hoping I was feeling brave. Bravery was not kicking in, but my hair started looking awful as it thinned. I began to wear my Pam Lucas scarves. I wore my *Survivor* buff that David had gotten me. That is what I hoped to be: a survivor.

What if the hair stopped falling out? Maybe I wouldn't need to shave my head. What if I shaved it all off, and it wasn't necessary? I wouldn't know though, would I? If it quit falling out, and I went ahead and shaved it, becoming a skinhead, would I have jumped to conclusions?

I was in denial. The shedding had to stop. It was gross. The clippers were waiting on me, but I wanted to feel glory.

25
Rock On In A Wig

I had invited Wayne over for dinner the night after I started dealing with preparation for shaving my head. The entire family had been jumping in to help Wayne as he suffered through his divorce. We all invited him to our homes for meals or to do things, not wanting him to be alone. His spirit was shattered, and we wanted to boost him up. He constantly watched and hoped he would see his daughters come up the drive. He continued working long hours, trying to catch up financially after his divorce and to find comfort in his work. With his full-time job, always helping others, running his shop, and having sleepless nights, he was on overdrive, physically and mentally.

As he walked in, his first concern was for me. "Connie, how ya doing?"

"Oh Wayne, my hair is falling out. Dinner is ready. I know you love roast and I made a cake, too. But no guarantee there isn't any hair in your food," I said as I removed the roast from the oven and poured him a cup of coffee as we chuckled.

"You need to remember why your hair is falling out," he said. "The chemo is working. You think about that and say to yourself, *die, bad cells, DIE!*"

We all sat down to eat.

"Well, check your tongue periodically and spit the hair balls out. Betty spits them out all the time," I said as we passed dinner. Betty, my wonderful fat cat, looked on.

"As long as it is your hair, I don't care," he said as he leaned over the table and gave me an affectionate hug.

And watching this hard-working guy eat dinner made my mood wonderful as he, David, Katie, and I sat, forgetting all our problems. I laughed as I told Wayne about Cathy and Tina calling daily to get a hair-loss report.

Cathy had owned a very cool, quaint gift shop in our hometown for years. Being a meter maid now, she knows just about everyone. With my years working in the public sector, and our both staying rooted in Delaware, Ohio, we know just about everyone. It never fails that when we go out; we bump into many friends and have grand conversations as we all catch up on each other's lives.

Her meter maid job is a thankless job, but with her personality, the ticketed victims usually don't give her a bad time.

I recall one night when we went down to a local bar, owned by our retired deputy sheriff buddy whom we had grown up with. I am not a barfly or an alcoholic. Cathy and I are both social butterflies, and of course where there is karaoke, I am eager to go.

Dan's bar, within walking distance from the local college, tends to draw in numerous college kids. Many kids from the East Coast attend our local upscale, expensive college.

A young, slightly intoxicated college boy walked up to Cathy one night.

"I know you from somewhere. Where in the hell do I know you from?" he asked her.

"I don't know," Cathy said as she immediately denied ever laying eyes on him.

He walked away.

"I give him parking tickets all the time. The dumb shit parks in the same illegal spot every day," she said. "Sometimes he leaves, comes back, and I get him again. Wouldn't you think he would learn?"

She scanned the bar for him. She always hates running into people she had to *ding* with a ticket. "Shit, here he comes again," Cathy said as he walked by us.

Minutes later, he returned.

"I know!" he hollered. "You are a cook at the school," he said. "I'll buy you a beer if you give me extra food Monday when I come through the line," he said as he laughed.

We talked and enjoyed his silly drunken humor. He turned to walk away and made an immediate abrupt turn. Cathy's eyes got big.

"Shit! Now what?" she asked him. "And no! No free food at school Monday," Cathy said.

He pointed his finger at Cathy as he swayed back and forth on his clumsy feet. "I just figured out where I know you from. You are that damn meter maid who gives me tickets!"

"No, that is not me. No way. I am not a meter maid," Cathy assured him as she lied like a rug.

"Oh yes you are. You have given me so many tickets. I park on Spring Street all the time, and you sometimes give me two or three tickets a day," he said as he shook his finger at her. His eyes got big. He towered over Cathy by six inches (everyone towers over Cathy, my oldest sister of five feet four inches).

He continued prattling on, determined that she would admit to being the meter maid.

"Yes, I am the meter maid," she declared. "Why the hell do you keep parking in the same spot that says very clearly ... NO PARKING?"

It was then that he walked away, came back, and was carrying a beer for Cathy. How happy this young drunk was.

"I just send the tickets home to Dad in New Jersey. He pays them for me," he said as he walked away.

Cathy said that she has learned to not look at the actual make of a car, for fear of recognizing a family or friend's car. She'd be torn about ticketing them. She zooms in on the expired meter or illegal parking and simply does her job. Many times as she is placing the ticket under the windshield wiper, a familiar face might approach her to get in their car. She just has to do her thankless job.

And as our dad warned her with a laugh when she got the job several years ago, "Cathy, I will park in the darn town wherever I want, and as much as I have done for you, you better NOT give me a ticket."

Sometimes it does pay to know the right people. My job in EMS helped me a lot. I knew every cop in the city and county.

I recall the attack on our great nation on 9/11, my birthday. Like Pearl Harbor, or when Neil Armstrong walked on the moon, or when John Kennedy was assassinated, we remember the shocking news report and exactly what we were doing during such sad historic moments. I will never forget the sadness of our entire nation. I grieved on my forty-fifth birthday like everyone.

I recall that day in 2001 being warm, with much sunshine; seemingly such a promising and yet such a horrifying day. I was off work and tired of being glued to the television, hearing all the sadness. I took off downtown in my VW Bug. The news was too depressing. My Bug, with its bright bumblebee color, is an immediate eye-catcher.

I was inside a restaurant, visiting my dear friend Teresa as she was waiting tables. My cell phone rang. It was Cathy.

"Connie, I see your car. The meter has expired. Get your ass out here and feed the machine. I will have to give you a ticket."

"But, Cathy ... I am inside the Brown Jug, visiting Teresa. My food is about to come."

"Well, only because it is your birthday, I will put the money in for you."

"You are the best ... SISTER. I owe ya," I told her.

Cathy called me right around the time I was shedding. She was determined that I come to meet her for pizza. We'd always kid about David and Jim sitting at home; couch tatterin' as they watched TV. We needed air!

The local sports bar near both our homes was a regular hangout for many middle-aged people. We felt welcome and not out of place, and always enjoyed good conversations and laughs.

Occasionally, the Vinntage Band (spelled with two Ns), which consists of my dear friends, plays in various local bars. I'd always try to go when "the Band" was playing, to show my support. Their old-time rock-and-roll was wonderful music.

"No way," I told her. "I am not going out. I just washed my hair, and it is so thin, falling out in heaps. It looks awful. I need to shave it," I rambled on as I paced with the cordless phone. "If I could get brave, I could wear my wig, but I dunno, Cathy. I am too scared to go out."

"Oh, c'mon. Your wig is pretty. People will just think you cut your hair. They won't even know it is a wig, unless you start runnin' your mouth," she said.

"I know! I have a good idea. Let's just meet next door at the convenience store and buy a gallon of milk or something. Kinda like a trial run. Why do something as drastic as going in a bar where we know so many people?"

"Oh, Connie, for God's sake."

"We can just run in and out of the store like a test run. You can watch to see if anyone stares or gives me that double take," I told her.

She wouldn't take no for an answer. I knew she was right again. Big sisters almost always know what's best. Either I needed to be brave and go out or I would become a recluse until summer.

As I entered the parking lot, Cathy was pacing the sidewalk, waiting for me. Just as I parked at the bar and got out of my car, a friend spotted Cathy and me. Linda, a humorous friend, was aware of my cancer and knew I was in chemo treatment. As usual, it was great to see her.

"I love your hair," she said as she immediately noticed the changed style.

I was sure she probably knew it was a wig, but was being her positive, wanting-to-make-everyone-feel-good self.

"Oh, Linda," I said as I ran my hands gently down my wig, "it's a wig! My hair is falling out, and I must shave it soon."

When I confided in her that I was nervous about walking in, she proceeded to tell me how I would be just fine.

"I told Connie to not tell anyone it was a wig. What does she do? Tells it already before she even gets inside," Cathy bellowed with a big laugh.

We all walked in, and I sat down at the first seat I could find. The bar was long and narrow. I did not want to walk toward the back; because people watched the newcomers enter. Inside the door was good enough for me. Cathy likes to be the door greeter, anyway.

As I looked around, scanning to see if eyes were upon me, I looked to my immediate left. Just as I noticed a woman with a thin covering of hair on her head, she greeted me with a smile.

As it turned out, she knew me from coming into a store where she worked. Sadly, I had not recognized her.

"I am, yes ... Connie Curry," I replied after she asked me if I was Connie. I gently put my hand on her hand and boldly asked her if she was a chemo patient.

"I am," she said. "I had breast cancer."

"See this thing on my head ... wig! It's a dang wig. Tonight is my first night out. I also have breast cancer," I told her.

It was then as if we had known each other for years. She jumped up from her stool and we immediately hugged. Her name was Kay, and we immediately felt compassion for each other.

I thought of how easily we cancer soldiers bond.

We talked on and on. We compared doctors, treatments, and chemo experiences, and talked about our feelings when we heard the big "C" word. She pointed to her eyebrows when I asked her if she had lost her eyelashes and brows. I feared this.

"These are tattooed on me," she said, as she held her index finger to her brow.

"Wow, I would have never known," I told her. "And they truly are beautiful."

She was a true fighter with a positive attitude. Her face radiated beauty, even though she had so little of her glorious hair.

It worried me when she proceeded to tell me how she had been fighting cancer for five years. First it hit her breast, then her lungs, and now it was in her bones. She chose to stop taking more chemo.

I noticed such spunk and fire in her as she danced with her friend to every fast rock-and-roll song. She smiled and laughed, and I knew she was living life to the fullest for as long as she was given this privilege.

We talked and laughed and continued visiting like we'd known each other for years. There were disruptions as people we knew entered the bar. I saw old firefighter buddies and old school friends, and I was feeling confident and comfortable.

"You cut your hair. Cool," my firefighting buddy of twenty years said. "What made you do that? Just wanna change?"

"Well, not necessarily," I said as I looked at Cathy.

Cathy swished her hands across her lips, using sign language to tell me to zip it!

"Ya know, we've been friends for years, worked many fires together. If I told you why I really got my hair cut, you might be depressed all the way home," I said, grinning. Cathy shook her head at me.

Seconds later, his wife walked up and said, "Connie, how are your chemo treatments going?"

It was then that he looked at my head, and I lifted my hand to the top of my wig, grabbed it, and jerked it up and down.

"I swear, Connie. You are such a shit," he said. "But I am sorry and wish you the best."

"Why didn't you tell me?" he asked his wife.

"I just found out today, and you were asleep on the couch, and then we had to rush out to bowl on our league," she told him in defense.

In came the Bug doctor, Paul, the body man who had restored my Bug and restored my soul when he brought such beauty to my car. Cathy and I were both very happy to see him.

He had already heard about my illness. I had known him so many years and we had always been good friends. He always reminded me of Wayne. A hard worker, very kind, a gentleman with a lot of family values, he had a big heart like Wayne. Women had taken advantage of his good qualities and generosity for years, too.

He is humorous, and very knowledgeable about cars. His business reputation in town is flawless. Customers return to him and speak highly of his work. And that is why I have the coolest yellow 1974 Super Beetle in town.

Paul never made it to the back of the bar to socialize with other people. He was thoroughly entertained by me, Cathy, and Kay. I was trying to hook him up with Kay, or at least for a dance. He doesn't dance ... like Wayne.

I had to live up to my reputation, so I raised my hand to the top of my head, and as I wiggled it, I said, "Look, it is a wig," as he watched my forehead move.

"Connie, STOP IT!" Cathy said.

I heard Paul tell Cathy that he thought my humor was my way of dealing with my situation.

That night out was the best thing I could have done. It restored my confidence, and I knew I would not become a hermit waiting for my glory of hair to come. I was accepted.

I didn't say anything, but maybe he was right. Humor has been with me since I was a child, and laughter comforts me.

I was the middle child. Wayne was also stuck in the middle with me, but he was special, being the only boy. Cathy, the oldest, had been born with a rare juvenile arthritis. She had many knee surgeries and required a lot of attention. Tina, the baby, probably got the least attention, since Mom had us all one year apart, except for Wayne and Tina, who are eleven months apart.

I thought I had to be the clown to get attention. The reality was, we all got our fair share of attention, and my childhood was perfect.

I had very positive days, and sometimes I thought about death when I thought a lot about my cancer. If I died, I would want people to recall my passion for words, writing, family, my VW, and music, and how I loved and talked to everyone. I talked to strangers and tried hard to always be helpful and thoughtful. I enjoyed smiling at older folks as we made eye contact.

I loved kids and made them laugh, and I gave people change at the checkouts when they were short of cash. I baked food and took dishes to my friends' parents' homes as they grew older and became dependent and lonely.

Oh, but I am not perfect. The nurse at chemo had it all figured out about me: "My goodness, you were born on 9/11. No wonder you are a hellion," she said.

I know I talk too much, and I did not apply myself in school. I was boy crazy. I gossiped too much in school. As an adult, I learned that gossip was a waste of energy, but I still enjoy hearing the latest juice on someone I know.

I am probably too competitive and outspoken, and I eat too much junk food. I blow bubbles and pop them in public. I was a yeller when I disciplined the kids. I guess they adapted. The kids knew my bark was far worse than my bite.

I am probably too demanding and want perfection a lot. But I love compassionately.

Many years ago, in eighth grade, I had an English teacher I thoroughly enjoyed. Mrs. Lucas was her name, and I truly learned more in that one year than in any other educational year. She was my favorite teacher, and I loved going to her class.

She made learning fun. We wrote sentences on the chalkboard, and it became an educational game. We literally dissected each word and learned how to diagram. It was challenging, fun, and competitive. Competition fired me up. We raced to finish our sentences.

English became my love, and Mrs. Lucas my idol. I learned the joy of reading, and to win a spelling bee made a perfect school day. I loved her very much and wanted to impress her and make her proud.

I'd see her periodically around town, and she was still beautiful and classy. She always remembered me and enjoyed seeing former students. She had such a warm smile and rarely forgot a student's name. I loved standing in the aisle of CVS, talking to her.

We started e-mailing each other after she and her husband retired and moved to Florida. Mrs. Lucas was enjoying her well-deserved golden years of retirement in the sunny state with her husband. She motivated me and encouraged me to keep writing as I shared many of my short stories with her.

When she came to town the weekend of my thirtieth class reunion, she stopped into the local restaurant where my reunion was. It seemed wrong to have a social drink with my English teacher, but I did. Mrs. Lucas was probably the closest to being perfect of anyone who had come into my life.

26
Hair Today, Gone Tomorrow

Sunday morning after the night out with Cathy, I needed to go to the grocery store. I got up and drank coffee to get motivated. My peer pressure night out with Cathy, which was just too much fun, had me moving slowly. My wig smelled of bar smoke. I had not read the directions on how to maintain a wig. I didn't want to put it on my head until I washed it properly. It was expensive, and I knew it had to last awhile, even if my medical insurance did pay for it. (All cancer patients should check their policies for coverage. Many policies pay 100 percent or a partial amount.) Anyway, Suave shampoo was not going to cut the odor and was a major no-no. Special shampoo is used for wigs, and they don't have a great fragrance!

I hate grocery shopping. Is there any fun in it? I spend a fortune, I haul groceries into the house, and then I cook. The snack aisle and frozen-food sections scream my name: "Buy me, Connie. I don't care if your metabolism has slowed down and your hips want to spread more. I love you."

David had offered to go to the store. He had been helping me so much since my illness. He had started doing chores he had never done before in all our years of marriage. His devotion and need to help me were appreciated. But I could and would go to the grocery store.

It was a typical lazy Sunday, and football, his passion, was on TV. He deserved his day off.

As I got in the checkout line, my nose began to run. I didn't have a Kleenex. I moved up in line, wiping my nose discreetly with my hand and down my pant leg as if I was a snot-nosed child.

It was ridiculous how my nose ran. I laid food on the conveyor belt, wiping my nose as I continued checking out.

People stared, or it seemed that way to me. I had my do-rag upon my head. It was an array of colors, with butterflies splattered throughout the pattern. My sweater matched the trendy scarf that was around my neck. My nails were painted, and my earrings stood out to take away from my do-rag. It was not working. People looked at me and were giving me the double take.

I wiped my nose as I placed the salad dressing up on the conveyor belt. My cold, which I had gotten when my white blood count had dropped, was gone. Why was my nose running?

My denim jacket matched my stylish jeans. I did not feel beautiful. My head looked flat, and my ears stood out like sore thumbs.

Bravery had not kicked in, and I continued to molt like Donald Duck. My mind raced as I thought about needing to shave my head. I thought that I should have worn the smoke-smelling rug. I knew that after I got home and put groceries up, I'd have to shave my head.

I wanted to scream at people, *"Stop staring. I have cancer. I do not have a biker dude in the parking lot waiting for me. I am shedding and I am almost bald. I am not trying to dress like a teen. I AM SICK!"*

My back ached. My Lumbar-3 and 4 had flared up again. I had taken it upon myself to move my office to Ryan's abandoned bedroom, pulling my back out.

Ryan had also abandoned me. His way of dealing with my cancer was to stay away. He had not come home since Christmas. I watched for him each night Katie had a basketball game, so hoping he would come to show his love and support to both of us.

I thought of him as I placed the steaks on the conveyor belt. He always loved steak. I wondered if he had been eating decent food, or if he was just binge drinking. At times, I would forget he was not living at home, and out of habit I'd start to set a place setting for him.

I wondered if he was still in the college-party mode and was using my cancer as an excuse to stay away.

I started to cry as I thought of Ryan and my nose. I should have worn the smoke-smelling rug. And then it hit me and I remembered. I recalled the words of a cancer soldier: "Wait until your nose hair comes out. Your nose will run like a coke head."

The mystery was solved. I realized that my nose hair had left me. I hoped Ryan would come home before the nose hair returned in the summer.

Shelley, my wonderful niece, called not long after I got home. David and Katie helped put the groceries away. Mom called, and I told her I was going to shave my head. Amber and Allie had called and were coming for a visit, too. My sister Tina was rushing through dinner to come and support me. "Remember," she said, "it is worth it to lose your hair, because we can't lose you." She began to cry.

The rumor was out. I wondered if they had all called each other because they knew I was trying to get the courage up to shave my thin-haired head. After all, I looked awful. There was no use in trying to salvage what little hair was left.

They were on their way to our home, and I was glad. I knew I could be courageous with them as my wall to lean on. We would do it!

My sweet Allie Girl had caught me demonstrating the large mass of hair I easily pulled out. "Look," I said to Amber as I grabbed a wad and held it in my hand, "I have to shave it; it is disgusting. It is all over my clothes and my pillow and is falling into the sink when I am at the mirror."

"I SAW that, Grammy. Grammy is losing her hair," Allie announced to all with the saddest look upon her beautiful face. She placed her chin in her little hand on the table and stared at me.

I reassured her that it was OK, and reminded her of our conversation a month earlier. She seemed to understand.

Allie's daddy came to pick her up for his shared parenting week. I would miss her. Amber and Paul were kind and talked, laughing together as they talked about Allie. Allie immediately told her daddy about my hair dilemma. His concern and sympathy were sincere. We were finally friends.

"OK, Allie is gone. Who wants to shave my head?"

There was a knock at the door. Judy, our wonderful neighbor, had stopped to check on me. I was very happy to see her and did not mind her sharing in our family skinhead party.

"You guys can all make a path down my head," I said. "Anyone want to?"

It was as if they all took a step back. No one wanted the nasty job but Amber. I had always wanted her to go to barber school. She has a natural talent with hairstyles and cutting hair. I would later think I was way off thinking this when she finished my buzz job. Ha!

"Wait," I said. "I need to drink a beer first." Hope, my friend and roommate of Shelley, sat down to drink a beer with me. Amber got out the liquor and grabbed the clippers.

The buzz of the clippers made me flinch. I was putting my trust in a daughter whose hair I had mutilated more than once when she was a child.

With Jack Daniel's in one hand and clippers in the other, Amber said, "Mom this is for all the times you cut my bangs too short and crooked.

"I can't watch this," Katie said as she walked into the family room. Cathy got out her digital camera. I drank my beer, fast. I wanted a quick buzz from the Bud Light and the clippers. I pulled my ears out with my hands and stuck my tongue out to Cathy as she took my picture. I wondered if she would use this picture as blackmail on my birthday someday (probably my fiftieth).

"You are going to look as pretty as Demi Moore," David said. I knew this was not true; but in his eyes, I would.

"I always wanted a bald-headed baby," Mom said.

Amber shaved on, and I looked down, seeing so much of my hair on the floor.

"I wonder how many battle scars I have on my head from you guys," I said to Tina and Cathy. "You guys were always so damn mean," I said as we all laughed some more.

I felt my head. "My God, my ears have grown!"

I knew Mom saw my beauty no matter what the outcome would be. I knew she would keep us all strong, and it would be a sadness turned into something positive. She has always been the rock.

As I watched the last of my hair fall, all eyes were on me. I thought of Wayne's words: "Every time you think about your bald head, you think how that chemo is in there, working ... killing that cancer. Die bad cells, die!"

My beer was gone, and my hair was gone. I had shed no tears. We had laughed, and that was a good thing.

I heard crying behind me, and I recognized the cry. Katie had come back out as Amber had finished.

Amber walked over to talk to Katie as she reassured her.

I walked over to my six-foot-tall beautiful baby daughter with the golden, long locks of hair. "Oh, Katie," I said. "It is OK. I am truly going to be. Don't cry or I will rub my knobby head on you."

And with that, she laughed and wiped her tears. I put my *Survivor* buff on. I wasn't ready to look. We had made it fun, but it would be days before I would look in a mirror.

27
Wigs, Wigs, Wigs

It was the day of my second chemo treatment, and I decided to stop into Hope Boutique to look for another wig. Katie had a home basketball game coming up the very next night. I knew that people in the crowd would be staring at me when I walked by. I was apprehensive. The shorthaired wig that I had gotten and worn with Cathy still did not appeal to me.

I also realized that with the buff on without the wig, I truly looked ill. I looked just like an obvious chemo patient.

I walked into Hope Boutique with every intention of buying a blonde wig.

I think the short wig, although styled much like the De cut, was too dark, and that was probably why I couldn't get used to it. Mom even questioned me and was surprised that I had gotten a much darker color.

After chemo, we walked into Hope Boutique. I knew that David was as eager as I was to go home, but he was patient with me.

I recall spending many hours shopping for the first wig. I was inexperienced in this kind of hair business, and my mood back in the beginning probably left me negative and hard to please.

This time was different, and I was spontaneous as my old self. "We just got in this new wig," the saleswoman said. "It is the only one we have of this new style," she said as she spun it around on her hand.

I loved it immediately, but it was cocoa brown. I made David and the wig woman hide their eyes when I took my old short wig off. I hid my face from the mirror as I placed the new style on my head. I then looked in the mirror to straighten it up. It was instant love.

As I looked at myself in the mirror, knowing De would have to trim the bangs, I started loving it more. A blue-eyed, cocoa-dark-haired woman just might be unique. I needed help. From the steroids putting weight on me, I felt like a fat, bald, ugly woman.

The style was similar to Jennifer Aniston's cut. I loved it more as I twirled around, looking in the three-way mirror. Bald Demi couldn't hold a stick to the Jennifer Aniston look.

"I want it," I said. "I don't care about the cost!" I picked that wig out, purchased it, and was out the door as quickly as I had picked the color for my VW Bug. Car paint is as plentiful as hair colors. There were about ten different shades of yellow for my Bug, but I knew what I wanted the minute I looked at the paint chart. Just like my Bug, this wig was an instant choice.

I knew I could walk into the basketball game feeling OK. I always knew people looked at my head and my chest. *Does she have her boob? Has she had a mastectomy yet? Wonder if her hair will fall out? Is that her real hair? Oh my, I wonder if that is a wig.*

Curiosity is normal, and I was aware that many times, people don't know how to react or what to say.

Game night came, and I decided to wear the short wig. Imagine that! I plotted and schemed. The following game, I would stroll in with the long, darker wig on so I could screw with the basketball parents and students. I laughed, imagining them saying stuff as they whispered. "Is that Connie?"

"No, that isn't Connie. She has long hair."

"No, she has short hair, I saw her the other day."

"But, I think she cut her hair right after she was to start chemo. That can't be her."

I thought later I would buy a Cher wig, or a Reba wig. I wanted to keep them all on their toes, and mess with their curious minds.

I realized how right my new cancer friend was when she advised me that I would not go bareheaded once my hair was gone. Bareheaded was never going to be me, I suspected anyway. But she had told me that being bald is cold. Heat gets lost via the head, but I never knew just how instantly cold my head was during the cold winter nights. My head felt immediately cold when I removed my wig.

After a week, I had still not gotten brave and looked at myself in the mirror. When I got home, I'd immediately take the itchy wig off and place the buff on my head.

I thought about how the kids would help decorate the Christmas tree when they were little. They would hang ornaments on top of ornaments, using the hooks like extending bungee cords. One ornament would turn into five, hanging almost to the floor vertically at great lengths.

I have always loved long, beady earrings. The bold, bright, dangle, rattle look had always been my style.

So maybe I would start a long dangle look with extending earrings down my lobes like the ornament style our kids had given our tree. Certainly everyone's attention would be drawn to the wacky woman's accessories instead of her naked head.

I wore my *Survivor* buff all the way to the bathroom to bathe. I would drop it as I was about to jump into the tub, and after bathing, put it back on my wet head. I would not go near the mirror, afraid I would be tempted to peek. What purpose would it serve?

When I was about to put my wig on, I would put it on blindly and then walk to the mirror to make sure it was straight.

Melissa, my wonderful next-door neighbor, had sent me a card. When I returned her call to thank her, she had told me how many times she had thought of me but didn't want to bother me. Cards continued to come in the mail to me. It amazed me how many good friends I had. It truly lifted my spirits.

"Well, Melissa, I am bald now," I said as I told her about my two new wigs.

"Ya know, I remember when my mom wore wigs in the seventies," she said as we talked on the phone. "I recall when she would have me get dinner out of the oven so her wig wouldn't catch fire."

"You know, you are the second person today to tell me about moms who wore wigs just for the heck of it. Why would anyone want to wear these scratchy things?" I said. "De just trimmed my new wig, and she told me about her mom having several wigs of all different colors that she would wear when De was a child. Her mom would be about the same age as your mom," I told Melissa as I jumped up to reread the directions on my new wig pamphlet.

"Melissa, it is 2005, and it still says to keep wigs away from ovens or hot areas. Maybe this can be my excuse to stop cooking."

"And guess what else it says?" I said to her. "It says, 'don't sleep in your wig.' Well, shit. Now I am disappointed. I love that scratchy thing and so looked forward to sleeping in it. Can you imagine sleeping in it?" I said as we laughed.

We talked on, laughing as I reminisced. "I remember a girl in eighth grade who used to wear a hairpiece. It looked totally ridiculous. I remember her hairpiece being an almost gray color," I said. "She was a beautiful brunette. She wore that hairpiece almost daily to school, tacked on the back of her head. She looked so two-toned and silly. Maybe that was my reason for having a hard time finding a wig to please me. Mary Jane has scarred me for life."

The next morning, after the ballgame (Katie played great defense by the way and scored ten points), I ran into the bank and then over to the drugstore to pick up my prescription. Chemo was turning me into a true drug user.

When I got out of my car and was about to shut my door, I noticed how windy it was. My wool scarf was blowing around my neck. I didn't know whether to grab my scarf or my wig. I pictured the wig blowing off and me chasing it through the parking lot.

As I walked into the bank, I was sporting my long black leather coat. I rarely wear that coat because, although it is beautiful, I tend to feel like all I do is untangle myself as I get in and out of the car. Cathy must have gotten tangled in it also. She gave it to me. No wonder most men sleep naked. I hate long nightgowns, too.

I also wore my sunglasses as I entered the bank. True incognito was going on.

The girls at the bank knew me, BUT they did a double take.

"Connie, I love your hair," the bank teller said. "It is so beautiful."

Well, I keep surprises like Allie. "It is a wig," I said. You can't tell?" I asked.

"Well, I wondered," Jackie said. "I knew you were taking chemo, but I wasn't sure if your hair had fallen out. How are you feeling?"

"Good. I am doing OK," I replied.

"You sure seem happy. It is great to see you still smiling. And your hair! I am serious. It is so cute."

"My sisters told me for years to go dark. Don't you dare tell me this color is better than my blonde weave I've had for years," I warned them as I handed them my check to be cashed. "Rebates are great, aren't they? Look at how much money I got back on the new fax machine I purchased. Anyway, as I was saying, don't tell me getting sick makes me look better," I jokingly said.

The three bank girls laughed as I strutted out, swinging my new long hair.

I turned the corner and almost ran into one of the basketball moms whom I had just seen the night before. Another double take and she roared with laughter. "Connie, only you can take something so tough and turn it into something fun and positive," she said.

"Wait until you see me at the next game, I'll be in this one; and then the next game, I am coming with the Dolly look, or the Reba look. The sky is the limit."

"I am just so glad to see you feeling better. I watched you a week before at the game. I could see you felt so bad. I was just telling Steve that it was so good to see you last night at the game, up selling 50/50 tickets and smiling," she said with so much sincerity in her voice.

She hugged me, and I went in the drugstore to look at fake eyelashes, just in case I needed them later.

Good white blood count, pretty wig, and a smile. What else does a woman need? I thought as I walked into the drugstore.

28
We All Need A Betty

Three days after my head was shaved, I realized I needed to truly liberate and bic it with a disposable razor; a Mr. Clean shave. The little stubs of hair that Amber left felt like pine cones sticking through my *Survivor* buff and my wigs. It felt like being pricked with needles. I'd had enough needles at the clinic; who wanted more? My head had begun to ache like it did when I was losing my hair. I doubt words can describe the pain my hair follicles had, but they truly were very painful, and this chick ain't no weenie.

The first night after I got my head buzzed, I realized that the pain was coming back; it awoke me as I tossed in my sleep, causing the buff to move, pulling on the stubs as they stuck my scalp.

David heard me groaning in my sleep, and my discomfort woke me too. Betty heard me.

Betty, part Maine coon breed, is the fattest, coolest cat and is full of personality. She is gentle, not a loner, and friendly—uncommon among most felines. She sleeps between my legs or near my hips. Prior to settling down for the night, she follows me through the house like a puppy. She watches me, knowing my routine, and even sits beside me as I go to the bathroom before going to bed. She sits on the sink as I brush my teeth.

As I get comfortable, turning on my reading light to read, she walks up to my face, sniffs me, licks my face, and hunkers back down for the night by my lower body.

Her eyes are as green as the skin on watermelon. She was named in memory of the famous green-eyed Bette Davis, one of my favorites.

During the night, when she sensed or heard me being a weenie about the hair pricks, she wobbled up toward my face. She began licking me. It was very unusual, because she moved her nose as she pushed my buff away from my head. She continued the ritual of licking me, smelling me, and rubbing her face across my face.

"Aww, Betty," I said. "I'll be all right." I rubbed her beautiful long hair. She truly was troubled about me. She would throw her head, pushing her nose on my buff like a dog burying a bone. She seemed to actually be trying to remove my buff.

David used to claim that he didn't like cats. I think it was some macho thing. He was taught to not like cats because his dad hates cats. We had cats, kittens, and sometimes two to three litters born just days apart when I was growing up. In the sixties, cat control was unheard of. It was common to drop cats off at the Van Brimmer house. We never were quite sure why people picked our house. It was almost like there was some sign on the mailbox that said: "Dump unwanted, starving cats here. This family will take care of them." And we did.

I remember once when two female cats became pregnant about the same time and delivered out in our old camper just days apart. The two mamas teamed together. They put the kittens together and took turns nursing them. We Van Brimmer kids raised smart foster cats.

David and I always had dogs for the kids, and I slowly eased him into having cats around the house. My kids all learned to love cats, including Ryan, who to this day adores cats.

Betty came to our home one summer day, uninvited and unexpected. Her long hair was mangled, she was starving, and she looked to have been neglected for a long time. She was not a pretty sight.

It is a mystery how she picked our home to be adopted into, but she did. I guess our home had that same imaginary sign that we had out home when I was growing up.

We will never know if she walked many miles or if someone dumped her at our home.

It was apparent that we would keep her, feeling sorry for her and knowing that she needed some tender loving care.

It was also apparent that my husband would demand that we not feed her so that she might give up and wander next door in hopes of a generous home elsewhere.

It was settled. We sneaked out and fed her at the back door. We brought her in to visit only when he was not home. In time, I knew the secret would be out and hoped he would accept her, knowing that the war would be four of us against him and we would win.

"Are you guys feeding that cat? You AREN'T feeding that cat, are you?" he would ask when he noticed her sitting on the porch stoop.

"Oh no, we aren't feeding her."

Weeks passed, and Betty started gaining weight. Her coat began to shine, and we cut and combed many fur balls out of her. The cat food was nutrition to this once-starved cat. She grew fond of us and began to trust us.

"Why is THAT cat still hangin' round here? You better not be feeding her," he would say in his authoritarian voice.

"I don't know why she keeps hanging around," I would reply as I looked at the kids, and we would snicker behind his back.

She waddled up to me one day. I hollered to the children. "Oh for goodness sake. She IS pregnant. Look at her belly! Your dad is going to have a fit." (She must have been pregnant when she arrived those few weeks before.)

With lack of interest and no fondness for the cat, David ignored her. She grew and grew and grew. I fretted about him discovering the mother-to-be. I knew it was just days away from the birth of kittens. How could he not notice her fat, pudgy belly?

We assumed he knew by now that we had been feeding her against his wishes, but he quit asking and probably wanted to avoid a confrontation. We would sit on the porch as she would walk up, and no words were spoken. The children and I would make eye contact and watch David to see if he noticed her pregnancy. Good golly, her belly almost dragged along the ground as she waddled, and he totally ignored her existence.

The day came. She gave birth. Where were the kittens? We watched her disappear, return, and repeat the cycle. I knew she was leaving to feed her kittens. The kids searched everywhere. Wherever Betty had hidden them, she had succeeded in keeping this grand hiding place.

About two weeks later, David headed out in the early morning for a fishing trip to Lake Erie, two hours north of us.

He always would make a day of it because of the long trip, pulling a big boat, and of course for the love of good fishing on the lake.

The water was calm, and the weather was perfect for fishing.

We had fretted that day because Betty had not been seen for several hours. We had searched all over the house, inside and out. The mystery continued about how many kittens she had and what they looked like.

David arrived home from fishing earlier than normal.

"Have you seen Betty?" I asked.

"Who is Betty?"

Silly question. He had no clue we had named her. After all, he wanted to believe we had not adopted her.

"Yeah, I found your damn cat AND kittens."

"OH, a little cat fishing," I said with a laugh.

"Funny, Connie, very funny," he said as I hollered at the kids to come see the kittens.

"We found Betty!" I screamed.

We later found out that he had towed Betty and the kittens unknowingly to Lake Erie, and it wasn't until he was out in the middle of the lake that Betty surfaced from under one of the seats of the boat. David heard the meow of kittens and investigated.

What if she had jumped out of the boat as he was towing it up the highway? The thought made me shudder, and I was so relieved they arrived home safely.

And that tough, macho man who hated cats so much was responsible for that safe trip back home.

"OK, you can keep her, but we aren't keeping those four kittens."

Today, Betty continues to be part of our family. We found nice homes for three of the kittens, and of course Betty was "fixed." She is wonderfully fat and lazy.

When we started making excuses about not being able to find a home for the fourth kitten and discussed what name to give him, David knew it was another hopeless battle.

Skippy, named in honor of his boat ride, also sleeps on our bed with the man who claims to hate cats.

And Betty? She sat on the edge of the tub the next morning as I bathed and rubbed hair conditioner on my head and blindly put the Bic to my head. I finished, rubbing my skinhead. I braved it for David, taking off my buff so he could give my head a second going-over as he shaved the hairs that I had missed

"Is my head snow white?" I asked him.

"Pretty white," he responded.

"Do I have any scars?" I asked curiously.

"Yep, there is one big one on the back of your head, and a big dent," he said.

And it was then that I knew it. My memory was still intact after thirty-six years of child brutality. That was the exact spot where Cathy had cold-cocked me with a plastic cup and had cut my head open years ago.

Dad was called to come home from work on this summer day because I was bleeding like a stuck pig. I remembered begging him to please not make me go to the hospital to get stitches.

I won. He put cold compresses on it, got the bleeding stopped, and headed back to work. Mom came home shortly after and was so angry that Dad did not have me stitched up.

He made an all-right decision. I did not suffer the fright of stitches, and the scar was hidden for years. And Cathy got in trouble.

I just knew I would continue to avoid mirrors even if David and the kids accepted my frightful look. Betty loves me. And I am rather jealous of her ... she has so much glorious hair.

Photo Gallery

Me with Dr. Linda

*I was experimenting with a scarf and trying
to get brave to go without a wig.*

*One of the many parades I participated in.
Yep, that's me. What a wig!*

*Ryan and me just days before I lost my hair.
David in background.*

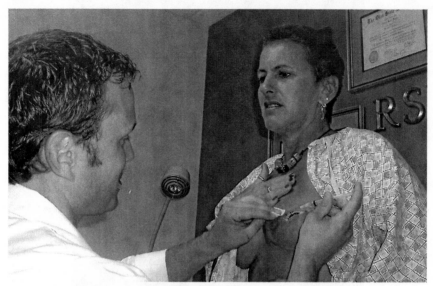

My hair is growing AND my silicone breast.
Dr. Houser injecting saline into the expander. Isn't he cute?

Carol Osbourne, Me and Teresa Evans
on our trip to South Carolina.

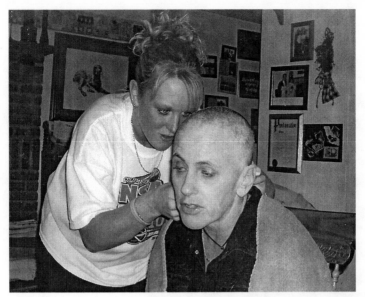

Amber shaving my glory away.

Me showing off my new blood purse. Days after my mastectomy.

Ryan and Katie

Big hair days! Me with my family in 1989.

left to right: Cathy, Tina, me and Mom. This was candle day years ago. We melted old candles and made new ones. What fun!

Me doing my favorite in Cocoa Beach, Florida.
I am sure I was singing, "These Boots are Made for Walking".

Sandi Briden came from Iowa just to see me and to see the famous Gourd show in Mt. Gilead, OH.

Katie at her high school graduation with Mom and Dad.

160

Amber always wanted to cut, shave, curl and comb someone's hair.
This was one of her first amateur hair cuts on her dad.

Left to right: Judy Byers, me, Karen, my cousin and Charlene
at the Relay for Life in Delaware, OH.
All bosom buddies making the survivor lap.

Katie the kicker right after a game.

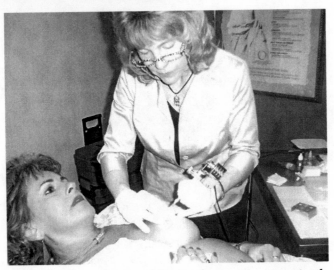

Elaine, the tatoo RN adding color to my new nipple.

Bonnie Kelly, Me and Teresa Walsh. I am so proud of this picture. They are the co-founders of Silpada Designs and this was a wonderful trip I won. They made me feel so welcome!

Margi and I in New York City

My dear friend Dave Hickson and I at our 30th class reunion. I didn't know then it would be his last.

Me and my glorious bug. Check out those chrome wheels.

Me, Cathy Luft and Dave Stevens. My crew and best friends.

Dad and Wayne

Our annual chick trip to Putinbay.
Front row left to right: De, Cathy, Val.
Back row: Me, Deb and Margi

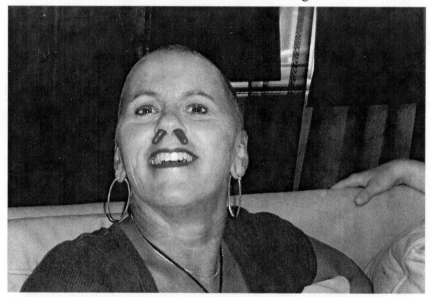

Guess who?

State Softball play offs in Ashland, OH. I sprayed my hair for team spirit. Behind me is Tammy Williams, Pam Bodager, Sister Cathy. Beside me is Sister Tina. All there to show support for Katie. David must have been off getting cokes.

Me with dear friend, Bob Curtis, father to our famous Ben Curtis (Class reunion)

Relay for Life walk with my family.
David, Katie, me and Amber.

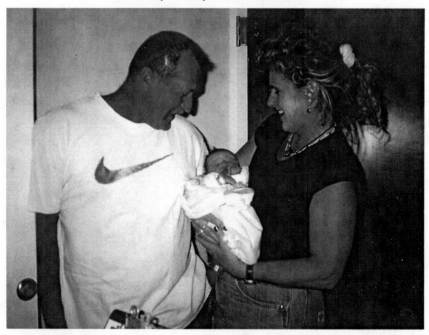

Our first view and touch as grandparents. My Allie Girl!

My first wig. Brittany had just trimmed the bangs.

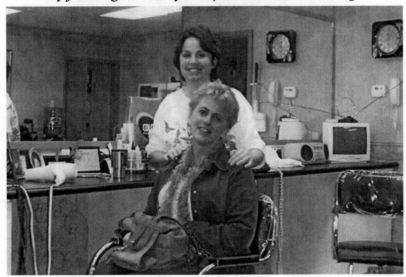

The day De opened the shop to cut my long hair off to prepare for Glory gone days.

Our wedding so many years ago. We look like kids.

Cocoa Beach. Tammy and I the day we fooled the silly boys with my two wigs. Check out the puffy steroid face. Ewww!

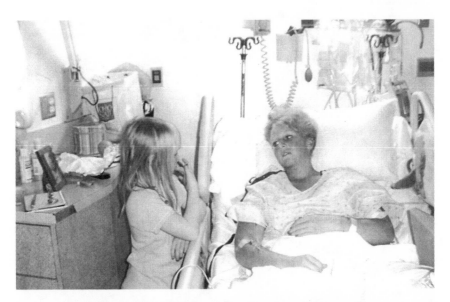

Allie visiting Amber after her horrible wreck.

My friend Charlotte and I who I met much later after my breast cancer. Her cancer came later.

Komen Race for the Cure. Me, Ryan, Derrick, Teresa, Samantha and Diane. Teresa saved me more than she'll ever know when she made me run. Ryan was my strength.

1960. Mom with me in front of her.
Front: Wayne, Tina and Cathy

Great Uncle Wayne with Allie
sporting a new hat he got her for Christmas.

Amber speaking at a high school with OSU Coach Jim Tressel and
Demetris Stanley about drinking and driving.

29
Contagious Vibes

It was chemo day and I was a pro with fewer jitters.

As David and I went through the revolving doors, I read the sign again. "Please use revolving doors to preserve heat." I wondered why, since they kept the chemo lab so damn cold. I thought they liked that chilly, shivering cold.

I looked to my left for no particular reason and saw a man and woman sitting in the waiting area. Sue Falkner. The mystery was solved and I could tell her thanks again. We all spent a lot of time sitting, waiting, and waiting more, and I'd talk to kill time. Dad always told me I could blow up a potato bag.

I saw a bright smile. She even recognized me in my new fake-do. I had hair; she did not when we first met. We were reunited as wig women.

I ran over to her.

"I am so glad to see you again. I have thought about you so much since we met. I didn't even realize I had not gotten your name until after you left last time."

She smiled up to me and touched my arm. "How ya doing? Wig?"

"Yep, I lost my hair ... like clockwork. Two weeks, and POOF! It began doing the let's-leave-her-head dance," I said as I put my hand out for an official introduction. "My name is Connie Curry. What the heck is your name?"

"Sue Falkner," she said as she shook my hand. Her face radiated such positive vibes and good attitude.

"Sue, I am a writer. You touched me and helped me so much; I rushed home to write about you. I am writing a book," I said. "When I make it big with this book and am cancer-free, I want you to know it is partly due to you."

I continued on. I was very excited to see her. "You have no clue how much you helped me that first day of chemo. I was so scared and negative. You restored my faith and hope. Hope Boutique didn't, though. Call me particular, but I didn't like that first wig I got," I told her.

"Well, you look great," she said as she checked out my second wig.

I looked over to see if anyone had called my name, since I was so involved in conversation and not paying attention.

"So, tell me ... how are you feeling? You doing OK too?" I asked.

Immediately she spoke, upbeat, always smiling, and without a complaint.

"We will be on the same schedule for our chemo," she said. "Try to get the early ones before they fall behind. You seem to get in and out sooner," she advised me. "And we can see each other."

It was then that they called her name to go in for her blood work.

"Wait, do you have a phone or e-mail?" I asked her. "I want to send you the chapter I wrote about you. Where do you live anyway?"

"Urbana, Ohio," she said as we stood up and began walking toward the nurse.

Sue quickly ripped a check deposit slip off her checkbook. "Here," she said. "I hardly know you, but take this."

"It's just a deposit slip," I told her with a laugh. "I like ya, but I am not depositing money into your account. BUT, if I get on the *New York Times* bestseller list, I just might make a drop for ya."

With that, I handed her my business card. I knew we would not lose touch again.

I went in shortly after her to get my blood drawn to check those unpredictable white blood counts. We always hope our count is good so the fight can continue. Postponing until the white blood count is back up is disappointing. We all just want to finish the rounds.

I looked in each room, wondering if she might be near me when we went to chemo lab. I sat down at the blood lab. The lab room is not private like most of the chemo rooms, which are chilly but bright and homelike, with televisions and comfortable recliners to kick back in while getting the drip. Some have two-seaters in them, and I would assume that if no preference was asked, one might be on the buddy system for several hours with a stranger.

The nurse came in, asking me questions about how I had done with my first chemo. Various questions were asked, and I rattled on, joking about my night out in my wig and how my daughter had buzzed me in revenge of crooked childhood cuts I had given her.

"Smell! It smells like smoke. My sister made me go in a bar. I am afraid to wash it. I haven't taken the time to read the directions," I told her.

As she was checking my blood pressure and looking for a vein, a young woman walked in with her husband.

She looked about thirty, and I read her face instantly. Fear. My sixth sense kicked in again.

She sat down in the blood-draw chair as she rubbed her hands together. Her husband and she made no eye contact, and no words were spoken. I am sure he was a concerned and loving husband, but they both probably felt confused, empty, and lost.

"Is this your first chemo?" I asked. My nurse looked over at the sad woman, waiting for her answer.

She threw her hands up to her face, nodded yes, and sobbed hysterically.

"Oh, it is OK," I told her. "Really, it is not that bad. Trust me. I swear ... you will be JUST fine."

She smiled through her tears and nodded.

"And it is OK to be scared. You are braver then I was. Ask the nurses here. My first chemo day, I walked out. I asked them to pull the IV, and I left. Just walked right out the door. Do you have breast cancer?" I asked.

She continued to cry. "Yes," she said in an almost-whisper.

"Well, I am here to tell you, you will get through this. I will get through this. I feel good and so much braver. You will be the next time, too."

"Connie, do you have any swelling anywhere?" the RN asked me.

"You mean other than from those steroids that have puffed up my ass? Does that count?" David, the new soldier who was crying, and the nurse laughed.

"And I never sleep," I said as I talked to the nurse and the new patient listened.

"My God, I have cleaned and done more work in the last three weeks than I have ever done. If you have wallpaper to rip off, get on it. When you start the steroids, there's no limit to what you can accomplish."

"I figure ..." I sighed. "See, I have lost my hair. Don't worry, though," I said as I looked at the new girl again. "Like my wig? Anyway, I figure I will be like Rip Van Winkle. When I am off these steroids, I will throw some fertilizer on my head, crash for months, and when I wake up like old Rip Van Winkle, I will have hair down to my bubble butt."

We all laughed and had so much fun as blood was being drawn, charts filled out, and medicine dispensed orally for our war against nausea before the cocktail drip was dropped slowly into our veins.

During chemo, my head began to itch from the scratchy wig. I had prepared like a good Virgo and had brought my *Survivor* buff and VW ball cap.

"Oh, just take it off," my nurse told me. "You are a minority around this place with that wig on. No one has hair. Just take it off." So I did and I placed my new headgear on. *Survivor! Yea!*

As we walked out that day, finished with another treatment, I knew I was halfway finished with chemo. I turned the corner to hit the revolving doors. *Save energy!*

As I twirled my wig on my finger, the receptionists were staring at me, grinning. "Check out the *Survivor* buff. Am I chic or what? See ya in three weeks! Ta-ta!"

The day was bright, with unusual warmth for January. The sun was shining.

If my heart had wings that day, I hoped the new cancer patient jumped on and I had helped her. I had made her laugh. And most of all, I thought of Sue Falkner, and how she had given me good vibes to help another fallen comrade who was sure to step back up to the plate.

30
Wigless Wonder

So there I was, the owner of two wigs and the reality is, they itch. No matter how realistic they look, they feel like head girdles, too.

I decided to be brave on my eighth day after my second chemo. As prescribed, I had stopped taking my steroids. Like my first chemo treatment, day six and seven were bad for me as I came off the medicine. They made me feel like I was crashing. Each step I walked felt like I was going though quicksand.

My stomach felt bloated and miserable. Day eight, I got up and felt on top of the world. I was thrilled to feel almost normal again. I had errands that I had wanted to do for days.

I put my makeup on, and dangling earrings, and picked out a cute brown-and-black outfit. I started to walk away from the mirror to take my *Survivor* buff off and put my wig on. *Oh, which wig,* I wondered. *Is it a long-hair or short-hair day?*

I am not wearing any. I am going wigless, I thought.

Cathy had just bought me the cutest trendy black hat. I call it my *Cold Mountain* hat; very similar to the hat Nicole Kidman wore in that great movie.

I placed it over my buff, looked in the mirror, applied more blush to my cheeks, and I cocked my head, looking in the mirror again. I adjusted the hat a little to the right.

It was a cold winter day with snow on the ground and sharp winds. I put my black leather coat on, with my brown wool scarf that I've had since eighth grade (styles do come back). The scarf covered my neck well for warmth and style. The buff was over the top fourth of my ears, which helped them look smaller. I truly liked the hat look.

My first stop was the drugstore, and then the post office. No one at the store seemed to stare at me or think I looked weird. I found that reassuring. I did notice many smiles, even from strangers. I smiled back.

No matter the headgear, cover stick covering the dark circles under the eyes, and blush adding a glow to the cheeks, a cancer patient without a wig stands out.

As I approached the post office entrance door, I was eager to see my postal buddies. Being a writer, and sending off many manuscripts, I knew each employee by name. Mike, a high school friend and postal clerk, was also one I was anxious to see. I had not seen him since our thirtieth reunion. My visits was always fun, with lots of laughs.

When I walked in the second door to the counter line, Mike came barreling from behind the counter to see me. He hugged me with such genuine affection. It was then that I knew he had heard.

"We are the bald and beautiful, Mike." (Mike's been bald since he was in his twenties.)

"Yea, we are," he said.

"No, Mike, you wear bald much better than I do. I am as bald as a baby's ass. It is just not a girl thing."

He asked me many questions about my health, and we laughed as I told him stories about the last couple of months.

As I was heading home from running errands, it occurred to me that this wigless style could do lots for women who don't feel like having an itchy day in a wig.

I realized how much extra help I was offered, and I got thinking that I could leave the house on my bad chemo days and still get a lot accomplished with the help of so many sympathetic people.

I remember that after talking to Mike and getting in the line for postal service, I was offered a cut in line. I think if I go wigless in the future, I could learn to lean a little on walls and counters and sigh in distress. This wigless thing just might be the ticket.

The following day was another good day. I had no CPMs to apply on patients, so I had the day off. I had the pleasure of babysitting Allie.

I decided to do another wigless day as we headed to the grocery store. The particular store where I buy groceries rarely has carryouts. Do any stores have carryouts anymore or is this a luxury of the past? Again, the wigless look worked wonders. I was offered help out to my car with my groceries. How grand and unusual. I accepted the offer, out of the ordinary for me since I am of an independent nature.

As always, Allie wanted to see Grandma and Papa Van Brimmer. It was nearing naptime for her, and out of habit, she wanted her blankee as we headed out home. Amber and Paul, her parents, had agreed to set some rules with Allie to encourage her to stop sucking her thumb and dragging the blanket everywhere. I agreed to abide by their wishes.

"Allie, remember that Mommy left your blankee at home. You can only have it at bedtime, since you are four and such a big, big girl."

"Oh, Grammy," she said with such a theatrical expression, "I am mad at my mommy, I am mad at my daddy, I am sad for my blankee, and I am sad because you have a balded head."

I drove on to Mom and Dad's, knowing that she would be sidetracked and happy once she saw Mom and Dad. I recalled many times hearing her panic and cry as she misplaced it, and looking everywhere for it.

What is it about grandchildren that make grandparents so soft-hearted? If I had had that blanket, I would have immediately handed it to her. I was aware she needed to stop sucking her thumb. I had already noticed she hadn't sucked her thumb when the blanket wasn't around. This new rule was good and just might be the trick to break her.

I didn't want this beautiful child to damage her mouth or teeth. We want them to have manners and good morals and be well-behaved. Discipline is the key, and I know this! But it is difficult for me to be stern with her.

I think now that I am older, I am more patient and wise, and yes, I am soft in my heart for this little girl.

She rules the roost when she is with me, I reluctantly admit. But I do know that kindness and patience are the keys to getting her to do what I want. I can always win with reverse psychology (most of the time that is).

When she was younger, and I watched her so much, I always tried to wash her blanket. Any parent who has a "blanket baby" knows how soiled and nasty the blankets can get. They drag them everywhere. They hold them as they eat lunch. They wipe tears, dirty noses, and hands and wrap the cat in them.

Allie always made me out to be the enemy when she noticed it was missing.

I succeeded in getting it in the washing machine most of the time. It would usually be dried or about finished when she would discover it gone.

I recall one day when she was about three.

"Grammy, where's my blankee?"

My heart raced! She was about to show me who was boss, and I was crossing into a battle zone. How dare I wash that blanket? How could I be so cruel to want to wash away a week's worth of Play-doh, ice cream, and the aftermath of a snotty cold? How dare I want to make her "blankee" smell pretty and look bright again?

She became suspicious, immediately sensing that she had not misplaced it.

Allie threw her hand up to her forehead like Scarlett did when Rhett Butler was leaving her, and as dramatic as Scarlett, she said, "OH NO! Grammy! You didn't! You didn't!"

"Yes, Allie, I did," I shamelessly said. "I am washing it."

"I can't bawieve you, Grammy! I WANT my blankee NOW!"

"I have a great idea, Allie. Let's go downstairs and look in the washing machine so we can see your blankee getting allllll clean."

As we walked downstairs, I started to think that I might just win this battle.

"Get it out, Grammy. I want my blankee."

And it was then that she threw herself against the washer, and tears the size of tennis balls starting falling as she hugged the washing machine. This brought to mind Scarlett again when she clung to the banister as Rhett walked away.

I was now on Allie's "hit list"!

"Allie, it won't be long. Grammy will have it all washed and dried soon, and you will be so happy when you smell it and see how pretty it looks. Just be patient. Do you remember what be patient means?" I asked her.

"One minute?" she sobbed.

The world came to an abrupt halt as we stood at the washer, waiting for the rinse cycle and final spin. When the washer stopped, she looked up at me with those big passionate, pleading eyes and said, "Is it done, Grammy?"

"Well, I guess it is done enough," I said as I took it out of the washer.

"Oh Grammy, I wuv you. It smells so good. Grammy washed my blankee," she said proudly as she hugged the wet blanket to her chest.

It was again brought to my attention that I have a soft heart. It also occurred to me that I was also going to have a wet but content child at naptime as she snuggled and hugged her wet best friend. David and I would end up with a wet bed too.

I was eager to see how this new rule would pan out, and if her parents would weaken.

As we pulled into my parents' home, Allie jumped out of the car, excited to see Grandma and Papa, totally forgetting her blanket.

That evening, Katie had a home basketball game. It was senior night for the girls' team. There was a short ceremony to honor the three seniors. Ryan had called earlier in the week. He actually asked me how I was feeling. I was so glad he addressed the issue, even though he briefly touched on the topic of my cancer. A few nights prior, I had talked to Sue in my writers' group about Ryan. She said that if a man can't kick it or piss on it, they don't know what to do. I thought how humorous and great her analogy of the male gender was.

Ryan was coming to the game. I was elated. Amber and Allie were coming too. I knew that Katie loved their moral support. After all, she had been dragged to every kind of sporting event for them since she was born. No wonder she played more sports then any kid at her high school. It was bred in her. Amber and Ryan had played many sports, and I remember the spring of Katie's birth, having her at the soccer fields when she was days old.

When I got pregnant with her, I was on a mission to find a certain baby carrier. No one had them, but in my mind I knew I had to have a white wicker baby basket. Baby baskets had gone off the retail market in the mid-eighties. I recalled a huge controversy over the varnish on baskets and them being a possible health issue.

I went to every basket store, wicker store, and baby store I could find, determined that a basket would be very practical for a newborn at soccer games.

It had to be a beautiful white, symbolizing spring. It needed handles for walking long distance at the huge soccer field complex, and it had to have a hood over it for shade. It needed to be big enough for a baby to be comfortable while sleeping. I found one! I was thrilled. Perfect and it was white. I then went to a sewing/craft store, which was an unusual place for me to shop. I am not crafty, nor am I a seamstress. To this day, buttons and seams are my limit. Cathy repairs all our clothes.

I bought a thick piece of sponge-like foam. I remember being on the floor almost ready to deliver, measuring and cutting the foam to fit the bottom of the basket. A receiving blanket tucked over and under it was perfect for the baby to lie on.

To this day, I consider that beautiful wicker bed a family heirloom. I remember walking with Katie in the basket. She was almost always lulled to sleep on the walks before the games had started. As we walked, I almost always wore pretty, cotton spring dresses, and sometimes a stylish straw hat. Katie was always in a pretty white bonnet.

We looked like the picture of health and full of spring spirit. Little kids would walk over to the basket, peaking in, curious to see what was in the basket. Katie slept through all the games, but she never missed a game to support her older siblings.

As I parked my car in a hurry to get into the game before tip-off, I looked in my car mirror one last time to be sure the wig was in place. I had decided to wear the long wig, and was running late because a dear friend's dad had passed away and I had gone to the funeral home before the game to pay my respects.

At the funeral home, I saw many old school friends, and although we were at a funeral home, the atmosphere was full of happiness. Marcia's dad was eighty, and he had lived a good life. The family was accepting of his death and celebrating his life.

Many people flocked to see me. Seeing me reassured them that I was OK, surviving, happy, and truly among the living.

I laughed and joked with each one as they hugged me. "Don't touch, don't touch the head," I whined in a high-pitched voice like Stuart from *Mad TV.* It was wonderful seeing so many old school friends, but I hurried out, giving Marcia a hug as I hurried on to Katie's game.

As I walked into the game, I felt all eyes on me. Everyone was already seated, and I had gotten to the game in the nick of time. My goal was to not make eye contact with anyone, but to get to Amber, David, Ryan, and Allie. Being in a different wig confirmed I was bald.

I was facing the crowd, removing my coat, and my eyes scanned upward to many of the basketball parents. I saw so many watching me, and the response was favorable, with warm smiles, laughs, and waves. I knew they loved my way of having fun with the wigs (even if they do itch).

Just as I was feeling so comfortable, I felt a hand (a small one) reaching upward to my head. Allie was about to grab my wig out of curiosity. "What is this, Grammy?"

It later occurred to me that she had not seen my wigs. With all the frequent visits, she always saw me in my buff. I had not even thought about the fact that she had not seen me in either wig. I should have prepared her for this transition.

To think my biggest fear was always worrying about the wig falling off, or someone hugging me and catching their wristwatch on it as they came downward. My granddaughter almost made a total spectacle of me in front of a huge mass of eyes, all in the innocence of a curious moment.

"Grammmmy, I just want to pet it," she whined.

"OK, OK, pet it, but gently," I told her.

I reacted quickly as I guided her hand. It amazed me how easily she accepted the wig on my head, and the entire situation ended as quickly as it had begun.

I sat for a while as the game started and then began my ritual of selling 50/50 tickets to the crowd. Cocoa Beach, softball, sunshine, and spring break were coming soon. Thousands of dollars were earned the entire school year to provide the expenses for the girls' varsity team to spend their break in Florida. Playing teams from all over the United States, preparing for their school season, and getting in shape were the goals. The Buckeye Valley softball team and Coach Carol Evans had a successful softball program. Money had to be earned, and I loved mingling with the crowd and selling tickets. I missed my calling and should have been in sales. I could truly push the tickets. Coach Evans loved the money we made at each home game.

I headed to the visitors' side, in an effort to sell more tickets. It seemed that most opposing spectators rarely wanted to buy tickets from their opponents. I had also noticed in the past that heading over to sell them and getting them to dig into their pockets for a dollar when the opponent was losing could be more challenging. My high-pressure sales usually worked. After all, if their ticket was pulled, they drove home with quite a bit of loot. I always reminded them that they could be the lucky winner.

Coach Evans and avid sports fan, has announced the games for years. The statistician's table was located in the front row of the visitor's side.

As I sold tickets to the visitors, Coach Evans blared over the microphone, "Don't forget to buy your 50/50 ticket from Connie Curry."

Unknown to her, I was up in the stands directly behind her, and I jokingly hollered down, "Excuse me, but Jennifer Aniston is here tonight."

"Correction," she bellowed over the mike. "Jennifer Aniston has your tickets."

I stood, waving across to our home side. What fun I was having! Thank goodness it was halftime, and Katie was in the locker room with her team. This would have been one of the many embarrassing moments for her.

At halftime also, the team came out early so the three seniors could be recognized and honored for Senior Night. As they came across the basketball court with their parents on each side of them, each was given a single rose by their teammates. As Rachelle accepted her flower and walked across the court, I saw her coming directly to me. She handed me her rose. "For you—get well."

I hugged her tightly. "Awww, thanks, Rachelle. God love you, girl."

I didn't know if I would ever get over feeling paranoid about the wig flipping off. But I held tight to that beautiful rose.

31
I Saw A Man In My Bathroom

In the past, I must have habitually looked in the mirror. I don't think I was ever prissy. It was just a habit every night when I bathed... I think. I smiled a lot in the mirror, searching for wrinkle lines. I noticed that if I displayed that frightened look, the crow's feet disappeared. I checked eyelashes for plucking and my skin for zits.

It had been five weeks since my head had been buzzed, and I still couldn't look in mirrors except with my wig or buff on while applying my makeup.

I remember days when I never locked the bathroom door. It was a waste of time, because the kids used the little screwdriver on top of the fireplace mantel, jimmied the lock, knocked, and bust on in. It was the social place where everyone seemed to gather. It never failed that when I wanted a quiet, private bath, someone had to pee. When someone had a question about homework or advice about a boy at school, they couldn't wait to pull up to the toilet seat. In her younger days, Katie, the roving reporter, had to come in to rat on her older siblings.

Ryan never came in. His questions could wait, but Amber and Katie always came in to interrupt my baths. So, between Betty the cat, and now Katie and Allie, Calgon never takes me away. After

I lost my hair, and being a little vain, I didn't like them to see me bald.

Becky, one of my best high school friends and now a professional photographer, had asked me repeatedly if she could take my picture for the cover of my book. My book ideas were exciting to me. I was so hoping I could muster the courage to allow Beck to take my picture.

As the day approached for my photo appointment at her studio, I turned belly up. I had every excuse to postpone the bald shots. Becky accepted my cancellation with understanding and compassion.

"Let me go to Florida, get some sun, get this steroid weight off, and I am sure when I get back, I can be brave. Becky, you know that if I am not comfortable with my bald head, I won't shoot well for the pictures. This book is so important to me," I pleaded to her as we talked on the phone. "Just remember, you might have to doctor up the pictures. By April, I may not have any eyebrows or lashes. I will just have to take the chance."

"Connie, we will do them whenever you are ready," she said, and that was that!

Why would I want a picture on my book of my bald head? It was important to me. I wanted the reality to be seen by many. I also hoped that we could bring out something positive for women to see that we can smile without our glory. I hoped that with some effort, a feminine look could be captured without hair. Even though I had down days and didn't feel like smiling, I smiled more than I frowned.

As I bathed that night, I locked the door, a new ritual I had began five weeks ago. I jumped in the tub with my buff on and removed it to shampoo and condition. Usually I would pick up the buff immediately from the side of the tub and stick it back on my wet head. (I just never knew if someone might try to jimmy the lock out of habit.)

I wondered why I shampooed and conditioned my head. Soap works fine on skin. I convinced myself that the conditioner was good for my hair follicles. I used it like a fertilizer so that when my chemo was finished; the follicles would feel healthy, wanting to burst out like spring daffodils ready to bloom.

I got out of the tub, dried off, and put all the girlie-smelly-stuff on, I routinely walked over by the medicine cabinet to brush my teeth and apply deodorant. I put forth much effort to ignore the mirror as I opened the cabinet door.

That night, as my mind was miles away, I forgot I had not put on the buff, and I looked up in the mirror. I saw a stranger staring back at me. I looked away as quickly as possible. I know it was a brief second that I thought I saw a man standing behind me. I knew this was impossible. David respected my privacy, and the door was locked.

What a stupid thought as my heart rate settled and I almost laughed at my stupidity. A man? No way. It was much like when I have jumped at my own shadow. The confusion only lasted for a few seconds.

It truly took me a second to realize it was me. I did not recognize myself. The image in the mirror horrified me. It made me mad that I had been careless and had looked. I vowed never to look in the mirror. I knew nothing positive could come of seeing it. It would only depress me, and I knew I was not beautiful like Demi Moore. I was absolutely right. I started to cry and I jerked the buff down over my eyes. I was so pissed off.

I was shocked how white my head looked. I wish I had been really brave and taken a mirror like my hairstylist has taught me to do, aiming the little mirror at the big mirror to see the back of my hair. I might have seen the battle wound from Cathy. But I didn't want to look again.

Fat is prettier tan, so I was looking forward to trying to get some tan on my head in Florida. How would I ever get the courage to sunbathe bald? Maybe the wine or strawberry daiquiris we drink all settled in at the pool sucking up sun rays would make me bold. Besides, many liberated people reside in Cocoa Beach. If Tattoo Mike, whom I met there years ago, could walk around with tattoos all over his entire body, sporting a parrot on his shoulder as he drank beer in the oceanside bars, I could be different, too. Maybe.

I started feeling a little pretty in the wigs when I had put makeup and funky earrings on. I noticed that I constantly made sure my fingernails were bright red and my lipstick always in place. I was probably overcompensating.

As I was getting dressed, the phone rang. It was Theresa, a dear medic-friend from my EMS days. I had not heard from her since I had gotten sick. I felt so blue. News had gotten back to me that she had put off calling me. She feared crying and was too upset about my cancer. I was sad to think she was upset. I felt disappointed because if I was being brave most days, I hoped she could be, too.

"Connie, I have something for you, but I don't quite know what to do with it," she said.

"What do you mean, Theresa? What is it?"

"I got ten inches cut off my hair for you, and I have it, but I am not sure what to do with it. It's in a bag," she said.

I immediately started crying. I recalled all the women in the waiting room at the oncologist's office. I shared so many conversations with them, and how we all expressed the same concern … our hair losses.

"Oh, Theresa. Of all the treatments, needle sticks, chemo, and thoughts of losing a breast, or women that have had mastectomies; we have such a hard time emotionally losing our hair. Thank you so much. The wigs truly do help us. You are a gem of a friend."

I was very surprised. Her long gorgeous, golden hair was beautiful. I was choked up that she had done something so generous for me. I knew I must find a way to use her special gift. She had sacrificed something very wonderful for me. And, like the saying goes, blondes have more fun, and I was always eager for fun!

The following day, I called around, trying to find out what we could do constructively with Theresa's hair. I found out that it takes three full haircuts to make one wig. But those ten inches had to be put to use somehow. Her sacrifice was too huge to go unnoticed or for her to not be rewarded.

I called her back. We decided to check with Locks of Love, a nonprofit organization that provides hair prosthetics for financially disadvantaged children in the United States and Canada. Most of the wigs are made for children who have long-term hair loss.

Many suffer with alopecia areata, a mysterious medical condition that causes hair loss. Just looking at the before and after pictures of the children on the Web site tugged at my heart. The bright eyes and big smiles topped with the locks-of-hair wigs on small faces warmed my heart. What a wonderful organization for these kids. Generous people and leaders had made this possible. I began a mission for those locks of love given in my honor by a good friend.

We would donate her hair to those precious children.

We found a home for that wonderful glory.

32
Under The Influence Of Chemo-brain

On February 2, 2005, I went in for my third chemo. I was counting down, and by the end of February, if all went as planned, I would be finished with chemotherapy. Yeehaw. Dr. Linda told me I would know more about possibly having radiation, a mastectomy, or another lumpectomy after my chemo was finished. I would not have radiation if a mastectomy was done. I was praying for radiation, even though I knew I would have to have thirty-five treatments. It would be a new, mysterious avenue to travel, but I was willing. I hoped it would be a walk in the park compared to chemo.

I was resistant and dreading going to chemo when I awoke that early, cold morning. Just when I was feeling well, it was time to get knocked down again. I was not looking forward to my blood count dropping again, which as a rule happens about eight to ten days after the chemo cocktail.

I managed to pick my spirits up when I thought about seeing Sue, my new optimistic friend. It was not her job to always cheer me up, and if she could be positive, I could too. I also wondered if I might see the new girl I had met at the last chemo treatment, who was so young and scared. I assumed she would be bald like many of us, and I hoped I would find her again.

I did not see her. I wondered, but had no idea if she was scheduled for later. Even if I knew her name, I knew the staff probably wouldn't give me information about her. HIPAA, a new privacy protection for patients, would prevent me from finding her, so I didn't ask. She may have been in a wig and I might have walked right by her, not recognizing her, anyway.

I saw Sue and it was wonderful. She was her usual upbeat self. Before we left for the day, we planned and scheduled a buddy room when we took our next chemo. The staff laughed at me. I had left my room and they were in search of me. I wondered if they thought I was GOA again. (Gone on arrival, as many patients were when I worked in EMS. The drunks who wrecked would scramble out of their wreckage and take off on foot to hide before the cops came.)

David directed my nurse to me. She suggested that Sue and I get a room together next time, as she stood holding her stethoscope, trying to get me back to my room. "We have already decided that," I said, smiling.

Another nurse was searching for an RN named Connie. Connie was nowhere to be found. "Connie. Hey, Connie." There was a pause and another shout, "Connie, Connie, CONNIE!"

"In here," I hollered. The nurse looking for RN Connie came in my room and stopped short. "She isn't in here. Not you, silly. You crazy woman."

"Hey, did you know there is a song by Brooks and Dunn about a Crazy Connie?" I asked her.

When Connie surfaced, I heard the nurse ask her if she was familiar with the Brooks and Dunn song, as they pointed at me.

"I do know that song," Connie said. "It is a great song."

"How does it go?" asked the other RN.

"Oh, I know it, but I can't think how it starts," Connie said as she swung her stethoscope around on her hand.

I then started singing it. "That's it, that's it," Connie said.

"I am a karaoke queen, and I love that song. I LOVE to karaoke. It is sooooo fun," I told them.

I had met Woody, the DJ for a local radio station in Columbus. Woody and I had e-mailed each other several times when I participated in the famous birthday pranks he pulled on people. With the help of someone, he'd call people on their birthday. He always wanted short-fused, hotheaded people to make the prank successful. He loved to argue with them on the air and get them fired up. They would be clueless that it was Woody, the DJ, since he disguised his voice so well.

With info given to him, phone numbers, and a scenario about something controversial the birthday person has been involved in, he sets a trap for them. I helped him set up some great ones, and he had pranked my sister Tina and Margi. If it is a good one, he broadcasts it over the radio, and they are always funny. Tina's was a huge success and hilarious.

With so much communication through e-mail to prepare these, Woody and I had become friends. About a year earlier, I had gone to a Dixie Chicks concert and he, along with his other DJ sidekicks, were in downtown Columbus for a concert.

I e-mailed him and told him I would be there. We met near the coliseum and had a blast laughing and talking.

It was not long after that when I had WCOL playing as usual on my kitchen radio. "Wake up with Woody," as they advertised on their radio station, and I listened religiously each morning.

As he started to play "You Can't Take the Honky Tonk Out of the Girl," he said, "Does anyone know a Crazy Connie? I do. I met her at the Chicks concert." And Brooks and Dunn broadcast over the radio singing the Connie song.

As my blood was drawn, we talked on and on about various birthday busts we'd all heard on WCOL. Woody is a true nut.

My blood count came back good, and it was time to get my cocktail. The IV was put in, and the drugs began titrating into me. I kicked back in my recliner, and David and I talked about my recent confusion.

I had read in many pamphlets about different side effects the chemo might cause. I'd read the pamphlet stating that sex could change. I decided I would not read it. Why ask for symptoms? Why let the mind wander and make excuses? My sex life had been healthy, full, and gratifying my entire adult life. I had not felt any changes, except feeling less attractive, but that didn't seem to be an issue with David.

It was never my sex life that was unsettled. It was the emotional part of my life, and the daily stress of family issues. After two chemo treatments, and a third about to begin, my body was still inviting and full of sexual desires.

But the memory loss plagued me. I worried. I had treated many patients with Alzheimer's disease and I knew I was too young to have the first stages of that sad disease.

"Ya know, I am going to ask the nurse about this memory thing," I suggested to David. I unplugged my IV pole and got up. I knew the IV pole had a backup battery and would continue feeding my vein.

As I walked out of my room, pulling my IV pole on wheels, I headed back to Sue's room, looking for her, and noticed a RN in her room.

"Hey, excuse me girls. Oh girls," I said as I pictured myself like the older folks in hospitals, IV in hand, and the other hand holding the hospital gown shut to prevent my butt crack from showing. Thank my lucky stars; we did not have to put those silly gowns on for chemo treatments.

I looked like a healthy woman, driving an IV pole with a mashed-potato memory.

"You're back, Connie," Sue said with a smile. The nurse welcomed me with a grin also.

"Sue, do you feel like your memory is scattered?"

"I do, yes. YES, I do," she replied instantly.

"Chemo-brain, we call it," the nurse immediately said.

"Well, I did read about it," I told them.

"You are kidding," Sue said. "So that is IT!"

"Yes, it is very common for the chemo to do this to you," the nurse advised us. "Your memory will come back, but they say it takes about a year once you have finished chemo."

"Oh my God, I am going to walk around with Stickum notes on my forehead," I told them. "I am a list-writer anyway. I now make a list and can't find the damn thing." We talked on, sharing and comparing our symptoms.

"I have had three babies, and I have never had that loose-bladder thing like many women. I can hold it forever," I boasted. "But just recently, I notice that I piddle so easily and can't get to the bathroom quick enough."

"Chemo! It's the chemo," the RN told Sue and me as we sat and took mental notes.

"Well, holy cow. That explains something." I told them. "Betty, my cat, has this ritual. She nestles down beside me every night. Prior to heading down to lie by my feet, she jumps up to my face to greet me, using her claws on my waterbed mattress. I cringe when I think about her sharp nails and all that water."

They listened attentively as I rattled on. "I got up the other morning, and my PJs were wet near my bottom. I assumed I had piddled again. I thought it was that chemo-brain stuff going on."

They laughed.

"I assumed I had forgotten to pee, or my bladder was misbehaving again. It was Betty's fault. It took me until the following night to realize that my bed was leaking and it was not my fault. The mystery is solved," I said.

Sue's treatment was about ten minutes ahead of mine. She was finishing as I turned to drive my IV pole back to my room. "I'll be over to see you before I go," Sue said.

"Cool! See you in a bit," I said as I put the IV in second gear and rolled out.

As Sue and her husband came over to tell David and me goodbye, Sue was excited to share some news with us.

"Guess what I found out today," she said. "Did you know you can get chemo-brain from the chemo and it messes with your memory?"

"Sue ... Sue. Helllloooo. It was me that brought that up and told you about it. I have now proven that theory. You have chemo-brain, just like me."

"It was you? You told me? Well, shit," she said, and we roared with laughter.

In defense of Sue's confusion and so many medical people talking to us, advising us, checking us, and filling our minds with information, it truly was hard to remember who told us what. But we shared a good laugh.

And I knew as we said our goodbyes that we would meet again in three weeks. I just hoped she and I would remember we signed up for a buddy room and would know each other.

After all, we were the temporarily chemo-brain women with mashed potatoes for brains.

Our brains would rejuvenate in a year.

33
Small-town Dreams And Big Friendships

Ostrander, Ohio. Bob Curtis. It was just an ordinary name and town. It seemed to be. Bob Curtis was the first boy I ever held hands with, my first kiss, and my first slow dance in junior high school. Ostrander, a rural community, is probably not even on Ohio maps.

I lay beside him in hay on chilly, fall nights when I went to the ever-so-popular Curtis hayrides. We were innocent. We were kids and had not a worry in the world. Our youth was our security in life and our happiness. Never a worry.

I remember the day in the spring of fifth grade, on the hill in grade school. Bob and Perry were meeting to have a fight over who would be my boyfriend. The kids crowded the hill to watch the outcome. I observed in an infantile way, appropriate for an innocent, young girl. I was impressed. The fight never happened, but my friendship with Bob and Perry is as firm as the hill and Radnor School forty years later.

I had not been out to socialize since my wig party with Cathy. Claire, my dear friend, and I decided to go out. We had a reason and a good excuse. Vinntage Band (spelled with two Ns, remember?) was playing at a local bar in town. Claire had been cooped up with sick kids. My blood count was starting to fall from my third chemo, but I was not going down without a fight. I was holding on for the celebration of life. The following week would be my down week, and I did not want grass growing under my feet.

We walked into the bar, and the crowd was abundant. I saw so many familiar faces and people who had sent me inspirational cards in the last several months. It was a wonderful, glorified night out with my glory wig on. The hugs and kisses were so welcome and sincere.

As they approached me, I used my typical phrase, "Hugs! But don't touch the hair." My fear stayed with me that something could get caught in my hair. I wiggled my fake scalp at them. They laughed and shared my humor as many chimed in with added conversation.

Jim, Bob, Rowena, Viv, and Dave, my best friend from the Vinntage Band and high school friends were among the wonderful crowd. I felt pretty. When I had looked in the mirror seconds before my exit from home, I knew I was satisfied with my looks and the wig. My blazer jacket hid my steroid hips.

I didn't want to chance a trip to the public bathroom, look in the mirror, and change my attitude, so I held my bladder for five hours. To look in a mirror with so much excitement and fun in the air would possibly have sent my mood into a plunge. The rock-and-roll music was superb, and Viv, Rowena, and I hit the dance floor first among all the people. Vinntage Band members smiled as they strummed, beat the drums, and sang. They knew I could get the crowd on their feet. I did.

Claire deserved a fun night out. She had done so much for me since my bout with cancer. We had cried on the phone together many times. Our work, families, childrearing, and the news of my cancer had been many of the troubled conversations we had had over the years. Claire, a free spirit and outspoken fighter, was much like me in personality. She is a long-lasting friend.

With a big heart and loyalty to me, she set up a schedule with many of my friends to have food dropped off at my home after my chemo treatments. My pride and independence had gotten in the way many times as so many friends knocked on my door with fresh dinners. I knew they did it to show they loved me, and it also made them feel good to give. Giving is truly a self-gratification given to the recipient and the giver. I learned to say thanks with grace, send thank-you notes, and let my pride relax. My memory and appreciation would always be intact for their gracious hospitality to my family and me.

As I walked off the dance floor, Bob Curtis approached me. "How ya doing, Connie?"

"I'm OK. I am as bald as a baby's ass, but I am OK."

"Well, you look good, and ya know," he said, "Connie, you have to beat this. You are too damn ornery to not win this," he said as he patted me with his rough, hard-working hands.

"That is just what my dad would say, Bob. He has said exactly that many times to me over the years when I was having challenging times."

His wife Janis, a quiet but friendly woman, listened, smiling as we talked about old friends and new adventures.

Bob and Janis are the town celebrities, but most would not know it. They don't walk it or show arrogance. They are full of pride and acceptance of a fulfilled dream that many parents can't even imagine. Yes, I suppose they're ordinary in their attitudes because they are like the many people I was fortunate to grow up with— hard-working, simple, middle-class people whose motivation had paid off.

Their field of dreams had come true the summer of 2003.

I was at a travel softball tournament for Katie's softball team in Dayton, Ohio. Many locals from my town were at the softball tournament. Our loyalty was with our teen daughters, but our hopes and dreams were with Bob Curtis that Sunday.

Parents had headsets on and the doors of their cars open as they listened to radios. They blared throughout the park. We cheered for the girls on their big plays in softball, and we huddled near the radio, listening for updates. Our hearts raced and we were elated. Ben Curtis, a small-town young man with discipline, commitment, and a passion for golf, was doing what no one expected. He was leading in the British Open.

I remember leaving the ballpark after the long, hot day with Katie all sticky and sweating from playing ballgames, and heading out home to see Mom and Dad. I couldn't wait to talk about the outcome. Mom had called my cell phone several times during the tournament. We listened together as Ben played many holes, making par, slowly pulling into the lead. Our voices cracked with so much emotion for Ben. I thought of Bob and Janis. I remembered when Ben and Nick were born. I had followed Bob and watched him show cattle each year at the county fair when we were in high school. I later followed Ben as he succeeded through golf tournaments all throughout high school.

He had gotten a full-ride scholarship to Kent State College. For a child to get a full-ride scholarship is pure joy. To graduate, go on, and become the British Open champion was more than any parent's imagination could grasp. Our county was beaming with supportive pride.

At the park, we all wanted to stand up and announce to all the out-of-town softball people that *this is our Ben, our town, our friend's son, OUR BOB.*

As I walked in the door at home, I ran to Mom and Dad. "Can you believe it? Oh my God. Ben! How grand is this, Mom, Dad?"

Our family had never played a lick of golf. Of all the sports my children had participated in, golf was not our sport. But Mom had always followed golf on television. To watch the British Open that day and to see Ben was her ultimate high.

"Well, Dad. You have done it now," I said to him in a joking voice. "Bob was my first boyfriend. I kissed him, hugged him, and held his hand. I dated him." I prattled on, laughing. "I minded my p's and q's. You threatened me about not having sex in school. Did I listen to you? Was I a good girl? YEEEESSSS, Dad. Now LOOK! My son could have been the British Open champion. See what happens when I listen to you, Dad?"

We roared with laughter as Katie shook her head at me. And of course, it was all said in a joke. I wouldn't trade Ryan, my son, for all the Bens.

I was just a proud friend.

34
Smells And Touches

I should have prepared and taken notes each day after my series of chemo treatments. Like clockwork, every three weeks, the side effects were exactly the same as I felt my white blood count dropping. Muscle aches, heartburn that felt like fire rolling down my esophagus, and stomach bloating all began about eight days after the chemo.

My right arm, which was fed the chemo, would begin to ache like severe sore muscles, and pain would radiate down my entire right side. My cuticles would become soft and peel like snakeskin. My fingernail polish became paper thin and pulled away from my nails in big pieces. It reminded me of the summer days when Cathy, Wayne, Tina, and I would take turns pulling big layers of sunburned skin off of each other's backs. We'd lay the big pieces down for safekeeping, seeing who could pull the biggest piece off without it breaking.

None of these deteriorations was my imagination. When I thought about it, it frightened me to think something so powerful was in my body, destroying healthy things. I would put my mind in reverse and remember that it was going to cure me and was also killing the bad stuff. We were just taking the long road to get there.

At my next appointment, I was curious to ask the nursing staff about my stench. I was sure it was not my imagination. Around day nine of each treatment, I started to smell a peculiar odor seeping from my skin. No one else in the family claimed they could smell me. They thought I had gone mad.

I bathed daily. I loved and used my girlie-smelly soaps, body oils, and powders. I sprayed myself with my favorite colognes.

I stunk. I smelled like chemicals. I was certain.

An unusually warm Sunday, seven weeks after my head had been buzzed, I got the badge of courage. I had gone off my steroids as directed and was feeling emotional. The steroids would throw me into an emotional turmoil as I was withdrawing from them. I felt like I was on speed for about three days after discontinuing them, and they put my moods in a high unpredictable gear.

I would cry at the drop of a hat. Many would be happy tears, but mostly I was an up-and-down roller coaster of mush.

I sat at my makeup table, looking out at the dirty old snow. The warm day was helping it melt away. It had been there for weeks. I loved seeing the sunshine warming the ground and slivers of green grass popping through. There was a promise of warmer temperatures and spring days. I applied moisturizer to my face.

I applied makeup and put on my lipstick and long dangling earrings. My *Survivor* buff was atop my head as usual.

I slowly pulled it off, not letting my eyes leave the mirror. I wouldn't blink because I feared I would turn away.

As the buff left my head, I looked at myself. It wasn't that man! Minus the makeup, earrings, lipstick, and cleavage, I was Wayne.

My heart felt warm. I didn't want to run out to the mall and enter a fashion show, but I felt at peace. I felt honored to look like my brother. His face is like his disposition ... kind, pleasant, and generous. His eyes are sparkly and big, full of life and gentle. His beauty is within and out. I was thrilled to see him though my eyes and reflection.

I was like a child who had just learned to walk. I became brave and almost comfortable as family and friends stopped over to check on me that Sunday. I wanted to share my accomplishment.

"Wanna see my head? I'll show ya," I told Shelley, my niece. "I looked today."

"Sure. Show me," she said as she and Katie looked up from the table. Katie had a look of apprehension, probably recalling her tears and how my skinhead party had frightened her.

"Wait, I want to show you something else, Shell." I scampered off to my bedroom. Shelley and Katie laughed.

Shelley sat at the table helping Katie with math homework as I began a fashion show, coming out in a wide variety of headgear.

"OK, here it goes," I said, walking out bare-headed.

"Aunt Connie, you don't look bad. You look like Sinead O'Connor."

"Wait. Is that a man or woman? Isn't Sinead O'Connor a basketball player?"

"No, Mom. That is Shaquille O'Neal." Katie nudged Shelley and they giggled.

As the day went on, I started feeling worse. My throat hurt, my stomach was a mess, and my legs felt as weak as a new lamb's.

Just as I put on a pot of coffee, looking for a source of energy, Wayne stopped to check on me.

Seeing him warmed my heart and made me feel better. He and I continued to adjust to our life changes and shared concerns for each other. My lost brother had resurfaced, and our entire family welcomed the old Wayne home.

"Wayne, oh my God. I did it. I looked at my head. Guess who I saw in the mirror?"

I walked over to pour him a cup of coffee. "Who?"

"You, Wayne. I look like you."

"Let me see," he said. "C'mon, Connie, I want to see it."

As I pulled my buff off, he immediately reached over and rubbed my head.

"Oh, Connie. Look how smooth your head is and shaped so nice. You look OK. Really," he said as he rubbed me.

"Oh no. Look here," I said as I spun around. "Here is the scar where Cathy cold-cocked me when we were kids. I can feel it."

His hard-working hands felt rough but soothing and welcome to my head. His love and acceptance brought instant tears to my eyes and I couldn't stop crying. David watched me, understanding the tears and my steroid–withdrawal outbursts.

By evening, I was feeling horrible. I did not want to let the blood count win. "Let's go to Wal-Mart, Katie. I don't feel like driving. Will you drive me?"

She started her car, and the radio was blaring pop music. Ugh.

"Katie, you're such a good driver. I am so relaxed when I ride with you." I leaned against the window, and I knew Katie was hot. She had turned the heat exceptionally high for me.

After our shopping spree for boring household necessities, I asked her to take me out home. She knew where home was to me. *Out home* was my safe haven, my childhood, my parents.

"But, Mom. You act like you feel so bad," she said. "You sure you want to go out to Grandma and Grandpa's?"

"I do. I need Mom."

As we walked in, Mom greeted us, knowing with a mother's sixth sense that I was having an off day.

I told her about showing my head to Katie, Shelley, and Wayne.

"I told you," Mom said. "The night Amber buzzed you, I told you that you look like your brother."

"Well, let me see," Dad said as he sat up from his hunkered-down nest on the couch. "I want to see it, too." He pulled his afghan off and stood up.

As I took the scarf off, Mom walked over to me. "Oh, Connie. Your head is so dry," she said and headed off to get Dad's hair moisturizer.

Dad stared at me and smiled. "HA! You DO look like Wayne."

"Well, Mom ... I haven't looked at it since we buzzed it," I told her as she walked out of the bathroom. "I rub my hands across it when I bathe, but I assumed the rough feeling was whisker-like-hairs. How the heck did I know it was dry skin since no one sees it?"

She stood to my side, applying the moisturizer. The rhythmic circular motion of her soft hands mesmerized me. I leaned my head into her stomach as I sat in the chair relaxing. Katie and Dad watched.

"So round, so firm, and fully packed," she said as she continued rubbing my head. "I told you your head is nicely shaped and you look cute."

I leaned more into Mom. I could smell her wonderful scent.

"Your head is full of stories wanting to be published," she said as she rubbed and lulled me.

Tears began falling from my eyes, down my cheek, and I couldn't stop.

"Don't cry. You are all right," Mom said. "You are going to be just fine," she said as she looked down at me. "What's wrong?"

I had no answer. I did not feel sick, sad, or happy. I felt content, peaceful, and loved.

I guess I just needed my mom.

35
Blonde Bombshell

A friend told me about the Susan G. Komen grant given through our local hospital for the benefit of cancer patients. The Susan G. Komen Foundation is a nonprofit organization supported through generous donations. The money is donated across the nation in her memory. Before Susan's death, she asked her sister to help fulfill her dream to not let breast cancer be forgotten. Susan believed in a cure and hope for the future. She died a young woman. And her sister honored her request.

I visited the Web site, knowing I would give a donation in memory of Susan G. Komen. Our income and medical insurance were sufficient, and I was blessed to be able to donate. I certainly didn't need a handout, and found this nonprofit organization amazing.

As I read about Susan and how her sister had worked so hard to not let her death be in vain, I was certain I wanted to help. Whether I could run, walk, or crawl, I would plan on participating in the annual nonprofit marathon in May.

That Monday, after my visit out home to Mom and Dad's, I called Jennifer Maynard, RN, the cancer program coordinator at our hospital. She offered to send me a booklet from which I could select various head covers, wigs, silicone breasts, nipples, bras, and everything imaginable to help us deal with a variety of losses.

Jennifer and I had known each other four years through our work. Her compassion, concern, and knowledge to help others were phenomenal.

The booklet arrived and I instantly loved all the beautiful scarves and the variation of how the models wrapped, tied, looped, and wore them. Their faces looked gorgeous and their styles classy.

I ordered a beautiful scarf and insisted on paying for it. "No, Connie. This money was given to us for people like you. You are a county resident and deserve it. If you feel compelled to give, just give donations to the American Cancer Society or the Susan G. Komen Breast Foundation *[www.komen.org]*."

Thanks to this wonderful foundation, I was now the proud owner of a new blonde wig, too. Jennifer called to let me know the wig had arrived. "Wait until you see this wig. It is so pretty and cut about the way I want my hair to look," she said.

"I'll be right in," I said eagerly as I headed to the garage to start my car.

I couldn't wait to see it. Jennifer allowed me the use of her mirror. I asked her to close her eyes.

"No peeking," I said as I whipped my wig off and replaced it with the new blonde one.

"Oh, Connie, it is so much blonder than I thought. It is really too blonde on you, isn't it?"

"Yeah," I said as I turned my head looking in the mirror side to side. "I think it is waaaaay too blonde for me. Aww Jennifer, I am sorry, but wow. This is just so hooker blonde."

"You know what? The more I look at you in it, the more I think I like it on you."

"Really? I don't know. I haven't been this blonde since I was eight years old," I told her. "I feel like such a nuisance not liking it, but I do love the curls and style. The texture is wonderful, too." I looked at myself again in the mirror and frowned.

"Well, take it home. Leave the tags on it play with it a little. Get an honest friend to give you their opinion. If you decide you want to return it, we can exchange it for a darker one," she suggested.

As I arrived home, I started dinner and jumped in the tub. I heard someone coming in the door but knew it wasn't time for David yet. As I heard the pitter-patter of little feet and Allie squealing my name to see me, she burst through the bathroom door. I threw my hands up to my head, covering it with the washcloth.

At four, she was inquisitive, and as much as I loved her, I didn't want her see my head. Children are boldly honest, and I wondered if she would say something hurtful and reject me. She adored me as much as I loved her.

Her persistence prevailed. I will always remember that day. I was still bloated from chemo and the steroids and excited about the new wig, and I was not feeling my best.

She immediately walked toward me. I saw no fear or rejection as she started taking her clothes off to jump in the tub with me. She picked up the body lotion near the tub and put it on my head, rubbing in a circular motion. Her gentle little hands brought acceptance, unconditional love, and comfort no medicine could give.

Tears fell down my eyes.

"Am I making you feel better, Grammy?" she asked as she leaned down to my face and saw my tears. "Why are you crying, Grammy? Aren't I helping?"

"Oh, Allie ... you will never know how much I love you and how much you have helped me."

So as I traveled through cancer, my Allie gave me strength. She turned my self-pity into hope and my vanity into being comfortable in my skin.

When she is an adult, I hope she remembers those cloudy days I had and how she brought sunshine into my heart.

She helped me live.

Katie came home, and there we were with the bathroom door wide open. Amber was sitting at the table, drinking a Diet Coke. Katie grabbed the camera and took our picture.

"Darn you, Katie!" I bellowed.

When the picture was developed, it amazed me that such a candid shot of a fat, bald woman in a tub with a beautiful, accepting child could speak volumes of unconditional love.

As Allie and I dried and dressed, I told Amber and Katie I wanted to show them something.

"I need an honest opinion," I said as I walked toward my bedroom. "Don't come in, Allie. Grammy will be right back."

I put the new blonde bombshell wig on and walked out. "Wow, Mom. Where did you get that? It's awfully blonde," Amber said. Katie just stood and stared.

As I started to tell her about it, Allie looked up from the picture she was coloring.

"Ohhhhhh, Grammy," Allie said with the most peculiar look on her face. Her dramatic expression with her hand gestures kicked in as she threw her hands up to her face. "You look AWFUL!"

Amber, Katie, and I burst into laughter. "Well! Jennifer at the hospital told me to get an honest opinion. I guess I better not pull the tags off, and put it back in the box to return."

I learned a lot from Jennifer the day I stopped for that blonde wig. I exchanged it for a darker blonde one that I favored and wore the most through my bald days.

Jennifer's knowledge about cancer was informative, and I found myself asking many questions about breast cancer. Being an advocate for cancer patients and doctors at the hospital, she finds her work fulfilling. It is depressing at times when she sees the patients deteriorate before her eyes, but her spirit in helping them always kicks in. She is rewarded when she brings a smile to those she helps.

Minutes before my arrival, a breast cancer patient had left her office. The forty- something female had just had a mastectomy and started chemo. She was deeply depressed and could not find the courage to look at her chest in the mirror. Her hair was just days away from falling out. The chemo was making her feel the typical misery, and she was thinking about discontinuing it.

"Connie, I wish you could talk to her. She needs cheering up and given a reason to fight this. You have the spunk and attitude and could help," she said as she confirmed my phone number to give to the patient.

"Oh, I will be glad to talk to her. I would love to help if she'll call me," I said as I took the blonde wig off and put my scarf and hat back on. "Is her name Judy?" I asked.

"Yes, it is Judy," Jennifer said with surprise that I had guessed who this troubled woman was.

"I heard about her from a mutual friend. Don, her co-worker, is my old high school buddy. He is the one who told me about this wonderful Susan G. Komen fund."

"I did bring a smile to her face today," Jennifer said. "When I handed her the silicone prosthetic for her bra and gave her the wig she'd ordered, she cried and gave me a big hug."

We continued talking about the different treatments as she expressed her experiences, opinion, and knowledge about the different treatments doctors use to aid patients with breast cancer.

Jennifer claimed that about 212,000 people are victims of breast cancer every year in the United States. Of those, about 1,000 are men, and 20 percent of these afflicted patients die. My heart fluttered. I hated hearing the percentage, but put in perspective, when the cancer is found early and proper treatment is given, most of us can survive this disease. I tried to be optimistic daily. "Mind over matter," they say, and I worked daily to add my humor, attitude, and love of my family and friends to make my mind strong and full of healing power.

As Jennifer proceeded to inform me, I listened intently. "Mammograms are not reliable or dependable in women under the age of forty. Because women under forty have *dense readings,* mammograms cannot see through the cloudy tissue to be read accurately. MRIs or ultrasounds are the key to getting a better view for proper diagnosis. But insurance companies balk and don't want to pay the extra cost for routine breast checkups using these more-expensive tests." Her phone rang. I waited for her to continue.

"Mammograms cost about $100 compared to $1,000 for MRIs," she continued as she hung up the phone. "Ultrasounds can find fluid-filled cysts, and many of these cysts are benign," she continued. "They also detect solid lumps, and those are the ones that can be cancerous."

"I have had dense readings my entire adult life. Why didn't my doctor order an MRI or ultrasound for me when I had that lump off and on for two years?" I asked her. I shuffled in my chair, uneasy and angry.

"Well, this is only my opinion," she said. "Never watch a lump. It isn't supposed to be there. Doctors should always remove them," Jennifer said as she hit the table with her fist.

I thought about my obstetrician/gynecologist. I had gone to her for eighteen years. I wondered why she had not done a needle biopsy on the lump or ordered an ultrasound or MRI. I had two insurance policies. I was over forty. I would probably never know and would always wonder.

Many of my friends also went to her for examinations and checkups. My name was coming up in conversations. She was concerned and asking my friends about me, knowing I was not going to return to her.

My periods had gotten weird and harder. I asked Jennifer if she thought menopause helped to trigger breast cancer. I suspected I was starting into menopause months prior to the cancerous lump that I had discovered. My last pap smear confirmed it. I learned I was in menopause and had cancer all within the same week. Talk about depression!

"Estrogen medicines doesn't cause cancer, but I feel it might have a connection and can help cancer cells to ignite and could be connected," Jennifer informed me. "Many women take estrogen for hot flashes, and if they get cancer, I suggest they discontinue the use of estrogen."

I advised her that I had tested positive for the drug Arimidex, an anti-estrogen medicine used for five years after cancer treatment is over. This medicine is taken daily if a patient tests positive for having estrogen receptors and decreases the chance of breast cancer occurring again.

I was suppose to feel lucky that I tested positive, but after reading the side effects and knowing I would be committing to this potent medicine for five years, I had mixed emotions.

36

Ann.com

In early March, just weeks before I was going to Florida, three of my bus driver girlfriends invited me to Myrtle Beach. Carol, Teresa, and Jalana had a Friday and a Monday off from school and were determined to take a mini-vacation. They all insisted I go. Their husbands were staying home, and they squealed with delight thinking about a weekend away with no cooking, cleaning, or husbands.

I was torn about going. As much fun as I knew these girls were, for the first time, I wasn't sure I could keep up with these vivacious women. I was plagued with pain in my hip and down my leg. The thought of traveling for fourteen hours cramped in an SUV left me skeptical and unmotivated. As I looked at the calendar, I realized the timing was perfect. My white blood count would be back up, and I would arrive home the day before I would receive my last chemo treatment.

"You don't even have to drive. We will. You can rest. We really want you to go," Teresa pleaded.

"I am not the Connie you used to know. I am a crabby, sick old woman, Teresa. I am fat, and I am bald. I ache."

"Oh go," David said. "You'll have fun."

They would not take no for an answer. After much persuasion, it was decided: I would go.

Carol, who owned a beautiful house near the ocean on a luxurious golf course, packed us in her SUV. She planned on taking us out on the town. I, the once-social girl, had slowly become inhibited since the loss of my hair. I found myself constantly forcing myself to go out into the social arena. I could not get over the paranoia of my wig falling off or someone staring at me, discussing the curiosity of my hair possibly being a wig.

We left on Thursday after they finished their bus routes, and drove all night. Before we had even left our county, the drinking began. Carol was our designated driver.

We talked, sang to the radio, laughed, and gossiped. By the wee hours of the morning, we reached our destination. The temperature was chilly, but the sun shone. The house was beautiful. We had three days to cram in sightseeing, manicures, shopping, and bar-hopping.

Carol, the official tour guide, knew all the hot spots. But after driving all night, we were all exhausted. Missing a night's sleep is not what forty-something women should do. We lay around all day in the house, sat out on the patio, drank coffee, and watched golfers (some seemed to be goofers with such horrid swings).

We talked about every subject women can chat about: kids, jobs, husbands, people we'd heard having flings, almost-flings, cooking, my cancer, sex, and people we all knew. Gossip! We laughed as we shared stories and reminisced about days gone by. Teresa and I had shared many wonderful times and enjoyed sharing our tales.

Carol, the tour guide, made us appointments for pedicures and manicures. Jalana had never pampered herself with such luxury. Teresa and I had only splurged once in this unnecessary pleasure in life. Carol was the pro.

We all showered, and a vote was taken on which wig I would wear on our Friday night out. They all tried to support me and gave me great compliments on how wonderful I looked in the wig. I was not so sure. Being a good sport, I put on my happy face and slammed down a beer, and off we went to the bar that Carol has been to many times in the past.

As we arrived, it was obvious this bar called the Crocodile Rock was the popular hangout for vacationers. The place was packed!

215

After waiting awhile, I found a great table for the four of us. There were two piano players and one drummer. People wrote down songs on a napkin as they handed them to the band, in hopes they'd play the requested songs. It seemed they knew every song requested. Sometimes they would change the lyrics to something dirty and funny.

They involved the crowd and brought people up on stage, pulling stunts that drew many laughs. They were absolutely crazy, talented, funny, and grand musicians.

"Connie! Where is Connie from Ohio?" The question echoed throughout the bar.

I slithered down in my chair as I glanced at Teresa, Jalana, and Carol.

"Who did this? How did he get my name? And what will they make me do up there?" I asked my friends as I shook my head no. "I don't want to go up there," I said.

"We want Connie," the piano guy bellowed across his microphone.

"I am going to kick all your asses," I said to Jalana, Teresa, and Carol as I stood up, leery of walking up on stage. As I walked over to the piano guy, I immediately pointed my finger at him.

"Do NOT make a fool of me. BE NICE!"

As he motioned for me to sit next to him on the piano bench, he began playing a familiar tune. I smiled.

"Baby face, you got the cutest little baby face ..."

As the song ended, he leaned over and kissed my cheek. It was as simple as that and I knew my friends had done this to bring me confidence and happiness. I also knew that they must have left a hefty tip just for my night of fun.

I left the stage. It crossed my mind to jerk my wig off for all to see my bald-as-a-baby's- ass head and so they'd know I didn't have a pretty little baby face. I decided to be good, and walked back to our table.

They all made several trips to the bathroom as my girlfriends consumed beer after beer. I began to notice that Carol and Teresa were going to the bathroom and gone longer than normal. They'd always come out laughing, but my mind drifted back to the entertainment as they sat back down.

I got up, heading to the bathroom. I approached the door and immediately heard a female voice singing within the bathroom walls. I walked on in and saw an older, short woman singing away as she tidied up the sink. The bathroom was clean and decorated in a lovely manner, pleasant for a bar.

I entered the stall and continued to listen to her sing the song that the band was playing. She seemed to know every word as she hit each lyric.

"Who are you singing to?" I asked as I finished up in the bathroom.

"Oh, to myself or anyone who will listen," she said.

As I swung open the bathroom door, she immediately approached me, handing me special hand soap. I opened my hand as she squirted it. I ran my hands under the faucet, washing, as she handed me a towel.

I noticed a beautiful variety basket of lotions sitting near the faucet. A candle was lit also. "You are welcome to use any of those bath-and-body lotions that you would like," she said.

We talked about bath-and-body products as I rubbed the lotion into my hands. She was so full of energy, happiness, and enthusiasm for life.

As I was about to walk out, I saw her walk over to a hardback chair where she sat each night while working the bathroom. I also noticed a tip jar to the left of the sink.

I placed a dollar in the tip jar and she thanked me.

As I walked back to our table, I commented to my girlfriends how nice this woman was and how hard she worked the bathroom job to get tips.

"Do you realize that each time I have to pee, I will have to pay a dollar?" I told them. Adding up the cost of a drink, a tip for the drink, and a tip to pee, I was looking to spend much more money. Once the bladder cuts loose, frequent trips to the john occur. Ever notice that? It seems we women can hold our bladder for hours. Once you let the bladder win, it takes advantage of you and runs you back and forth.

"Her name is Ann, Connie. She's a local and I met her a couple of years ago. I always come in to see and visit with her in the bathroom," Carol said. "We talk about going to lunch sometime."

I found this so refreshing to hear from Carol, my wealthy friend. Three beautiful women and it seemed they enjoyed social hour in the john more than the men who were abundantly around us.

We found so much humor in Ann. "Oh crap," Teresa said later in the evening. "I have to pee." She dug in her purse for a dollar. "Well, shit. All I have is a five. Maybe I can sneak in fast and out the door without tipping her."

We continued listening to the band. The music was seventies and eighties disco. Some rock, too.

"Does anyone have a dollar? I have to pee," Jalana said as she stood up. "All I have is a ten, and as much as I like Ann and her singing while I pee, I am NOT leaving a ten-dollar bill."

It was contagious. I had to go again, too!

"Maybe if I don't use her lotion and grab a towel before she gets the chance to hand one to me, I won't have to tip," I said.

Each time I entered the bathroom, I felt obligated to leave Ann a tip. I wondered if she needed the job or was just a retired woman who was bored and liked to stay busy.

"I have always liked to sing," she had told Carol and Teresa earlier. "So I sing in the bathroom and get paid, too."

Once, when Teresa walked out of the john, she had asked Ann if she had a song request. Teresa was going to put in a request for Ann. Our seats were so close to the band's stage that by this time, Teresa was in like Flynn with the lead singer/piano player. He was making eyes at her. A song for Ann was possible.

The band started playing, "Joy to the World." As the lyrics demanded a pause, Ann could be heard from the bathroom. A little off mark with the lyrics, her voice amplified through the bar. It was full of sheer pleasure. I pictured her in the bathroom, wiping spattered water off the sink, shining the chrome, and flushing toilets or picking up tampon papers off the floor as she danced and sang.

The band was playing their last set, and the hour was late.

"Here comes Ann. She must be finished for the night," Teresa said.

She came walking toward us carrying her basket of lotions.

"I just want to tell you girls goodbye," she said as she swung her basket of lotions on her hand.

"Do you have an e-mail address?" Teresa asked her.

"No, I don't have e-mail yet," she said. "I'll have to learn how to type so I can get a computer."

"I know just the address we can make for you when you connect to cyberspace," Teresa told her. "Ann@wipeyourhootchiewashyour hands.com," Teresa said as she roared with laughter.

Ann laughed and laughed.

As we waved goodbye, she slipped out the door.

"Good! I can go pee for free now," Teresa said as she scooted her chair back quickly and jumped up, heading to the john.

Without her knowledge, I sneaked into the bathroom, waiting in Ann's chair.

I listened to the flush of the toilet. As she opened the swinging door, I instantly squirted soap on her hands as I turned the faucet on. She laughed as she washed her hands. I held out my hand, waiting for my dollar tip.

"You talked to Ann so much, I doubt she noticed you sneaked by a couple times without tipping her," I told her. We roared with laughter as she dried her hands.

"Can you imagine having a job like that?" I told her. "What a wonderful attitude she has, too!"

"When we come back next year, we will look up Ann, the john lady," I told Teresa, "and you better bring some dollars to doodle."

37

Dinner For The Temporary Misfits

One day as I put one of my Pam scarves on, I thought again of the day Whitney gave them to me. My thoughts traveled to Jim, her widower, who had to adjust to many changes. I continued to worry about Whitney's struggles with the loss of her mom.

Not only was he trying to fill the shoes of a mom and a dad, but he had his handicap to adjust to. Jim suffered a CVA one year to the day prior to when Pam was diagnosed with Hodgkin's Lymphoma. The doctors said it was one of the biggest strokes to happen to such a young man of forty-four. "The silent killer," they say, but Jim survived against the odds.

Life had been free and easy for this family. Jim had started his own successful electrical business, and Pam set out to find a new job with benefits to cover medical insurance for their family after she quit working for me. Jim's business was booming, and Pam loved her new job.

"Hand me that screwdriver, would ya?" Those were the last words Jim recalled the day his life changed as he fell to the floor after losing consciousness and was rushed to the hospital. His dream to have his own business slipped away that day, when his life was almost taken, too.

Pam never complained or felt sorry for their family hardship. She pampered him, but made him try to be strong again. She was patient, but would not let him give up and ordered him to try harder when he did his exercises to strengthen his left side. She stood tough and firm, determined that Jim could rehabilitate back to being the man he once was. As she was going through chemo, she pushed herself to go to work. Pam was always optimistic, smiling, and never complained. Without her job, they would have been without medical insurance and what income they had left. She fought with courage and determination to not lose these two important necessities.

The electrical equipment and tools lay unused. Jim wasn't ready to throw in the towel and sell his business. He continued doing rehabilitation exercises, and his courage helped him to hold on as he showed slight improvement daily. Disability benefits were slow in giving aid to a man so deserving, and one who had worked his entire life.

Slowly, his health improved, but it was obvious that he would not be able to run his electrical company, and he sold most of the equipment to help feed his family. Pam continued working, and Whitney helped with household chores as Jim went daily for rehabilitation.

When Pam was diagnosed with Hodgkin's Lymphoma, I questioned it like many probably did. Why? How could one family handle so much grief and challenges? I questioned how God let something like this happen to one family. Why oh why would God take Pam away when Jim and Whitney needed her now more than ever? She had fought too hard and had deserved to win.

I would never forget the day Jim called to tell me she had died suddenly. I had planned to go visit her again, but isolation had not been lifted and I was waiting. I never got to see her again.

I was in pure shock and enormous appreciation when Jim would pick up the phone to check on me regularly since my illness. I had him and Whitney over for dinner. We compared cancer stories, and his positive attitude for me amazed me. How do people regain faith in health issues, doctors, cancer, and life when cancer kills a loved one? Through it all, Jim found God and the strength to carry on.

So as I put that silky soft scarf on, I thought of the Lucas family again. My mind had been troubled since my last conversation with Jim. "This is no way to live, is it, Connie?"

His moods were typical of someone missing his wife and good health. Although most of the time he was positive, that day left sadness in my heart from that simple, strong statement of his true feelings.

"Of course it is," I told him. "Whitney needs you. Pam has to know you will look out for Whitney."

Several weeks after that conversation, I spontaneously picked up the phone and called him.

"Hey, Jim! What are you doing?"

"Oh nothing ... just watching TV," he said in a sober voice.

"Do you have plans for tonight?" I asked.

"Nope, just staying home," he said in his monotone voice.

"I have a great idea. David and I are going out to eat tonight. Do you want to go with us? I have a friend who is bored with no plans. I am going to ask her to go, too. Wanna come along?"

Immediately he replied, "OH, NO. I don't want to go."

"You are depressed today, aren't you?"

"Yep, I am."

"Well, then go out with us, Jim. I am not trying to fix you up with Tammy. She is such a dear friend, and so fun to talk to."

"I don't want to go, but thanks."

"Jim, you just said you had no plans. Tammy had four fingers amputated from a horrid disease. I am bald and fat from steroids. You have a limp. We are all misfits, but what should we do? Ya think we ought to curl up in fetal positions, stay home, and feel sorry for ourselves? C'mon. We all can share in good conversations and good food."

The phone was silent. I waited.

"OK, I will go. What time?"

As I hung up the phone, I dialed Tammy. I smiled when she said, "Sure, I will go."

I smiled even bigger when I told David my plan. He shook his head as he read my mind, knowing how persistent I am and how I love to hook people up.

My original plan was not to match-make. But it occurred to me that they were about the same age, with big hearts, and hands that were warm but just a little clumsy.

Jim and Tammy were both rusty in the dating arena. It took Jim over a week to call Tammy and ask her out to dinner after we'd introduced them. They talked for approximately three minutes, just long enough for her to accept.

The night they were to go out, she called me an hour before he was to pick her up. She had a deep desire to puke. Her nerves were those of a nervous schoolgirl. Jim probably wanted to belt down a drink to calm his nerves, but he was rusty in the alcohol-social scene and had given up alcohol after his stroke. If I could have known, I would have given him advice like I gave to Tammy as we spoke on the phone.

She was pacing, watching for him out the window, wondering, and blaming me for getting her into this new adventure. I hoped it would be a good one.

"Just be the Tammy I know. Talk, share your stories like you do with me; that always makes me laugh," I said as I coached her. "I know you can't help being shy, but I forget you are shy. I wish he could see the Tammy I know."

"I swear. I am goin' to puke," she confessed. "Why am I even going out? You KNOW my luck with men."

"Call me when you get home. I will stay up to hear how it was. And if nothing develops, maybe you two can just be friends. Maybe keep each other company and build a good friendship. Both of you are wonderful people who could use some companionship."

Later, my phone rang, and it was Tammy. It was not a good sign as I looked up at the clock. They had gone to dinner and on to Tammy's, and he asked for a kiss as she was about to get out of his car. With a peck on his lips, she was in her house and PJs by 9:00 PM when she called me.

"Have you seen that movie, *Ten Ways to Lose a Guy*?" she asked me. "I'm a pro. I can lose a guy in one way," she said as she told me about dinner.

They had talked a lot. Jim spoke about Pam, and Tammy told him about her disastrous marriages and her last relationship. I wondered if they would go out again. I was curious if Whitney knew about the date and how she felt, since she had told me she wasn't crazy about her dad dating since the death of her mom. I knew this was the typical feelings of a child.

Tammy and Jim both had lost significant others in different ways. Both of them were possibly not ready for a commitment. Time would tell, I thought as we hung up.

I ran my bathwater and laughed, thinking about Tammy, and grew excited thinking about our trip to Florida, which was just weeks away. Both of us, being cold-blooded, craved warm temperatures and to be near the ocean again.

I hesitated in pouring the aromatherapy lavender bath crystals in my water. Amber had bought them for me when I had my lumpectomy, and I had stopped using them. She had the same thoughts as De, my hairstylist friend. De had traveled several times to England. The English belief is that lavender helps soothe the nerves and helps patients to relax. De had made me a sachet of lavender to hold and smell when I was going through all my tests. I had taken the sachet with me the day I had my surgery.

I remember the day they did the lymph node study and how upset I was, wondering and worrying about my recent diagnosis of cancer. I held the sachet in my hand as the radiologist ran tests on me. I feared the cancer was in my nodes as I lay on the cold table. The girl had no idea I was crying because I tried to hide my emotions. I sniffed and cried quietly.

"What is that strange aroma I keep smelling?" she asked me. "It is a familiar smell but I can't figure out what's in here," she said as she repositioned me on the cold body-size tray for more tests. Good ole EMS days always comes back to me. The tray I laid on reminded me of the trays we used to put dead people in as we slid them into the morgue.

"Lavender. It is lavender you smell," I said. "My friend De gave this to me."

I assumed the bag resembled a pot bag. (I think they used to call them dime bags.)

"De claims that all the hospitals in England have lavender smells throughout their hospitals. Studies have shown that lavender scent helps one to relax. I guess it is not helping me," I said as I held it to my nose to smell again. She saw my tears as I got choked up.

Amber's kind gesture and generosity had pleased me. As my water ran, I kept reflecting back to all those tests and how scared I was heading into the unknown. I found myself not wanting to ever smell lavender again. I didn't want Amber to know that the smell brought back such horrid memories for me. The lavender bag had also been in my hand the day the first surgeon had told me that they did not get a clear margin, my nodes were infected, and I needed a mastectomy as soon as possible.

I decided to pour the crystals in my water. I wanted Amber to know I appreciated her thoughtfulness. I watched the crystals swirl and dissolve under the faucet as the tub filled. I stood naked, looking in the mirror at my breasts. I looked at the lumpectomy scar and lifted my armpit to see if I had any armpit hair yet. I remember always having to shave, never wanting armpit hair. I wanted to see hair. I wanted to keep my left breast. I dreamed of hair ... anywhere on my body.

Three weeks and three days had passed since my last chemo treatment. It was time for hair to start growing, and it was not going to grow fast enough to suit me. The only obvious place that I had found new hair was in the middle of my eyebrows. Go figure! I hadn't had to pluck since I had started chemo. Although I worried about losing my eyebrows and eyelashes, it was nice not having excess hair to pluck.

My lashes and brows had thinned out, but with mascara and an eyebrow pencil I was able to keep them looking relatively nice. Using an eyebrow pencil was a new experience, but with the help and guidance of my friend Teresa, I learned how to give my brows a natural look.

I thought more about Cocoa Beach and smooth legs. No shaving!

Cocoa Beach had been an annual visit for me during school spring break since Amber had made varsity when she was a freshman. David didn't have enough vacation time and hated Florida. He traveled to Florida to watch both of them their senior year, but preferred saving his vacation for hunting. I remembered teasing Katie when she became a freshman and varsity tryouts were about to start.

"No pressure, Katie. But ya know how I hate the cold and love Florida. You make varsity as a freshman and I am off to Cocoa Beach again for four years."

This would be my seventh year to go with the high school team. Tammy had gone with me Katie's sophomore year and loved it very much. The condo that I had always stayed in was a hit with Tammy. Shops everywhere, including the famous Ron Jon Shop at our back door, along with the ocean a stone's throw away from our room. We knew it would be another wonderful week. One week in a condo together would be delightful again, since our friendship was so incredibly strong. No doctors, no chemo, and no worries until I returned home. I vowed to erase all worries and enjoy the Florida sun, even if I would be bald and would come home to an appointment with my oncologist, Dr. Linda, my breast surgeon and an oral surgeon. (Seems chemo likes to pick on teeth and gums also). I would dread my return, even though I'd be eager to see Graham, my wonderful golden retriever. David would be eager for good home-cooked meals and clean socks and me!

I planned on reuniting with my publisher, whom I'd met at Cocoa Beach years prior. He owned a newspaper, and I had worked for him as a humor columnist. We'd only communicated through e-mail or phone since he'd hired me. Derold, a Georgia resident, consequently had business in Cocoa Beach the week Tammy and I would be there. It was going to be wonderful to see him again.

Linda, my high school friend, had relocated to Orlando, Florida. We planned a day at Cocoa Beach. I pictured a spectacular lunch at a restaurant with an ocean view. Maybe we'd be daring older women and get something pierced or tattooed.

I planned on taking many scarves and hats. The vanity was slipping away. I knew the wigs would be hot in Florida and scratchier when the sun pelted down on my head as I watched the girls play softball. I decided I was going to be bold and skip the wigs, wearing my bandannas, scarves, and hats.

38
Hairless Vacation

Florida was approaching. I was helping Katie gear up and get packed. Sunscreen, ball socks, softball equipment, shampoo, emergency pack of tampons, disposable camera, money, and more money were on the lengthy list. A hairbrush, blow dryer, curling iron, and shampoo were not on my list.

Tammy couldn't wait to hit the Florida sun again. I had mixed emotions. As much as I wanted to be positive and feel good about myself, I found myself wishing for the warmth, but stressed about my lack of energy. I hated my appearance.

I tried on my spring clothes. They were all tight, and I knew blaming it on the steroids was an accurate theory, but I was also angry with myself for not working harder to get the weight off. I refused to buy new clothes. I wanted to suffer through them and not make it easy by purchasing comfy, bigger clothes.

Being frugal, I was tempted to hit the thrift stores for last-minute spring clothes. Although I am not a shopper, I love the bargains at the secondhand stores. People never would guess that most my clothes come from my sister Tina's leftover yard sales and thrift stores. I accessorize with my chucky sandals and wonderful big earrings, bracelets and necklaces. Voila! My outfits are three-quarters the cost of new clothes and are stylish.

Since my first chemo, I started having a severe pain in my right buttock that radiated down my entire right leg. After each chemo, the pain would subside, always returning about two weeks after the chemo drip. I was in constant pain each time it erupted, and slept in short intervals. Walking to get the pounds off was not in the cards because I hurt so much.

I knew I should call Dr. Rhoades or Dr. Linda, and they would give me something for pain and to help me sleep. I wasn't playing the tough-girl role; I just wanted to keep as much foreign stuff out of my system as I could. I feared becoming drug dependent. Just hearing the word "Vicodin" puts me in a rage. I have personal knowledge of several people who had been addicted to Vicodin. Although I have never liked taking medicine, I still worried about how easy it would be to just swallow those little pills and sleep the physical and emotional pains away.

As we readied ourselves for Florida, my hip continued to plague me. I wanted to walk beside the ocean with hair and in comfortable clothes. I knew none of this would happen. My hip brought worries. *Now I must have bone cancer,* was the thought that tortured my mind. I chose to ignore it, wait it out, and postpone calling my doctor. I feared he would have me tested and my Florida trip would be ruined or cancelled because of bad news that I was not prepared for.

Chemo almost always throws women into menopause, and their menstrual cycles stop. My periods had not stopped, and Dr. Linda was thrilled. She was planning another MRI when I returned from Florida. She was the first doctor who had told me the importance of MRIs being done one week after the first day of a woman's cycle. She was a firm believer that the MRI readings were clearer and more accurate if timed properly around a woman's menstrual cycle.

Going away during spring break would not interfere with my medical treatment. My period was due the week I was to leave for Florida, but the chemo was still in my system, so the MRI had to wait. Dr. Linda wanted an accurate, clear reading. I no longer needed to take all the medicines and was happy to throw the rest of the steroids down the toilet.

Dr. Linda planned an MRI on my return, when my next period would be due again. The chemo would be working to leave my body as I awaited my period and my MRI on my return home.

Then, just as I was due for my period, it stopped. The chemo had finally thrown me into menopause, and I was saddened. To think I missed my period and hoped for it each month seemed silly, since I had always hated them. The MRI would be scheduled regardless, since Mother Nature and chemo could not be controlled. This MRI would be the most important one, because a decision would be made about whether I needed a mastectomy or another lumpectomy.

In my depression at losing my period, I started my ritual of listening to songs on the radio and making a list of the ones I wanted played at my funeral. The friends I had chosen as pallbearers were added to the song list for easy reference for my family to notify when needed.

I had so many wonderful songs chosen for my funeral. They were powerful, with spiritual messages. I was being ridiculous, but I couldn't stop worrying.

I pictured Don, Paul, Jed, Don C., Dave, and Mark carrying me as "Spirit in the Sky" played. I imagined them all looking at each other, nodding and smiling as they thought of me, my spirit for life, and my choice of songs.

I packed my too-tight clothes for the trip, and found my mood lifting as I listened to Tammy's excitement. A week with her would be medicine to my self-loathing soul. We shared such a wonderful friendship.

We arrived in Cocoa Beach in pouring rain but warm temperatures. By the time we had our rental car and had checked into the condominium, the rain had stopped and the sun radiated in the Florida sky.

I called Katie and found that the ball team had arrived safely. Katie was eager to play softball. We started unpacking our clothes, and I knew that being with Tammy and watching Katie catch would make me happy. I was curious to see how good the softball team would be.

I also realized how comfortable I was going wigless in the condo while rooming with Tammy. My head was warm for the first time in months, and my comfort zone was easy with Tammy. I kept a scarf nearby in case another softball mom popped in to visit. But wow! It felt so wonderful to not have to wear any headgear.

Like every year when I return to Cocoa Beach, the bar next door to our condo reiterated the celebration of spring break. The patio on the ocean side of the bar was packed with partygoers and amplified wonderful rock-and-roll music. Each afternoon and on into the evening, great bands play the entire week of spring break.

Tammy and I decided to walk over. It was late afternoon, too early for us to be drinking, but we were on spring break and the laughter echoed up to our balcony. "Let's go over for just a drink and listen to the band for a bit, Tammy," I suggested.

I freshened up my makeup, squeezed into a pair of capris, and put on my short wig. As we walked, the music became louder and the laughter and dancing of the crowd promising. I readjusted my wig and flattened my belly, and we found seats near the band. I noticed the locals that I recalled from year to year. Mike, the tattoo man, was there, but the parrot that rested atop his shoulder while he sat at the bar each year was missing. I wondered if the parrot had died. Mike, the man covered with more tattoos than I had ever seen in my life, would never die. I just knew it.

It saddened me that he did not recognize me like he had for so many years prior. I knew the cancer had played havoc on me, and he had reminded me by not recognizing me.

Sitting at the table next to us were construction workers. They drummed up a conversation with us. They were from many parts of the United States. They had been working in the Cocoa Beach area since the hurricane that hit months earlier, causing extensive damage. We found out that their jobs take them all over the nation. What a life for these young, single men!

The more the band played, the more the construction guys drank. Tammy and I sipped our drinks. We laughed at their drunken states and behavior. The sun began to set, and we decided to run over to the condo, shower, and go have dinner. Tammy headed over first as I stayed behind listening to the band and the drunken construction guys. (I was saving the table and not wanting to miss a song the band played.)

Tammy returned, and I headed to the condo. "Come back," said one construction guy as I walked away.

"Oh, I'll be back," I said. As I walked over, it occurred to me how much fun it would be to mess with the drunken construction guys.

I showered, put fresh clothes and makeup on, and put on the long dark wig. As I approached the table, I saw Tammy snicker. She knew what my intentions were. She also knew that the drunks would play right into my hands.

As I sat down in the exact seat I had before, the construction guys checked me out as if I was new meat coming to the bar. And just as I thought, they liked the new girl and had forgotten the shorthaired one in the time it took to drink one beer and for me to shower.

We never did leave for dinner. We drank entirely too much. As we walked back to our room in the dark, I twirled my wig in my hand, and Tammy and I laughed as we recalled the wild construction guys. We hoped they found their one-night stands, but we knew it wasn't going to be with Tammy, Connie, or the longhaired woman who took my place.

Linda, my high school friend, came and we had a great lunch, almost like the one I had visualized. We never made it to the tattoo shop, but shared wonderful conversation and laughed as we reminisced about so many days gone by.

Derold, my publisher, came to visit me, and the entire week was full of sunshine, laughter, and competitive softball games. The high school team headed back to cold Ohio with a 6-0 record. Tammy and I flew home to a snowstorm. Our tans were obviously very out of place. But Ohio was home, and I had reality hitting me in the face. It was time for doctor appointments and a verdict about my life.

39
Back To Reality

It was time to unpack, catch up on sandy laundry, find a place for all the accumulated seashells, and call Dr. Linda's office to schedule my appointment.

My MRI was scheduled for three days after I got home. Dr. Linda was not going to wait to see if I would have a period. Not only did I fear the results, but I was not looking forward to the test. I had had so many MRIs since my diagnosis, and to lie perfectly still for almost an entire hour in a long tubular machine was difficult. My hyper personality and the tight quarters played havoc on my mind. Give me needles any day over an MRI!

I knew the importance of an accurate reading. The day-and-a-half wait for the results was emotionally straining.

The following day before I got the MRI results, I had a follow-up appointment with Dr. Rhoades, my oncologist. I decided to tell him about my sciatic pain and to face the music. I was sure he would order some kind of test. A bone scan was ordered for the same day I was to hear about my MRI.

An IV was started, and I was injected with something that probably was not so grand for the human body, but the importance of the bone scan outweighed my concern of the injection.

I was to wait three hours and then return for the bone scan. As the test was being done, I tried to get the technician to give me information about what she was seeing on her test screen. Although she was not a doctor, I knew she probably could read my results as well as Dr. Rhoades. She was not talking! (I knew she would not be at liberty to divulge the results, but I was very worried and looking for reassurance.)

As I arrived home following the bone scan, my phone rang.

"Connie. It is Dr. Han [Dr. Linda to me]. I have your MRI results."

Immediately, I began to cry in the phone. "I am so afraid of what you might tell me," I said to her.

"I have good news, Connie. Your MRI looks cancer-free. The chemo looks as if it did its job. You do understand, though ... we need to do another lumpectomy, and I highly recommend radiation after the lumpectomy," she said.

"Oh, Dr. Linda, I am so happy. I was so afraid. Thank you so much. And yes, I am willing to do radiation. I get to keep my breast! Yaaaaahoo!"

We said our happy goodbyes and I thought about the bone scan. I knew I was over one hurdle.

I had grown tired of going to Columbus, but had to return to Dr. Rhoades for my bone scan report the next day. It was not even the end of the week and I was pooped. I continued to work in between my appointments. Katie continually showed concern. I still rarely heard from Ryan. Amber was working, going to school in the evenings, and wrapped up in her own life.

We watched Allie in the evenings while Amber went to school. I hoped this new firefighting career that she desperately wanted would happen for her. She needed a job to give her self-worth and a better income for a single mom.

David insisted on going with me. I tried to act nonchalant about the test and preferred being alone (or so I thought). I had already imagined the worst and had kept my thoughts to myself. *I will not go through chemo again. I will not become one of those cancer victims who just keeps crumbling away and misses out on quality life.*

So although it was probably selfish of me, I wanted to hear the results alone. I wanted no pressure from anyone, and I wanted to decide the outcome and decision.

As I waited in the examination room, I became frightened. I paced back and forth in the room, alone. I kept looking at my watch. My appointment was at 9:40 AM and it was 10:30. I opened the door and peered out. I paced more.

As I stood at the door, I noticed Dr. Rhoades and Connie, his assistant, walk by and into the conference room. I thought the worst. I just knew they were looking over my bone scan and trying to decide how to give me bad news. I remembered Connie from a prior appointment so many months before, and how she seemed to be in charge of dealing with bad news and the emotions of the patients.

She had not come into my appointments with Dr. Rhoades on recent visits. All of a sudden, she was back.

As I waited, I thought about all the family and friends who had offered to go with me. I knew having their support and someone to converse with would have made my wait much easier.

I thought of the beautiful spring day and the sunny skies. I was cooped up again in a doctor's office, and the clock was crawling. My palms were perspiring and my chest felt tight.

Dr. Rhoades and Connie walked in together ... finally. He immediately apologized for keeping me waiting. I burst into tears.

"Dr. Rhoades, I know why Connie is with you. I just know you have bad news. I saw you two in the conference room. I can't take any more bad news." I rambled on, not giving either of them time to say anything. "I worked in the medical field for years. I saw what cancer did to many patients. I want a quality life." I pointed at Connie. "I know why she is with you. She brings bad news to patients. She did way back when I first got sick."

"I am always with him. I am his right-hand man," Connie said jokingly.

"Have you had your second lumpectomy yet?" Dr. Rhoades asked me.

"I have not gotten it scheduled yet. I am not having it if you are bringing me bad news, Dr. Rhoades. I won't!"

"Well, I think you need to have it; your bone scan doesn't look bad, but … "

"But what? But what?" I started crying again.

"There is a rather large spot on the bone scan right here," he said as his hands lay just above my knee. "Have you ever had an injury there?"

"I am sure I have. I played many sports, and I was injured years ago snow skiing. I don't remember if it was that knee. I slid into bases playing softball. I was a tomboy. You are scaring me," I cried out.

As he began to talk, I interrupted him. "Dr. Rhoades, that knee does not hurt. I have healthy knees. It is down the side of my leg and my sciatic nerve that hurt so bad."

"Well, that is a good sign," he said as he stood up straight and flipped through my file, which seemed to grow by leaps and bounds on each visit.

"Tell me straight up. Do you think I have bone cancer? Just tell me. And what about the pain down my hip and side?"

"I honestly do not think you have bone cancer. There is much pain with bone cancer, but I would like to get an X-ray and try to see a different view of that area," he said.

"You mean I have to wait more days, not know today?" I asked. "This waiting is worse than the tests!"

"No, no," Dr. Rhoades said.

"I am escorting you to X-ray now," Connie said, "and we will have the results today. Is that OK?" she asked.

I stood up, implying my consent.

As I waited again in the examination room for Dr. Rhoades to look at the X-ray, I grew impatient. Four hours had gone by since I had walked in that morning for my appointment. The sun was warmer and the day felt like a beautiful spring day. I craved the warm temperatures and wanted to escape.

He walked in, carrying the X-ray. He sat down beside me. As he held the X-ray up for me to see the huge dark spot above my knee, he said, "I want to send you to a specialist. His name is Dr. Bos, and he is an orthopedist who deals with many of my cancer patients."

"Oh, Dr. Rhoades. Don't take this wrong, but I am so tired of doctors, appointments, waiting, and more tests."

"I think he might want to do a needle biopsy and send it off. We just want to be sure it is nothing. In the meantime, let me give you a prescription for that pain you are having."

"I don't want Vicodin or pain medicine. All that shit does is cover the pain because it'll make me sleep. I don't want to sleep more."

He proceeded to explain to me that the medicine was a more potent anti-inflammatory than the over-the-counter medicine I had been taking. He denied the pain could be nerve damage from the chemo. I wasn't sure, but I thought the timing was odd.

"Isn't it possible it is an internal birthmark, an old childhood injury?" I asked, looking for reassurance. "Maybe it is nothing."

"Yes, it is very possible," Dr. Rhoades replied.

His staff made my appointment. I would wait another week before I knew the results of another test. My heart felt heavy as I left his office and went out into the warm sunny day. I said a little prayer as I got into my VW Bug. I knew my doodlebug would lift my somber mood. After all, it was Bug weather and I had a spring season to enjoy. And I had a softball game to watch.

40
A Sorta Lucky Day

I was feeling great, knowing I had finished chemo, and I felt on top of the world. My blood count was stable and I was looking ahead to better days. Katie had an away softball game that happened to be the furthest-away game on the schedule. The school was located in a rural isolated area. The drive took me through many small country villages. David would go straight to the game from work.

It was a pretty spring day. Bug weather! The girls won, and I climbed into the Bug for the long drive home. Trick Pony was blaring from my CD player. My windows were down, and my hair was not blowing in the wind. A blue bandanna was atop my bald head. I decided to take my headgear off and feel the wind.

As I entered a small town, I recalled it being known as a speed trap. Another mom was behind me and had followed me for the first twenty-five miles. Just as I entered town, I let off the accelerator. As quickly as I tried to abide by the traffic laws, I saw a policeman running radar. His lights came on. I was busted!

I watched Shelly, the softball mom; pass me as I pulled over to obey the cop. As he sat in his cruiser, I pulled my registration, driver's license, and proof of insurance out. I wanted to impress him, but I also thought this might look like I was very experienced in being reprimanded for my driving. I had been a very experienced, lucky speeder, but my record was clean. I decided to place them back in my glove box.

I was irritated and worried as I waited on him to walk up to my car. Just as I looked in my rear view mirror, I noticed another police officer in the passenger seat with him as he opened his door to approach me.

There I sat, looking not trendy, and much like a pathetic chemo patient who wondered how stiff the fine would be.

"May I see your license?"

I reached over, opened the glove box, and handed him all three documents.

In a very sweet, innocent, shocked voice, I asked, "Why did you pull me over? Did I do something wrong, sir?"

"We have you locked in on radar, miss. You were going forty-eight in a thirty-five."

"Oh my. I was? Are you sure it was me and not someone else, Officer? I never speed. You did look at my record didn't you?" (I knew he had checked my record prior to getting out of his car.)

"We know it was you, miss. Why the hurry and were you wearing your seat belt?"

I happened to have worn it that particular day even though since getting cancer I had been careless about wearing it. "Oh yes, I always wear my seat belt," I said as he handed me my insurance card and registration. "I didn't mean to speed. I just have a long drive home."

He stood looking at me and he did not react. I tried harder.

"I will be right back, miss." I watched from my mirror as he got back in his cruiser. As he walked back toward my car, I noticed the other policeman walking with him. I realized immediately that she was a female officer. My heart felt hopeful. She would have compassion and sympathy. I giggled internally. My mind raced, thinking and determined to get myself out of a hefty fine.

I also wondered how soon the high school softball bus would swoosh by me and see the mess I had gotten myself into. Katie would tell David, who had left ahead of me. My Bug stood out like a sore thumb, and everyone recognized me from miles away. The vibrant yellow stood out on it, and the excellent condition of it caught all eyes.

When they reached my window again, with as much tenderness in my voice as I could muster, I said, "You really aren't going to give me a ticket, are you?"

"Do you have cancer?" the female officer asked. "My aunt just died of cancer."

Well that sure is not reassuring, I thought.

"I have breast cancer. Look, I am so sorry for speeding."

"OK, this is the deal. We are only going to give you a warning but please stop speeding," the male officer said as he handed my license back to me through the window.

"OK, I will. I promise," I said as he handed me back my documents. "Thank you so much. I guess I will be on my way and thanks again."

"Have a good evening and good luck," the female said.

I put my seat belt on, put my car in first gear, looked out my side mirror for oncoming traffic, cranked up Trick Pony, and headed for home.

"You are a lucky woman, Connie Curry," I said to myself aloud as I hit fourth gear. I looked over to find my bandanna scarf on the passenger seat. It was blowing in the wind.

41
A Mountain To Climb

I went to the ortho specialist, and the minute he walked into the examination room, I liked him. He was so full of personality and down-to-earth. Dr. Rhoades had told me I would like Dr. Bos, and I did ... instantly.

"I can tell you right now, Miss Curry, you do NOT have bone cancer."

"Dr. Rhoades told me I would love you, and I do already," I said as I walked toward him, giving him a hug thirty seconds after laying eyes on him.

The spot on my knee remained a mystery, and he would keep an eye on it, having me come in again in six months to X-ray it, just to be sure it had not changed. He gave it a huge medical name that I don't even recall, but it basically translated into nothing!

Two weeks later, I was being carted into surgery again for my second lumpectomy. I wasn't as nervous as I had been months before when I was so inexperienced in medical treatments, and my fear of being put to sleep had subsided some.

I would wait again for the pathology report. What was to be three days of waiting turned into one week. The more days that crept by, the more I feared bad news. Work, softball games, and Mother's Day had gone by. Dr. Linda had not called, but each time the phone rang, I was sure it was her with the report. I picked the phone up several times to call her, only to hang it back up. *No news is good news* were my thoughts.

Katie's high school softball team was winning game after game. They were looking to win the district championship. Amber had dropped out of firefighting school. I was sad for her because she had tried so hard. My life was an emotional roller coaster. Ryan was not dealing well with my illness. His continued silence troubled me. Amber rarely called me and never called just to check on me. It hurt me so.

On Tuesday, almost a week after my second lumpectomy, Dr. Linda called. My heart raced, and I instantly knew she had bad news. I had that sixth sense kick in that morning when I awoke. I had talked to Mom on the phone, crying and telling her that the news just had to be bad or Dr. Linda would have left a message on my home voice mail or my cell phone. I had left both phones on for days. I knew she was trying to speak directly to me.

And I was right. "Connie, it is not good. Your cancer has spread throughout your breast. You have a second kind called evasive lobular carcinoma. I need you to come into the office."

My mouth went dry and my chest felt tight as she continued. I sat up in bed, where I seemed to want to be many days. I'd curl up in a fetal position, wanting to sleep away my worries. On sunny days, I would close the curtain, hating the sun for being so beautiful.

"The chemo apparently did not do enough, Connie. The cancer is worse. We tried."

"So I lost my hair, and my leg and hip never stop hurting. I've gotten fat, and you now want to take my breast," I screamed into the phone.

"We can't know for sure that the chemo didn't do something. We just know it did not do enough," she said.

"I don't want to have a mastectomy. Is this the only choice I have?" I cried into the phone.

"Connie, yes. We need to get you scheduled, get this cancer out of you. We can make you a beautiful breast. Dr. Houser works with me. He is a plastic surgeon and does marvelous work."

"How soon? How soon must I do this?"

"We will get you scheduled, but please come in to my office tomorrow. We will go over the pathology report; I need to check your incision," she said in her calm, gentle voice. "OK? Connie? Will you come in?"

"OK, I will come in," I sobbed into the phone.

When David came home from work, I was sitting by the living room window, letting the sun hit my back. My heart ached and my head hurt from crying. He knew without asking that the news was bad.

He walked over to me, kneeling between my legs, rubbing my face. I bellowed with tears, sobbing, unable to talk. He held my breast in his hand and kissed my forehead.

As I left Dr. Linda's office the next day, I headed home to prepare for an hour-long trip to a softball game. Surgery had not been scheduled until they got dates available from the plastic surgeon to coordinate with Dr. Linda.

I remembered the football game seven months earlier, when I found out I had breast cancer. How ironic. I put on another happy face and went to cheer Katie on for a victorious game that made them the district champs for 2005. This time I wasn't alone, and David's presence comforted me.

As I watched the game, my cell phone rang. I looked down and my heart sank. It was Dr. Linda's office, and I ignored it. I wanted to enjoy the game. My mind wanted to procrastinate about any information having to do with a mastectomy. A message was left on my phone.

My curious mind wondered what the message was. As I played it, I felt nauseated. "Connie, please call the office as soon as possible. We need to schedule your surgery."

I knew the responsible thing to do was to call, so I did.

"We can do it this Friday."

"Friday! That is two days away. I need to think. I need time to accept this," I said as I paced, walking away briefly from the game. "Wait. I can't. My brother needs me Friday. I am committed to him."

"Well, if we don't do it this Friday, the two doctors can't do it together for three weeks. Connie, you really ought to do it, and not wait. I know it is hard on you. You need to just get it over with," the receptionist said.

"Can I talk to my husband? Call you back tomorrow, please? I need to think."

"Sure. You call us tomorrow."

I hung up and rushed over just as Katie was up to bat. I looked at David and back up to home plate. The discussion came later. I knew my brother needed me alive more than my support for a battle he also was about to fight. I also was aware that waiting three weeks might be risky. I would never know that for sure, but anticipating and sulking for three weeks was not emotionally healing either.

I started accepting the fact that a lost breast was not the end of my world, but the possible beginning of a second chance of life IN this world. I also knew that I was loved for my inner beauty and kindness to mankind. My feeling of physical self-worth would come later when my hair continued growing and the art of plastic surgery would make me physically whole. My emotional being was starting to gather and mend.

Besides, I had some more softball games to cheer on. Katie was heading into regional tournament play and, like her team, Wayne, and me … we all had mountains to climb and triumphs to celebrate later.

On May 20, 2005, I would climb to the top of that mountain of my once-easy life. My left breast would be removed.

42
Susan Komen
Lifted Me Back Up

What poor timing it was when I got my bad news about needing a mastectomy. Just when I felt optimistic, I'd get down again. It was just two days before the Susan Komen 5K race. I had signed up many weeks prior to participate in this annual fundraiser. I solicited to collect money from friends and family for this wonderful nonprofit organization. I had collected almost $800 in just two weeks. How could I not participate when I sent a letter out to so many, telling them my desire to run in it?

But I felt fed up and defeated ... spent. It had been almost eight months since my diagnosis. My sciatica continued to hurt, and I was so depressed about my cancer and having to have more surgery. I was discouraged, mad at myself, and skeptical if I would ever be a survivor. I felt like doctors dictated and owned my life. My calendar for anything else had to be worked around checkups.

I questioned myself about not letting Dr. Number Two go ahead and do the mastectomy months ago when he told me straight up, "You need a mastectomy." He was right. I played with fire all in the name of vanity. Was I wrong to switch doctors because I didn't like his bedside manner? Did I search too long for a doctor, looking for one to tell me what I wanted to hear? Dr. Linda was so sure she could save my breast and the chemo would possibly kill the cancer. She was wrong. I felt angry with her, too.

I had been healthy all my life, and I thought I could be cured quickly. I always bounced back so easily from minor illnesses. I should have trusted him.

Most of all, I was full of hate. If the chemo were something I could hold in my hands, I would have kicked it, punched it, and squeezed it until it was miserable. I wanted to shake it and scream at it. *Look what you did to me. See how I feel!*

I hated it even more because I couldn't take my anger out on it. It had dripped so slowly into my body on each visit and was still leaving its aftermath on my body.

It took so much from me. *We don't know that it didn't do something; we just know it didn't kill the cancer in your breast.* I kept hearing those words that Dr. Rhoades had said to me. *Dr. Number Two was right. He knew what he was talking about.* I said this over and over to myself. I felt responsible for putting my family through more because of selfishness. I wanted them to blame me, but they didn't. David never once gave me a "See I told you so," or, "You should have listened to him."

I curled up in a ball and felt like dying. I didn't tell any friends about my mastectomy for days. I called no one unless they called me. As usual, the phone rang continually. Sometimes I would ignore it, screen calls, and not want anyone to know I was going to have a mastectomy. It seemed like such an embarrassing thing.

I confessed the truth when Teresa Evans called me. As usual, she called every day to check on me, and I cried when I told her I had to have my breast removed. She was saddened with me.

"But you need to do the race with me," she said. "You are going to be a survivor. It will do you good to go, Connie."

"I don't want to run in it. Besides, Teresa … my sciatica is killin' me. I can hardly walk. I am so out of shape and all I do is cry. I feel eighty."

"Connie, you be at my house tomorrow morning at 7:00. Ryan and Derrick are going to race with us. Samantha and her mom are going too. Diana is a cancer survivor, and hell, she runs around in

T-shirts without even wearing a prosthetic. Maybe you can talk to her. She can help you feel better."

As she talked, I continued to feel no desire to go to it. I sat holding the phone in silence, wiping my nose occasionally as she rambled on, trying to cheer me and get fight back in me.

"Be at my house in the morning. I mean it. We are going!"

And with that, she hung up.

I thought about Ryan, my weekend party son who had ignored and denied my illness. He was actually getting up on his day off from work on a weekend to go run in a 5K race in honor of me.

Macho, bodybuilding Derrick, Mr. Cool who had been wearing the pink bracelet in my honor and hope, was running. He had bragged for days about coming in first place and beating Ryan.

Teresa always there for me, and Samantha—who ran it every year with her mom since her mom was diagnosed five years ago—was always concerned about how I was.

I knew cancer survivors would be there by the thousands. They would all have positive attitudes; many still in treatment, some cured, happy, and once again healthy. As the evening got later and my mind thought of all these things, I dug my tennis shoes out of the closet.

At 6:50 AM, with a mug of coffee in hand, I knocked on Teresa's door. At 7:10, the six of us headed for Columbus to join 26,000 other people for a run that put the fight back in me.

I felt an instant bond with Diana. We talked about our cancer and shared opinions and views as we headed south. She had a great outlook on life. Ryan and Derrick harassed each other, laughing and betting about who would beat the other to the finish line.

Teresa ran this annual race for four years, probably never thinking she would run for me on her fifth year participating. Diana and I were wearing our pink shirts, symbolizing our breast cancer history. Ryan, Teresa, Samantha, and Derrick donned their 2005 Susan Komen white shirts.

We each had a race number that was about five-by-seven in size pinned to our backs. Room was left for runners to add names of fallen victims and survivors. Teresa, Derrick, and Ryan took markers and in bold writing added my name and Diana's below their numbers, showing their personal involvement in the race. I was honored to see my name on their backs, as I knew they would leave Diana and me in the dust when the race began. I kept thinking about 5K being equal to about three and a half miles. My God. How would I accomplish that distance?

In memory of: I added Kathy Peachey, a friend's sister-in-law whom I had never met but felt empathy for when she died a young woman, a victim of breast cancer. In honor of: I added Sue Falkner, my friend from the James Cancer Clinic whom I had taken chemo with and who would always be my friend.

Just as we were about to lock the car and head up to the starting line, my cell phone rang. Two of my good friends from high school had decided to run. They were on the grounds, and as I talked to Rowena on my cell phone, I searched the parking lot, looking for her. With so many thousands of cars parked and parking, I wondered if I would be able to locate them. I did.

I ran over to greet Viv and Rowena as they were helping pin their numbers on each other's backs. I saw my name on their numbers and my heart felt warm.

We walked toward the starting line. The crowd amazed me. I saw people of all ages. Some were pushing wheelchairs and strollers. I scanned the crowd, looking at all the pink shirts upon the backs of so many women. Our eyes met, smiles were exchanged, and silent words of compassion and understanding were exchanged through eye contact.

"We might leave you guys," Teresa said. "But we will see you at the finish line."

"Oh, thanks a lot, buddy," I said. "This is total bullshit. Who was it who MADE me come today and now you are abandoning me?" I joked to her.

I wondered if I would be able to make the entire distance. My hip was killing me. Diana and I looked at one another. *I have to finish this race. I collected all that money. I promised to run. I can do this*, I thought as I stood listening to the National Anthem play minutes before the crack of the starter's gun.

"See you at the finish line," I said, watching my name become smaller and smaller on their backs as they raced ahead in the massive crowd of runners.

Teresa, being an avid walker and in shape, was keeping up with Derrick and Ryan. I later found out that Derrick felt threatened by his mom. "No way is my mom beating me, Ryan. Run faster or I am leaving you behind. I won't ever hear the end of this if she beats me."

I jogged, walked, ran, and walked some more. Runners passed by me. Diana tried to keep pace with me. I needed a familiar face near me too. I slowed, waiting for her, but my competitive nature wanted her to hurry. I didn't want to come in last.

The humidity was high, but clouds threatened rain. Drizzle fell but we walked on. I wore no headgear. My bald head symbolized my fight. I felt the rain hit my head. It was refreshing. I lifted my head and let the raindrops fall on my face. I licked my moistened, rainy lips. Sweat ran down my breasts. Bald women ran by me, and I ran by other bald women. Men, young boys, and older folks walked or ran. We all cheered each other on.

Flat-chested women with no prosthetics ran proudly in their pink T-shirts.

People lined the sidewalks, cheering all the runners on. Water was offered along the sidewalks as we passed.

Youthful guys and girls from various Ohio State fraternities lined the corners, supporting us. Some held signs telling us how far we had gone. Bands played along the way as we continued on. Their spirit mesmerized me. It put the seal of approval on mankind. People care.

Adrenaline, determination, and my competitive nature kicked in. I looked behind me, unable to see the end of the racers. So many had passed me, but it seemed that Diana and I were in the middle of the pack.

"We can do this, Diana. I am NOT coming in last place or toward the end," I said as I got a second wind. I picked my feet up higher with firmness and strength in search of the finish line. Magically, I felt no hip pain. I felt strong. I ran.

Just as I thought Diana could not keep pace with me, I saw the finish line in the distance. "Look, Diana. We are almost home," I told her. "We can do this, and look behind us," I said as we both looked back, not missing a step forward. There were thousands behind us.

It didn't matter where we finished. I knew this. Deep within me, I wanted Ryan to be proud and remember the mom he always knew to be so strong and healthy. It appeared we would finish respectably in the middle of the pack.

As I hit the finish line, I looked to my left. I followed Diana, who knew why we veered left. I wondered why. Teresa and Diana had failed to tell me that breast cancer participants had to cross a bridge.

As I walked up the plank, I noticed women in front of me, stopping briefly to speak into a microphone. People cheered on each announcement.

"Mary Stevens, eight years."

"Jane Lowry, twelve years."

"Diana Young, five years," she said as she walked across the bridge. I realized they were saying the amount of years they had been cancer-free.

"Connie Curry," I said as I continued on.

As we reached the end, walking in single file, a rose was handed to each of us. As I took my rose, holding it up to sniff the wonderful fragrance, I saw Teresa, Ryan, Derrick, and Samantha.

They had finished the race about a half hour ahead of us and had been waiting and watching for us to cross the bridge.

I felt happy, strong, proud, and even healthy.

And then it hit me. All my emotions turned to tears as I looked up at my son and friends.

Teresa, my dear, longtime friend who never cried, was sobbing. Macho Derrick, a young man, so physically fit, trying to hide his tears. Samantha, who had fought the war with her mom, cried for Diana. Ryan—there he stood, my six-foot-tall son, crying and finally seeing reality.

I walked over and kissed each wet cheek of those who had given me strength to face my next step in my cure. Their embraces were in love and good vibes for me.

"Connie Curry, one year." Those will be my words at the next Susan G. Komen Race for the Cure.

43
Winners Prevail

I will never forget waking up the morning I was to be admitted to the hospital for my mastectomy. I was furious with the world. I wanted and NEEDED coffee. I had hours to wait without consuming any liquids or food. I had no desire to get out of bed.

I hated removing all my sterling silver jewelry again. I refused to go in without my makeup, even though the pre-op papers stated: no makeup, contacts, or fingernail polish. I needed to feel like a woman. I compromised. No mascara.

Most of all, I was scared. I was truly scared to the point of nausea, and I shook with fright. I thought of Wayne. I knew my family was already at the courthouse, preparing for a long day in a jury trial. David didn't make coffee. He knew the aroma would beckon me to the coffeepot. He went without his morning kick also just for me.

We arrived fifteen minutes ahead of my 11:00 AM appointment. Katie was excused from school to be with us. Her regional softball game had been rained out the night before. I was also sad because it was rescheduled for the evening of my surgery. I would miss the game. Her plan was to be with me until Cathy, my sister, came to take her to the game. Cathy would be her replacement for family/moral/cheerleader support.

When I walked into the pre-op room, I started crying. A gown, head covering, and paper slippers were on the bed for me. I was instructed to remove all my clothes and to put the cotton gown on. I slid out of my sandals and as I lifted my leg out of my jeans, I stumbled. I was shaking so badly, I was weak, dizzy, and unbalanced mentally and physically.

"I am so scared," I pleaded to the nurse. "I am just sooo scared."

David and Katie were in the waiting room until I was settled in. I would never settle, I was sure.

"I know this is hard. Let me get someone for you," the nurse said, and out the curtain door she went.

A woman came in and immediately began to help me take my clothes off. Her touch was slow and tender. Her voice and words gave me inner strength. "Look at how beautiful you are. You have the most beautiful eyes. Your face is gorgeous," she said. "Losing a breast is tough. I have not had this tough experience. But I work with all the breast cancer patients, and I assure you, you will get through this." She helped me put my feet in the cloth slippers. "Dr. Houser does beautiful work. You will be so happy when he reconstructs your breast." She rubbed my cheek and handed me a Kleenex.

"Now, let's tie that gown and get this cancer out of you. I am sure you have many people who need you around for a long time."

And she was right. I needed to be brave for Katie. I needed to show David that I believed him when he said I would always be beautiful. And I needed to get the surgery over, because I had to find out if Katie's team would get the chance to play in the state competition.

And most of all, I needed to be brave and send strong, positive vibes to Wayne as he fought to win also.

For a year, my family and I had talked about Wayne going through the worst divorce in history. I told Mom that if we even tried to tell people the things he had endured and lived with for twenty-seven years, they would think we were crazy and making up stories. His life would make a horror movie.

For many years, I had suspected all the things that finally surfaced. Wayne, a very private person, worked hard to protect us and to not involve us in his personal life. His pride, independence, and beliefs that a marriage is forever made him hide his life from us. He was embarrassed.

He had married young and had never known a loving marriage with excitement, partnership, respect, or passion.

Divorce, bitterness, and revenge surfaced, and things escalated. We feared for his life and safety because she was so miserable without him taking care of her. She was more amok than when she was married to him. She framed him, and because of young, inexperienced deputies, he was arrested. A guy who had not done anything wrong is his life and had an abundance of friends and respect in his community was facing possible prison time for something he did not do. If he were sent to prison, his job of almost thirty years would be gone. His home business would suffer, his heart would be broken. We would be lost without him.

From the long, drawn-out divorce and observing the court system, we all worried and had lost much faith in the judicial system. Wayne refused to plea bargain. He knew something had to go his way, and he would not admit to something when he did nothing wrong. His record was as clean as the person he was and is today.

Court dates were postponed three times. Months went by with sleepless nights for all of us who adore him. Wayne, a somewhat naive but pure, honest man, slept little and worked lots. The financial empire he had built was gone, and the kids were gone too. Lawyer fees and the divorce settlement had left him for the first time in his life starting over and rebuilding. I wondered if he would ever be totally happy if his kids didn't come back. I found some peace in knowing that they were hurting themselves, missing a dad who had given them everything, coached their softball teams, let them have horses, built them show wagons for the horses, and loved them unconditionally.

So when I agreed to have my surgery on May 20, I knew this day would or could change two lives. As Mom said to me when I was trying to decide whether to have my surgery or wait three weeks, "Wayne knows you will be there in spirit. Don't wait. We'll be with him and David will be with you. Wayne would be furious if you waited."

Dad and Mom were consumed with fright and determined that the truth would set him free. They worried about my health.

I wonder how a parent can rationalize telling horrendous lies about the other parent, brainwashing the children against another parent. Shouldn't a divorce be about two adults who can't live together anymore? The relationship is severed, but most good parents never wish to sever the relationship with the children. I felt anger many times because the kids were old enough and smart enough. "Someday, Wayne, just hold on. They will figure it all out. Hold on to that," I assured him.

My surgery lasted about three hours. Dr. Linda took away my breast and Dr. Houser started rebuilding. I'll never forget the day I met Dr. Houser. Young, with a friendly, handsome, youthful face—I instantly liked him.

"Dr. Linda, will I like him? Will he make me a pretty breast?" I had asked her as I wiped tears away.

"No, he won't make you a pretty breast. He will make you a spectacular breast. He is one of the best."

When I awoke from surgery, I was back in my room. I didn't recall being in recovery, but the first thing I remembered was thinking of Wayne, wondering what time it was. Then I wondered about my chest and if I would have the courage to look at it.

I felt the tube in my side used for the drainage of blood. David, Cathy, and Katie stood at my bed. "How is Wayne? Is it over?" I asked Cathy.

"I left to come here when they broke for lunch," Cathy said. "I don't know anything yet, but it sure looked like it was going Wayne's way," she said.

"We have to find out," I said as I tried to sit up. A nurse appeared checking, fixing, measuring, and asking me questions. My blood pressure was taken.

"Mom, my game was rained out again," Katie announced. "They are going to play it tomorrow."

"Is there a chance I can be discharged tomorrow?" I immediately asked the nurse. "My daughter's team is playing a tournament game. They have gone further than any team in the school's history. I really need to get out of here."

I wanted to look at my chest. I feared what I might see. I felt a harness-type bra on me, and as I looked down at my chest, it appeared to bulk up. I knew this couldn't be possible. I had seen pictures of mastectomies.

I lifted the blanket up and took my right arm, lifting the cotton harness-girdle bra up as I peeked into the middle of my left chest area.

A vision I will never forget hit me. I saw cleavage. I was thrilled. I slid my hand down to the inside of my left cleavage area. It was numb, but I felt tears fall down my cheek. The small mound gave me hope. I knew my breast had a long road to look perky and pretty, but I was willing to sacrifice the pain, appointments, more surgery, and whatever it would take.

"C'mon here, you guys. Look, look," I said as David, Katie, and Cathy all leaned toward me. "I HAVE CLEAVAGE," I squealed. They all laughed. I heard pieces of conversation about how all I talked about in recovery was Wayne. Everything was hazy.

I tried to talk to friends who stopped in, but I fell into and out of sleep. Flowers were delivered, but the world was hazy. Surgery had knocked me for a loop. I fell into a peaceful sleep.

When I awoke, I was alone and it was late and dark. Amber had stopped in and brought me flowers and a card. Ryan did not surface. As I became more alert, I thought of Wayne again. I reached for the phone. The pain would not allow me to reach it. I hit my button and a nurse came in.

"I need the phone and I can't reach it. I have to call someone. I have to find out about my brother."

I dialed Cathy, and as she answered, her greeting to me with so much energy was, "NOT GUILTY!"

We laughed, cried, and cheered as we talked on the phone. "Connie, they were practically laughed out of the courtroom. They got so tangled up in lies, and all their stories were so different."

I called Tina, who was traveling with Jared, her husband, on a trip out of town for the weekend. They had postponed leaving early to be in court, showing support for Wayne.

"Tell me everything. Don't leave out anything," I said to Tina as she began telling me from her cell phone. We prattled, we babbled, and we interrupted each other as we celebrated Wayne's victory. It was as if my mastectomy was forgotten and we didn't care. Wayne was free and would maybe sleep again. The next day, I didn't recall much of my conversations with Mom, Tina, or Cathy. My world had still been full of haze and garble from surgery.

I later heard from Mom, and she had told me how proud I would have been of Wayne. "He took the stand, well-spoken, speaking only the truth, and it was so simple for him. The truth is easy to tell and no one can trip up a testimony when the truth is told," Mom said.

At 10:00 PM I was out of bed, taking a sink bath, brushing my teeth, applying makeup, putting my contacts in, and calling Wayne. I was alert and my mind was clear.

Wayne and I talked for an hour. And then I walked the halls. I carried my blood tubing with me and I wanted to jump for joy. The nurses looked at me like I was a crazy woman, but they smiled.

"I am not a winner; I just did not lose," Wayne said. I knew what he meant. It was a sad day in court when Wayne's own daughter took the stand and told lies about the man who had given her so much. In all the stress, money spent, pain caused, he still had hope in his heart, kindness in his words, and faith in his future.

"Are you going to be OK?" he asked me.

"We are going to be just fine, Wayne. They can kick us when we are down, but we always get back up," I said. "I love you."

I felt his love through the phone as I hung up. And I also figured out why my surgery happened the same day as his court hearing. It was to give me strength and fight.

And it did just that!

44

Miserable Medicines

I was discharged early the next afternoon, as I had hoped. David and I had enough time to get all the flowers home, check on our dog that I had missed horribly, and head back south for the tournament game. I couldn't wait to put my sterling silver jewelry back on and take a real bath.

I was wired for coffee, adrenaline, and drugs. I felt on top of the world, knowing I had survived surgery. Prior to surgery, my sixth sense told me something might happen. I pictured me having a stroke, being left a handicapped wife and mom, a burden to all. I prayed for a clear margin. After all, I sacrificed my entire breast.

I was given an antidepressant prescription about a week before my surgery. Dr. Linda told me it was a no-brainer, since it could help me in two ways.

I had never experienced or ever knew how bad hot flashes were. I'd heard women talk about them. I, being a cold-blooded woman, laughed and welcomed a surge of heat. Or so I thought.

Since the chemo had thrown me into menopause, the hot flashes were becoming more frequent. I would wake up during the night on fire. I kicked blankets off, stripped clothes, and thrashed in and out of sleep. I was having about ten to fifteen a day. Hot flashes are much like going from 98.6 to 120 in body temperature in 1.2 seconds flat. I was sure I was smokin' out the top of my head. My hip pain continued to plague me too, and I was always exhausted but tried to push on. I had not slept solidly in months. I would be thrilled with four to five hours of uninterrupted sleep.

Not only are antidepressants used as psychiatric drugs; they are also quite effective for hot flashes. So the no-brainer, in Dr. Linda's opinion, was that the medicine would help with my emotions as I was trying to deal with the mastectomy and hot flashes. I yearned for sleep. An antibiotic and a pain medicine were added to my list.

I walked out of the hospital in a rush to make good time and to see Katie's game. I called her cell phone as she and the team were heading to the tournament. David was driving his typical S-L-O-W speed, unlike me, who always speeds. (Except never again through that one small, speed-trap town)

"No promises, Katie, but I am discharged and we are trying to get home in time so I can come to the game," I warned her. "If I don't make it, good luck and win. If you win, I promise to be at the championship game. Kick butt, Miss Katie."

As I hung up, I looked at all the flowers on the floor of the truck around my feet. I felt blessed to have such thoughtful, generous friends. I realized that I was not going to be able to go to the game. The bumps along the way hurt me as I tried to hold my chest to relieve the pain. I felt very tired.

I greeted Graham, my goldie. I was too tired to bathe, and David helped me to bed and headed to the game. My pillow felt like heaven, and I knew I could get a rundown of the game when he and Katie returned. I fell into a deep slumber with Betty, the cat, beside my head and Graham beside my feet.

The team won and would play the regional championship game three days after my arrival home. Katie had a big hit, scoring two RBIs. As she stopped at second base for her double, I later found out she said, "And that was for my mama."

I had time to heal, and knew I would not miss the championship game. The team had just broken a school record. They were 24-4 going into the championship game, and we were all very proud. Our local paper gave them great media coverage. More fans started coming to the games. Our young underdog team was about to go further and make us even prouder.

The days that followed, I began having horrible side effects from the antidepressant. As I waited for the game, and again for the pathology report, I developed a yeast infection. Dr. Linda found my sarcastic terminology funny when I referred to it as a fungus. I was a mess.

The day of Katie's big game was the same day Dr. Linda called me about the pathology report. It brought back all the fears I had before when I waited for results after the two lumpectomies. "Connie, we have a clear margin." I didn't feel the urge to celebrate. It seemed so strange; because although I felt relieved, I was not ecstatic like I would have been months prior. Dr. Linda was happy to finally give me this news. I didn't want to rain on her parade. *Well, I would hope it is a clear margin. Look what you had to do to get it. You took all I fought to keep.* I kept those thoughts to myself because she seemed sincerely happy.

"I also have a little bad news," she said.

I instantly grew tense.

"Now what? My God, now what, Dr. Linda?" I asked. "You are scaring me again."

"Connie, I have never seen so much scar tissue from your lumpectomy. I scraped and cleaned it up for almost an hour after I did the mastectomy. I could not see well enough to feel it was safe to pull the nodes I needed. I did not want to do nerve damage to your arm."

As she spoke, I already suspected what she was about to say.

"I was able to get very little of some nodes. They did test negative for cancer, but ..."

"Well, that is good, isn't it?" I asked, swirling my foot across Graham's neck as he lay by my feet on the living room floor.

"Yes, that is good, but I am thinking you might have to see a radiation oncologist and do radiation just to be sure the cancer is not anywhere else or in your lymph nodes."

I knew so little about radiation. I was tempted to rebel, but I was not in the mood to argue. I needed time to heal and think. All I knew was that thirty to thirty-five treatments, daily with weekends off, sucked.

I went to Dr. Houser, my plastic surgeon, for a follow-up and was given another prescription to fight the yeast infection. He was not happy to hear I might need radiation. Dr. Houser, being an artist as he built my breast, found working on radiated skin a more complex job. He wondered if I would have to have my breast radiated or just my armpit, clavicle area, and neck. I wondered also.

"So what do you think of it?" he asked me as he opened my gown to examine me.

"I love my cleavage, but I have not looked at the entire breast," I told him as I turned my head away. "It took me weeks to look at my bald head. I doubt I will find courage anytime soon to look at my boob."

"I had one patient who didn't look for three months. She has the record," he told me. "Your breast looks good, except it is still a little too swollen for me to inject saline. You should look at it, though."

"Nope, I am not ready. You just make the prettiest breast you can," I smiled and said. "But, wait ... I just thought of something," I said as I closed the gown. "What if you make it too perky and it rides higher than my right breast? I am not braggin' BUT my breasts were pretty full and not sagging. You even said that, didn't you? But this new one already looks like it is going to be as high as a twenty-year-old's."

Dr. Houser grinned. "I think when the swelling is down, we'll know more."

"I did have nice breast! I don't anymore," I said. "Not YET, but I have faith in you. Anyway ... Oh, I wish you could add saline today. I want all of this completed. I am so impatient, I know."

"Let's just get your breast back to a C cup slowly without causing any problems. Then we can always do some work on your right one to get symmetry," he said. "You really ought to look at it. You have an A cup now and it looks quite good. Your incision looks great. It is healing nicely and you still have your areola."

"How do you make the nipple?" I asked.

"Oh, it is a secret trick I do," he said as he grinned.

"Hold the flood gate, Captain. I wanna know what you do or use," I insisted.

"Oh, it is very simple. See," he said as he opened the gown back up. "Look here,"

"Nope, can't look," I said. "Maybe later, just tell me."

"We just cut here," he said as I vaguely felt his touch on my breast. I held my face away to the right, looking at the ducks on the pond picture hanging on the wall. I hated the numb feeling. "We cut it open, swirl the skin and shape it and bunch it up, and it truly works fabulous," he explained.

"Well, that sounds rather brutal," I said as I jumped off the examination table. "My Lord, I can't believe I have to carry this blood purse around with me another week."

"Well, you see Dr. Han [Linda] in a couple of days. Continue measuring it when you empty the bottle, and if it has decreased, she can remove the tube," he said.

So I left his office with an A cup on my left side and a C cup on my right. Although I was disappointed, I trusted his decision. I was learning to not question or rebel against my doctors.

Thoughts of Nicole entered my mind, and although I hurt and had trouble sleeping, I refused to take the Vicodin. That particular drug has a bad reputation with me, and I feared becoming an addict. I thought of Pam, and although it sounded crazy at the time, I felt like I was being disloyal to her. Vicodin had almost ruined her life, and it did ruin and take Nicole's. My friend Pam would never be the same after the loss of her beautiful young daughter from a Vicodin overdose. Pam was bitter at careless doctors who were allowed to feed Nicole's bad habit.

As a chubby, bald woman with one breast and a yeast infection, one would wonder why I worried about sex. I did. Sex has always been fun and enjoyable for me. Orgasms flowed through my body as easy as one-two-three. Since taking the antidepressant, I could not have an orgasm. I was furious and troubled.

I had bookmarked the *Physician's Desk Reference* book on the Internet, and I went immediately to it. Sure enough, the common side effects for Effexor matched me to a tee.

Nightmares, dizziness, and lack of ejaculation and orgasms were on the list. I was relieved to know it was caused from the medicine and not from some physiological problem that I was having since the loss of my breast.

I was disappointed with Dr. Linda, and wondered why she would give me something that would play havoc with my sexual world. She looked much younger than me. She knew I was now in menopause from chemo. Did she think sex was unimportant to a woman of forty-eight?

On my next visit for my follow-up with Dr. Linda, I immediately called her on the carpet for prescribing Effexor to me.

"Dr. Linda, you gave me a prescription for crap that keeps me from having orgasms. We cannot have THAT! I stopped taking it. It did take the hot flashes away, but sex is pretty darn important to me."

"Wait. Was this sex by yourself or with your husband?"

"Dr. Linda!" I shook my head at her. "I feel fortunate to have a man who wants me sexually. I about killed him trying to ... well, you know."

"Oh, Connie. This has only happened to two or three women that I prescribed Effexor to. It works so well for hot flashes."

"Is there another kind you can give me? The night sweats were so bad and it did help. I wish for sleep, too." I threw my index finger up at her, "But don't be messing with my orgasms. Y'all took my hair and my boob; I'll be damned if you are stealing my orgasms. I have enough to deal with," I said in a joking way.

She grinned. "Let me get you some samples of Zoloft to try," she said. "I'll be right back."

Afterward, she removed my drainage tube. I wondered if it would hurt when she pulled it out. It was wonderful! It felt so good as it came out of my skin. It had begun to make me itch inside, and the relief as it came out was soothing. I no longer had to walk around with my purple purse, holding blood. Woohoo! I could go to Katie's regional championship game feeling free and not looking like the American Red Cross with B positive hanging on my side.

I headed for home to get back on the Internet to read about Zoloft. They had the exact same common side effects as the Effexor.

I threw them onto the counter, unopened. I decided to double up on my vitamin E instead.

I had only been off the Effexor for four days. I noticed my happy moods and energy level were dropping. I cried about everything. I saw a Kodak commercial, I cried. A raccoon ran across in front of me as I was driving home. I cried after I braked to miss him. I hate raccoons. Years ago, a raccoon had killed my cat. They tip the lids up on our garbage cans and make messes. They are a nuisance and carry diseases. And there I was ... crying over a stupid raccoon that survived my lead foot.

It was time to get ready for the game. We had to win in order to go to the state competition. And these young girls were just the ones who could do it.

David arrived home, we discussed my appointment, he showered, and out the door we went to get to the game on time. Mom, Dad, Tina, and Cathy met us at the game. Ryan rushed there from work.

As we walked toward the bleachers, I started to cry ... again. The crowd that had come to support the team surprised me. As I scanned the stands for a seat, I saw many familiar faces. Jackie, a softball mom and good friend whose daughter had graduated three years prior and had played softball with Amber, was there to show support. Jackie had stopped by one day to show me her magnetic pink ribbon she had put on her SUV in my honor.

Jerry, a high school friend of mine who had graduated from Buckeye Valley, was there with his granddaughter. He no longer lived in our district but must have read about it in the paper.

Many students came by the heaps. Posters, chanting, and whistling could be heard all over the softball facility.

As they announced each team member on both teams and called out their record, I felt very proud. I cried as I stood cheering and clapping for each girl.

I leaned down to Jackie, whom I sat with at many games when Amber and Tammy had played softball together, and said, "LOOK at me. I am an emotional mess. What the heck will I do if these girls win? I will drown. My heart is racing. I am going to blow this expander out of my chest before my boob is even finished."

"Oh, Connie ... WHEN they DO win, you just holler and cry. I have some Kleenex in my purse."

We all stood for the National Anthem. I cried. I looked out at the girls all standing in unison with their hands on their chests, erect and in a vertical line along the first-base line. I sniffed as I stood at attention.

I saw Katie look up at me. I wondered if she thought, *My God, Mom is crying again. Now why? We haven't even played or won yet.*

David touched my back to try to settle me. It made me more emotional. My nose was running. As the song ended, Jackie turned and handed me a Kleenex. We laughed.

And so it was ... that day our Buckeye Valley girls won 4-2, breaking a countywide record in softball. We would head to Ashland College in Ashland, Ohio, for the state tournament in four days.

And I was no longer a minority. The entire team and many fans, players, and family cried tears of joy.

When we got home, I undressed as my bathwater ran. The bathroom door was half-open as Katie and I reminisced about the game. I slowly shut the door as I unzipped my girdle/harness bra that I continued to wear for comfort. My armpit hurt from all the probing to find lymph nodes. I remembered what Jennifer, my RN friend who had seen so many breast cancer chests, said, "Connie, you should look. It is the best-looking mastectomy and first-stage reconstruction I have ever seen. It looks wonderful. It looks more like a lumpectomy."

The mirror began to fog up from my hot, steamy bathwater. I opened the door again to clear up the mirror. "Don't come in here, Katie."

"Why?"

Walking in and out and never giving me privacy was the norm. "Just don't ... OK?"

I opened the bra and slowly looked up into the mirror. I immediately looked at my right breast, so full, round, and hopefully healthy. I sighed and looked square on at my entire chest.

I cried.

45
Give Me Breasts

As quickly as my mastectomy was done, an expander and seventy cc's of saline were put in my chest cavity, to begin the stretching of my skin. Dr. Houser had spent more time reconstructing after the mastectomy than it took to remove my breast. I was happy that the procedure was started immediately.

After surgery, I would lie in bed, uncomfortable, tossing and turning. My chest felt rock-hard, and in the dark I would run my hand across my once-healthy breast, thinking how unnatural it felt. I knew I would not expose it when I made love. I felt weepy and cried sometimes.

Sometimes it felt like a bolt of lightning in the area where my nipple once was. Sharp pains seared through the areola. I was glad Dr. Linda had salvaged my areola, though, and very surprised since I was originally told it would have to be removed too. The pain and tightness in my chest from the expander made me want to explode, so I could feel freedom to breathe easier.

I remember when I was in my third trimester with my three kids. My stomach and skin felt like it could not stretch another inch or it would burst. I started feeling this claustrophobic tightness again in my chest. Lying down would make the expander feel as if it was pressing into my sternum. I felt short of breath. The pressure pushed against my ribcage, causing back pain. It hurt so. I started having stings that felt like burning through my chest, commonly called stingers caused from nerves trying to rekindle.

In spite of the pain, I was still excited for my next visit with my plastic surgeon. Dr. Houser was like warm, fuzzy slippers, and our visits were always full of compassion, laughter, understanding, patience, and reassurance. I couldn't wait for more saline to be injected. I knew the pain was a great sacrifice for a future attractive breast.

I changed into a gown and sat waiting for him to come in. I felt silly, but I had a crush on this wonderful young man who could easily be my son. The curtain was drawn. I heard a tap on the door. As he peeked around the corner, I saw his warm, down-to-earth smile. Without giving it any thought, I quickly opened my gown and flashed him.

"I want more boob," I said.

"In my years in practice, you are the first to flash me," he said as he laughed.

"It is not like you have not seen them before," I replied.

"You are a nut," he said as he walked over, looking at my breast like Monet looked at his art.

"It looks good," he said as he palpated it, feeling the hardness. I flinched. It was very tender. "Well, you ready for more?"

"Wooo doggie, I am," I said. "Inject me, give me boob, baby!"

I watched him prepare and put saline in a huge syringe. "Is this going to hurt much?" I asked. The first seventy cc's were given in surgery, so this was a new experience for me, being alert and conscious.

"You are going to feel pressure. See this handy-dandy little stud finder? I am looking for the port under your skin," he said as he glided it across my chest.

"I bet when you need to nail stuff at home, you look for breasts with your stud finder, don't you?" I said as I watched him load the syringe.

He laughed, blushed a little, and came toward me with that big old syringe.

He immediately began pushing the saline in. It was painless but uncomfortable. I felt my breast getting tighter. I couldn't look. "How much have you put in?" I asked.

"Fifty cc's. Do you want me to stop?" he asked.

I looked at his face and down toward his hand as he stopped pushing the syringe of fluid in.

"Hmmm, give me more," I said. "Maybe just a little bit more."

As he injected, we talked about a mutual RN friend, his children, and his sister who is also a doctor. "Whoooa, look at that," he said. "You may only have to come one or two more times to get your C cup."

As I looked down, I couldn't believe how my breast contour had grown. It looked so round and pretty. My nipple area was still covered with gauze from the incision-healing process. I could pretend there was a beautiful nipple under the dressing.

"Stop," I said. "Wow, that is sooooo tight, but look at that boob," I said with so much happiness.

"I gave you ninety cc's," he said. "Most women take about thirty. You are a tough woman, or just crazy. I think you are about a B cup already."

As I left his office after making my appointment for the following week, I wondered if I had lost my mind. It hurt so badly. How in the world would I make it home in the late-afternoon traffic in a big city? One rear-end collision and I would drown in saline if I hit the air bag.

Sleep was restless and painful. It hurt to turn my head to the left, and my ribs hurt. *Forgive me, Pam. I have to take a Vicodin,* were my thoughts as I slithered out of bed and grabbed the prescription bottle. *I promise to not be dependent on them.*

The following morning, I awoke to a humid June morning. Typical Ohio weather! I had enough cleavage to wear tank tops without wearing the special left-side padded bra, compliments of the Susan Komen organization. I felt brave enough to put my swimming suit on, so it was decided....

I picked Allie up, and off to Tammy's pool we went for a day in the sun. Allie was very happy to see me, and excited to go swimming. She adored Tammy, and Tammy—still not having the privilege of being a grandmother—doted over Allie. She called herself Allie's foster grandma. The way she bought clothes, toys, and sandals for her, she fit the part of a generous grandma.

With the pain in my breast and the high humidity and temperature, I realized I was not the Connie I used to be. Tammy always understood me and sympathized with me as I decided to cut the first swim day short. The heat exhausted me quickly. Allie, being a redhead, was covered in sunscreen and had had enough, too. She was content to head for "Grammy's house" until her mom was off work. After all, she had a bike to ride, Graham to visit, Katie to pick on, and Popsicles to eat. David would be thrilled to see her when he got home from work.

Amber came and we laughed talking about Dr. Houser and my saline dose that I had gotten the day before. "I am a B cup now, Amber."

"Well, if that was me, Mom, I would be finished. Wish I were a C cup."

"The next time you go to Victoria's Secret and they ask you what size you are, tell them you wear a 160-cc cup," I told her jokingly.

It would be twelve days before I received another dose of saline. I postponed my appointment as Dr. Houser's suggested because I hurt too badly. I would receive more saline five days later. Tammy rode along with me that day. Dr. Houser thought we were both crazy women.

He warned me that the expander procedure would get tougher as I started radiation.

I guess I would find out soon enough.

46
Relay For Life

I Walked
I walked around a track today;
I walked to help a disease go away.
I walked because there is a need;
I walked that bodies could be freed.
I walked to give a small child hope;
I walked to help someone cope.
I walked for a husband or a wife;
I walked to help prolong a life.
I walked with my head held high;
I walked for that one about to die.
I walked excitedly not demure;
I walked to help find a cure.
I walked for everyone to see;
I walked for you, I walked for me.

Jeannie Davis,
Harding Co., Texas

My wonderful family and friends continued to stop and check on me. Tina was working diligently, with heart and soul, collecting money for the Relay for Life, an annual walk held in many cities to raise funds for the American Cancer Society.

She sent out a letter promoting donations in honor of me and my battle against breast cancer. Cathy and Tina had participated every year. I knew I would take the first relay walk with all cancer survivors, kicking off this all-night event.

Tina called me one day, excited to tell me about the outpouring of donations she had gotten in my honor. It thrilled me. She was emotional, excited, and full of enthusiasm for the upcoming event. Tina reminisced about how touching the event is each year. Luminaries with names of survivors and those who lost their battles to cancer would line sidewalks and be lit at dusk. Tina had bought luminaries in years past, in memory of Uncle Eddie and Uncle Joe, who died of cancer. She had collected almost $1,000 for this one. Amazing.

Teresa called me faithfully. Pam, my dear friend in southern Ohio, sent me e-mails and called me, always concerned. Pam and I found solitude in each other through our tough times. Pam had gloomy days like me. Her spirit would be up, then down. I found my battle a smaller one to fight than hers. She was grieving the loss of her daughter. It had been two years, and the emotional turmoil was something I sympathized about, but I could not begin to know the depth of her pain.

I just knew my heart ached for her. I also missed Nicole. I would dust my house, look at her beautiful face in the framed picture on the buffet in our living room, and be saddened at such a terrible loss of a beautiful daughter, granddaughter, sister, mother, and friend to many. I remembered when she was a toddler atop her pony, how fearless she was. Her beautiful, big brown eyes were so full of sparkle and life. Her laugh was contagious.

She was not a victim of cancer, but I thought of her as Tina talked to me about the luminaries.

Nicole had everything life could offer. She excelled in high school and was what many girls dream of being. She had intelligence, good looks, was physically fit, and was a cheerleader and homecoming queen. Although her parents divorced when she was a toddler, she continued living the traditional family life. No child could have more in the blessing of two fathers that adored her. Her stepdad took her under his wing, loved her unconditionally, and accepted her as if she was his biological daughter. There was never a doubt that his love and devotion was doled out to her as much as to his two biological sons.

Pam, her mother and one of my best friends, had emotional ups and downs raising Nicole. We shared our sorrows, disappointments, and sadness about our teens. We also laughed and shared warm moments bragging about our children.

Somewhere along the way, Nicole faltered. Because of a prescription drug, her world changed. It became the most important thing in her young adult life and was becoming a death sentence.

Her family tried over and over to help her.

Pam and Bryan sent her off to one of the nation's best drug programs in California. She agreed to go, wanting help. Her young children could not comprehend why their mom had left. We all had high hopes that she would return to be a good mother again. She wanted to be cured.

After three months in the drug program, Nicole was flown back to Ohio with a new attitude, drug-free and happy again. Or so Pam thought.

Just months after she left the facility, she was found dead from a drug overdose. Nicole left behind two small children... Hannah, the spitting image of her mom, and Michael, just a toddler, too young to later have memories of his mom. Pam's world crumbled.

I heard the sad news just hours after and ran to Pam's aid. My words could not help. There are no words of comfort when a mother loses her child. I will never forget the pain in my dear friend and how helpless she felt and how helpless I was in comforting her.

It turned my stomach when my doctors offered to prescribe the same drug for me after my surgeries and going through the tissue-expander procedure. I feared an addiction. I thought of Nicole.

The night of the Relay for Life, I was in a lot of pain. I had just gotten more saline in my expander, and the elasticity of my skin was being affected by the radiation. I hated each trip to the radiation clinic, and they tired me.

I looked forward to my visits to Dr. Houser's, knowing my breast was showing promise. I teased him about placing a watermelon in the lining of a jellybean. I had filled my prescription but decided I could be OK without it. I would tough it out for the relay.

David, Katie, Amber, and I headed out for the worthy occasion. It was a beautiful June evening with a clear sky, a warm breeze, and perfect temperatures. Tents were scattered around the track, and purple balloons were tied together on the starting line, forming an arch that blew beautifully in the sky.

Many members of my family were there along with friends. I walked up to the registration table to sign in, knowing I would be given a gold shirt like the other cancer survivors got.

A woman was in line in front of me. Our eyes met, and immediately we recognized the similarity in the length of our hair. I couldn't help but to look down at her chest, wondering if she'd had breast cancer. It was obvious. She stood in line, happy and without prosthesis. I was amazed and felt immediate respect for her. I wished many times I could be more accepting of my recent mastectomy.

She was probably not in pain like me, as I was stumbling through reconstruction.

"I love your curls," she said. "Look at mine! It is so poker-straight."

"Thank you," I replied as we moved up in line. "I have never had curls this tight ever in my life."

"When did you finish chemo?" she asked.

"March. It was March, and I am so glad to be finished with that stuff," I told her.

"I finished in March, too," she said.

"What is your name?" I asked as I begin to think she might be Judy who I had talked to on the phone. Her voice sounded familiar.

"Judy Byers," she said. "Wait a minute! Are you Connie?"

It was then that we jumped up and down, hugging and screaming with joy. Our bond was instant, and we talked rapidly, laughing, sharing cancer stories, and laughing more as the relay volunteers handed us our pretty yellow shirts and we put them on.

We all started walking along the track, and I spotted Karen, my cousin, decked out in her yellow relay shirt. She had helped and guided me so many times when I was first diagnosed. I always felt better after we talked. She called me or talked to Cathy ... always concerned about my progress. It had been three years since her mastectomy.

I always thought of how fortunate I was to have good medical insurance. Karen, a hard worker, was not so lucky. She was making payments and would for many years. She envied me that I would have a choice and could have my right breast lifted if necessary. She had reconstruction but couldn't afford a lift on her other breast.

Her silicone implant had sprung a leak four years after the original was put in. She was faced with more medical payments after she had to have it redone.

I remember the night I had stopped over to her house when I was still carrying that damn blood tubing. She had laughed and was surprised that I felt up to running around with my blood purse hanging off my shoulder. We had lifted our tank tops on that warm summer night and compared our boobs. At that time, I was only one week post-surgery, and she was very impressed with how good my reconstruction was in the early phase.

I checked out her fake nipple, which looked very real.

As I walked toward Karen at the relay, she jumped up out of her lawn chair and came running to me with open arms. Karen, tall and attractively thin even as a child, had kept her thin, fit figure. It was always wonderful to see her. Her humor was always very refreshing.

I introduced her to Judy, as David and Katie stood listening to us ramble on and on.

What a small world we live in. Seems everyone knows everybody in our hometown. Judy and Karen had known each other years ago. The three of us walked up to the survivor line.

As I walked, I read the names on the many luminaries that lined the track. I searched for my name, knowing that Tina had gotten one for me. I found it.

The National Anthem kicked off the event, and then a volunteer read two poems over the intercom as all the survivors lined up to take the first walk. The poems were fitting and powerful. I felt

Judy's hand touch mine and we held hands. Immediately I started to cry.

"Cathy told me this was wonderful and I would have fun," Karen said as she also grabbed my hand. "Look at me. I am a crying mess."

"Survivors go! Take the first walk and remember … you are survivors," blared the intercom. How I wished Nicole had been a survivor. I also thought of Pam, so alive with an open wound in her heart. I thought of Pam Lucas, my dear friend who had died of cancer. I thought of Pud.

Like the Susan Komen walk, people lined the entire track. I saw Mom, Cathy, and Tina a distance away, awaiting our walking by them.

Judy, Karen, and I held hands and walked as people clapped and hollered motivational things to us. I felt very connected and close to Karen and Judy. The weather was perfect, with bright blue skies and fluffy clouds.

As we rounded the corner, I saw Mom, the rock of my family. She was very emotional as she watched me walk. Tears of hope, courage, love, and support were among my family. Amber sobbed. Katie, my six-foot-tall daughter with the golden locks of hair, was also crying.

We walked on, still holding each other's hands. We were all full of smiles, and I know they thought as I did: *We are so happy to be alive.* I felt on top of the world as people continually clapped and cheered us on.

Caregivers were asked to take the next lap, and my family all jumped in for the walk. David, Amber, Katie, and I walked in a peaceful silence.

The relay lasted throughout the night. I opted for my own bed and we went home. Cathy and Tina roughed it, spending the night to celebrate the gift of life, warm skies, and generous help to make the annual drive a huge success.

And like the Susan Komen run, I knew I would return yearly to be a part of the relay and always hope for fewer victims and more cures.

Connie E. Curry

Relay For Life – CANCER NEVER SLEEPS

A cancer patient endures months and sometimes years of treatment and life-changing issues.

Staying overnight at the Relay is one small way that we symbolize and support the struggles of cancer patients and their families.

The light and darkness of the day and night parallel the physical effects, emotions, and mental state of a cancer patient while undergoing treatment.

As the evening goes on, it gets darker and colder, just as the emotions of the cancer patient. Often patients become exhausted, sick, not wanting to go on, possibly wanting to give up.

As a participant in the Relay, you may feel much the same way. Just as the cancer patient cannot stop or give up, neither can you.

You must continue.

The morning light brings the warmth of a new day, full of life and new beginnings.

As a participant, you feel the brightness of the morning and know that the end

Of the Relay is close at hand, however you know that...

There is no finish line until we find a cure.

Author Unknown

47
The Barbeque Pit

Nine months went by, and we were in the middle of a record-breaking, humid July. I had always been cold-blooded. For some reason, the heat affected me more than it ever had. Hot flashes and night sweats were a big contributor.

I was in the middle of daily radiation. It seemed to be the longest six weeks, going daily at 9:00 AM to reach my thirty treatments. I teased Dawn and Carol, my technicians, telling them they were barbequing me. I didn't like going alone, but found it ridiculous for David to miss work for a ten-minute appointment for six weeks. Many of my friends offered to go with me, but I didn't want to be an imposition.

I was given weekends off to rest my body. Boy, did I need it. Although radiation wasn't as hard on me as chemo, it wore me out. I became terribly depressed, which probably added to my exhaustion. The pain in my breast was constant, and I continued going to my chiropractor two days a week with not much improvement of my sciatic pain. My MRI showed more deterioration of my lumbar three and four discs.

Dr. Mellon had been my friend and doctor for many years. I had hopes that he could straighten my back out like he had many times. I was growing impatient and feared possible back surgery. I stood firm in my belief that the chemo had hit my weak spot.

All five of my doctors disagreed with me. "The timing was just a coincidence," they said.

Dr. Linda prescribed a different antidepressant medicine. The new one was a hefty load, and I attributed my tiredness to it also. I felt like an unemotional zombie when it started working in my brain. I had taken the new medicine for two weeks and hated the side effects more than the depression and hot flashes. Orgasms left me again. I discontinued taking it.

A high school friend had died of cancer. He was diagnosed and died within two months. My dear friend Claire had precancerous cells that showed up in a gastric intestinal test. I was sick with worry, waiting with her for the pathology report. If she had esophageal cancer, the success rate for a cure was only 10 percent. Claire did not start her family until she was in her thirties. Many times she had commented about wanting to be able to live long enough to raise her children. She had helped me so much, and I knew I would be there for her.

Another friend had a second cancer appear in her lungs just after she finished chemo for her first diagnosis. She was in stage three, and I knew her prognosis was not good. I called her, sent her cards, worried for her, and wondered about me. (I didn't even want to go there in my mind.)

Where in the hell was all this cancer coming from that was hurting and killing so many people?

Tammy, Pam, and Teresa continued calling me on a regular basis. Their invitations were thoughtful and helped me as they pushed me to go away with them and not vegetate.

David asked me to go places and do things. I had no desire. Just to bathe or shower seemed like physical labor. I felt ugly and fat, too.

I disciplined myself to walk each night with Graham, my dog. He loved it, and I needed the exercise. I hurt on each step but tried because Dr. Mellon and my mom, who had suffered some with sciatic problems, thought it would help.

I felt sorry for myself and grew resentful. My sisters called less, and my brother was in a new, refreshing relationship. Life was moving on for my family. I hid my depression, and it was easy because they were busy living their own lives. At times I felt jealous, and I hated myself for that.

I felt that they assumed I was well because I had hair and looked healthy. My pain was not visible. I continued to push myself. I wondered if I would ever be pain-free.

Ryan did not come home to visit much and had still not enrolled in college to finish as he had promised. Katie left messes all over the house and lived the typical teen life, running with friends and not having much time for me.

Amber and Paul argued and procrastinated in getting Allie registered for kindergarten. I worried. How could Allie continue living in a shared parenting situation and go to school daily? How could she live in two different homes every other week and feel secure and be rested for her education? Their homes and jobs were miles apart. Why couldn't I just have the pleasure of being a grandma and not worry about her? I wanted to have faith in their parenting.

My work had slowed down. The medical company I worked for had less business, and I missed traveling to the hospitals and taking care of patients, even though my energy level had dropped considerably.

My writing became my salvation, and Allie lit my world up when it felt so dark.

We celebrated her fifth birthday. Her happiness and our mutual love for each other were comforting for me. Her caring words helped. "Grammy, I wish my hair was curly like yours," she told me one day as we were driving down the highway heading to Tammy's pool for relief from the heat. "I am so glad you have hair now, Grammy."

We put on our sunglasses and rocked and sang to "Red Neck Woman."

"Grammy, you are so fun," she said. She gave me spurts of happiness and energy.

The majority of people who lived in Tammy's condo complex were senior citizens. We usually had the pool to ourselves. It was wonderful.

My breast hurt terribly as usual that day. I took my swimsuit top off and hid under the water. The water felt very good as I moved slowly in it. I hoped Allie would not notice.

"Grammy!"

She dog paddled toward me. "Let me see it."

"No, Allie," I said as I squatted lower in the water. "It is gross."

"Connie, don't tell her it is gross," Tammy said. "It is NOT."

I slowly lifted up because of her persistence.

"Well, that one isssss gross," she said. "When is it going to be better, Grammy?"

Tammy and I burst into laughter. "Ask a child and you will get the truth," I said.

By mid-July, Dr. Houser had finished with the expansion of my breast; 260 cc's of saline had made the C cup. It would be much later when he removed the expander to replace it with silicone.

Dr. Houser and my radiation oncologist disagreed on each other's treatments of me. It seemed I was in the middle of a war between two doctors who didn't want interference with each other's work. I wasn't sure which doctor's advice was right, and I wished they would communicate with each other more.

Dr. Houser told me that the elasticity of my skin over the breast area had changed because of radiation, and he needed to get the area stretched as quickly as he could before radiation was finished. My radiation doctor said it was making the treatments more difficult for them and obviously for me, too, because of the pain involved with my radiated skin being difficult to stretch.

I was very discouraged when Dr. Houser told me that the surgery to remove the expander could not be done until my skin healed from radiation. "It might take up to six months before we can take it out."

"No way, Dr. Houser. I am miserable. That is a half a year," I bellowed. "At least tell me maybe three months but not six!"

"Let us wait and just see how your skin does with the radiation. One step at a time," he assured me.

And I did go one step at a time. I started feeling more alive and seeing a light at the end of the tunnel as I counted each visit for radiation. My energy started returning. The antidepressant was out of my system, and I vowed to never take any again. I smiled and joked, and as one of my friends said, "Oh, I have missed the old Connie. You are coming back."

My radiation doctor was foreign, and his accent was strong. "Too big, too much breast. He need to stop," he said to me when he would examine me weekly. "It look big enough."

I came to the conclusion that by having both procedures done at the same time, it caused an inconvenience for the radiation staff. Because my breast size was changing, it caused chaos; causing the targets they had marked for the radiation to become inaccurate. It was time-consuming for them and me and torturous too. Each time they had to remeasure the targets to hit with radiation, I would spend about forty-five minutes lying still as they re-marked me. My expander always pushed into my sternum when I lay in the supine position. I dared not move.

The first day I visited the radiation clinic, an hour was spent marking my breast area and armpit with a blue semi-permanent marker. When I walked out that day, I cried and was furious with looking different again. Although I had hair growing (that was spring-loaded curly and gray) I was just starting to feel feminine again.

"You have to leave these marks on you throughout your treatment," Dawn said.

"You are kidding, right? You mean I have to walk around with these bold marker lines all over me?"

That was when I learned about targets and measuring, amounts of radiation, and looking like a freak. And I visualized myself wearing turtlenecks on the humid summer days.

The marks were long, bold straight lines with x's through them. One was above my left breast, one at the left side of my breast, one at my cleavage, and several were below my left breast. A bull's eye blue was on my areola. I looked totally ridiculous. My tank tops were definitely not designed for the blue Sharpie look.

I tested this new look on the first day I was marked up by Dawn and Carol. We had just left Allie's first tee-ball game and were treating her to ice cream at Dairy Queen. It was a typical humid

Ohio evening. As we stood in line, I noticed people looking down at my chest. I heard a child whisper as she looked at my chest. I was sure she was wondering why I had tic-tac-toe all over my chest.

"I never want to see another blue marker," I announced to Carol and Dawn one day. "Please, can't we at least take this one off that is right in the middle of my chest?"

Dawn came at me with an alcohol swab as I lay on the radiation table. "We can trim this one down a little, but we need to leave all of them because it is important to hit the areas we measured."

So I learned to dab my skin in the blue-marked areas when I bathed and I grumbled to myself. I wore tops that covered my chest. *To hell with it,* I later thought, as I slowly began wearing tank tops more frequently. I added big necklaces, which helped to hide the marks.

The first treatment was scary. I wasn't sure what to expect. I cried just like I did that first day of chemo. I was sent to a locker room to change into a cotton gown that opened in the front. I had to remove clothes from the waist up.

I was undressing, putting on a gown, and having to open it wide for all to view anyway! They had to look squarely down at my breast as they worked. Why the fuss about hiding my breasts for a brief walk from the locker room to the radiation room?

By about the third daily visit, I discovered a shortcut. I walked back to get my radiation, throwing my top up over my head and slipping my arms out of my bra as I walked to the radiation table. I was comfortable with Carol and Dawn, and privacy was never in the cards anyway.

"Am I the only one to come in here so bold, stripping?" I asked.

"Basically ... yes," Dawn said.

I could tell she truly did not care and found it acceptable, practical, and a time-saver for them and me.

I dreaded foreign stuff being put in my body. The doctor had warned me that I might develop scars on my lungs from the radiation. I watched Dawn and Carol run behind a wall to hide from this stuff that they were shooting into me.

Am I crazy and gullible? Why am I lying here on a table about to have high dosages of radiation shot into my body when they are running away?

I had to lie perfectly still, with my left arm placed high above my head resting in a sling-type contraption. It hurt my arm when I had to extend it because the expander left my mobility limited and pressed into my sternum. I had gotten stiff and lost muscle tone from the lymph node dissection, too.

Three different angles of radiation were given to me. I had nothing to do, so I would watch the machine slowly approaching me, humming and creaking to reach its destination above me as I lay on the cold table. It would make a big clanging noise and then hum like thousands of bees as it worked its way into my body. I counted fifty-five seconds and then heard another clang. Silence. The big rectangular monster would roar above me again to move to the second location. I would count silently again, not moving a muscle ... thirty-six seconds. Dawn and Carol came in and out on all three trips, electronically moving my bed to the precise location and removing big metal plates, sliding different ones in and out of the machines. Big red fluorescent lights shone in various locations around me.

I thought of quadriplegics and how they must feel in halo traction, only being allowed to move their eyes. I knew I was fortunate and would move again and walk out.

"We will be right back. Don't move."

"You are almost done" (the third and last... 1,001, 1,002, 1,003... forty-four seconds, I'd count).

"You can move your arm down now, Connie." (They told me this as soon as possible because they were aware of my discomfort and knew I couldn't wait to lower it.)

"Have a good day," I said as I rushed out.

"See you tomorrow, Connie."

I heard these comments thirty times through a speaker behind the wall that kept the "barbeque sauce" off Carol and Dawn. They could see me through a small television.

Once a week, I met with my radiation oncologist to discuss how I felt, and he would examine my breast and skin. Special lotion was given to me to apply to the irradiated areas. Each night after my bath, I would soak my breast and armpit in it.

The bold blue Sharpie marks would smear into my bras. My breast hurt even when I applied the lotion.

The exterior of my breast was numb. I wondered if I would ever feel the lotion falling downward onto my skin. To touch or rub it, though, sent me into a whirlwind of pain and wincing.

I remember one night as I examined my hair in the mirror, I picked up the lotion as I had done for weeks, squeezing it as it poured on to my breast. I continued looking in the mirror. It wasn't until I felt a cold, watery liquid go down to my stomach that I realized I had poured contact solution on my boob.

On some weekends, David had to redraw the lines as they faded away. Even if my new Medical Mutual breast aroused him, he knew it was off limits because of the intense pain. My appetite for sex had decreased for many reasons.

A Friday, my twenty-seventh radiation, Dawn announced to me that she was leaving on vacation. "I won't see you for a while, Connie. But, I will see you again when you return for a checkup," she said as she headed behind the wall for shot number two. "Be right back, hold still," she said again for the twenty-seventh time.

And on that twenty-seventh dose, I finally got burned. It felt just like bad sunburn under my left breast. I knew I only had three more to go and I felt fortunate. I got to know two women who both were always in the waiting room each day as I was finishing my radiation. Their appointments were always after mine. We talked briefly each day and became friends.

They were both burned horribly early on in their treatments. I saw their blistered burns as we shared our symptoms. I felt such sympathy for both of them when I saw the obvious burns. I had been lucky.

I remember lying there after Dawn told me she was going on vacation, hearing the clang and hum. Tears fell from my eyes. I wasn't allowed to move so I felt them fall slowly down into my ears. Dawn did not know I had gotten all weepy. I had mixed emotions. I felt sentimental because I had almost conquered the end of radiation. I also felt a bond with her and Carol.

"Dawn, I think you have become my friend." I placed my bra down over my breasts, climbed off the table, and reached over, giving her a big hug.

Dawn, a woman of about my age and height, was gentle, pretty, and kind. I think she was a little like me in her day. I guessed she might have been somewhat of a rebel, an ole hippie who liked to socialize and loved people.

She had worked in radiation facilities for twenty-five years. She had so much caring and no sign of being tired of her job, and I had grown to enjoy her. We shared tales about our children and life. She admired my jewelry each day I came in.

Carol, more reserved, shy, and quiet, was harder to get to know. Her age was a mystery because she was totally gray, but her face was youthful-looking. I hated how much gray hair had crept up on me when it began to grow. She wore her gray with style and was so darn cute. She was compassionate and understanding. In time, I learned to like her as much as I liked Dawn.

A guy named Gary came to work while Dawn was on vacation. They probably wondered if I would be as bold walking into the radiation room, flopping my bosoms out.

I think he had Bell's palsy, a disease that affects the face muscles and causes paralysis on one side of the face. I was curious, because I always found medical diseases and health issues interesting.

He was shy and seemed self-conscious of his minor flaw. When I would converse with him, his voice was serene and his smile warm. I loved his hair and found him attractive. I wanted to say to him many times, *Gary, don't be insecure. You are a handsome man.* He was so genuinely nice but reserved.

I liked to mess with them when they left me to turn the radiation on. "I'll be right back," I would say as they headed out. "You can take your arm down now, Connie," I hollered over the intercom after the last dose.

"Yep, you can, Connie," Carol said to me as she came back in to let me escape.

On visit thirty, a Wednesday, I was on a natural adrenaline high because I was driving into town for my last treatment. Hallelujah. Steve, my boss, had called, and I also had a CPM to apply for a patient way north of home. I needed the money, and I was looking forward to work.

I also got to see Allie, and took her to lunch. The humidity dropped and the temperature was mild. It was a wonderful day.

Tammy and I went shopping the night before. I picked out four perfect simple gifts to give to the radiation staff. I found the perfect tiny picture frames to give to the girls. They were bright, multi-colored replicas of what else? Flip-flops! I bought Gary a bottle of cologne. I wrote inspirational messages inside cards for each one, tucking their small gifts inside.

Like many times, I had that warm feeling of how wonderful it feels to give and not receive gifts.

"I know I talk a lot," I told Carol as she read my note card with surprise and happiness. "But that picture frame is perfect for you. Every time I talked to you guys, you would be heading out, telling me you would be right back, or telling me to hold still. And you girls always noticed all my colorful flip-flops."

Gary was pleasingly surprised and humble when I told him how much I enjoyed meeting him, too. "I bet you won't ever have another woman in here who rips her top off as easily as I did, right, Gary?"

"I think you might be right about that, Connie."

On the third dose of radiation, I couldn't resist celebrating as the machine moved away from me and became silent.

We had communicated many times through the intercom. I knew it was on.

"Woohoooooo," I chanted loudly as I got up, dressed for the thirtieth time, and gave each one a hug when they stepped back in to the barbeque pit for what I hoped would be the last time.

48
Boob Job Or Bust

Three weeks after my radiation was completed, I had a routine checkup with Dr. Rhoades, the oncologist. I dreaded going, because it always brought back memories of chemo days and all the tests I had when I found out I had cancer. I feared the thought of Dr. Rhoades possibly doing more tests and me going through the mental anguish of waiting for results. I didn't want to see bald women in the waiting room.

I found out Dr. Rhoades was behind, as usual, on appointments. I decided to venture down to see my favorite nurses in the chemotherapy office next door. They gave me a double take, amazed at how curly my hair had come in.

It was a majority opinion that I looked great. I was sure they compliment every patient. We all need tender loving care as we go through all our delicate stages.

"Check out my new boob! And look how perky it is. But it's like having a new Porsche parked in the garage and you aren't allow to drive it," I said.

I tilted my right shoulder up and showed them how I have to walk to boost my right breast to match the young one.

I visited too long and later found out that a nurse from Dr. Rhoades's office had called my name to come in and I was GOA (gone on arrival).

After the search and rescue, I entered the examination room and hopped up on the dreaded scales.

"Don't tell me what I weigh, just tell me if I lost," I told the nurse as she scribbled down my vital signs. I had lost four pounds, and because I had just come from lunch with a friend, I knew I probably had lost five. The sterling silver bangle bracelets I wore, the big chucky flip-flops, and the cell phone clipped on my side were certainly another two pounds.

"And let's deduct one more pound for my big belt buckle," I joked. I had lost, though, and was optimistic. Walking Graham, my goldie, was paying off.

The visit was simple and easy. Dr. Rhoades asked me if I had any questions or concerns and asked how I felt.

I knew he would talk to me about taking Tamoxiphen, the prescription drug that I tested positive for. Tamoxiphen, a hormonal agent taken once a day, is usually prescribed for five years post-cancer. I had heard other cancer soldiers talk about taking it and speaking about the horrid side effects. I knew it was potent, but studies had shown that it prevented the reoccurrence of cancer by almost 50 percent. It was a no-brainer. I had to take it until I was almost fifty-four years old.

Studies had shown that Tamoxiphen increased the chances of getting uterine cancer. Strokes and pulmonary embolisms could also occur. I was scared to death of this medicine and hoped it would help and not hinder me.

I found daily excuses to not go to the pharmacy and pick it up. I knew the pharmacist had filled it. By day three, I grudgingly went to the drugstore to get my prescription. I laid it on the kitchen countertop for two days, not wanting to be reminded of the possible side effects. Although all medicines list a wide variety of side effects and warnings, I was aware that Tamoxiphen was powerful, and I dreaded what might happen.

"You'd better take it," Cathy said to me one morning on the telephone. I resented her demand, but I also knew it was due to concern.

On day two, I picked it up, opened it, and popped one in my mouth before delaying this new life's ritual that was inevitable and added to my list of morning medicines.

I took my vitamin A daily for hot flashes, which seemed not to help much. Each morning I would get up, drink my coffee, and ingest Synthroid, Ibuprofen, and now Tamoxiphen, which might cause weight gain, sore muscles, vaginal dryness, and loss of sex drive. *Great! Just fucking great,* I thought to myself. My sciatica already was killing me and my weight troubled me. The hot flashes continued to set me on fire numerous times throughout the day and evenings. Night sweats were a bitch!

Sex ... a powerful pleasure or duty to sustain a marriage. I never wanted to view it as a duty. I smelled like a frying pan anyway. Each night after my bath, I would soak my breast and armpit in pure cocoa butter. My skin was tight over the expander, caused by the radiation. When I was pregnant, I would always drench my stomach with cocoa butter. I believed that it was what prevented me from getting stretch marks across my swollen belly. It was my belief that my home remedy might help again. Time would tell as I drenched my breast.

Due to the lymph node dissection, I was still not able to stretch my arm outward or high above my head. This was an inconvenience when I went through the bank drive-thru for fast cash. I nearly took my mirrors off each time, as I pulled closer to the machine. I wanted the flexibility back in my arm. I continued the exercises, placing my left hand on the wall and climbing up the wall as I reached higher and higher to stretch my arm.

The radiation had discolored and splotched up my skin. The splotching was also on my back, near my shoulder blades. It amazed me how powerful the radiation had been to shoot and blow through my back.

I was counting down the days until my visit with youthful, good-looking Dr. Houser. I was eager to find out when he might consider doing my surgery to remove the expander. It would be the only surgery that I was eager to have. I needed a date to feel optimistic and give me more hope of comfortable days.

I hated the expander and the discomfort it caused me. As much as I despised it, I knew I would ask to take it home as a reminder of my saline days.

The day came for my appointment, and I was so excited to go. I knew we would discuss surgery. Our time together was always professional but social, too. We fed off each other's humor.

"Oh, Connie … you look pretty good," he said as he observed my breasts through my tank top.

"I left this shirt on because it's new and I wanted you to see it. Isn't it cool and soooo seventies?" I said as I pulled it up and off. (I bet he was born in the eighties.) The tank top, a silky tie-dye, was very colorful. The V-neck was a little low, with a hint of cleavage. I loved being able to wear it and not look deformed.

Because I was not permitted to wear underwire bras with the expander in, I cut a small hole in my left breast cup and pulled the wire out of one of my bras. This little improvising helped to give me an even-balanced look. The left breast under construction was hard as a rock.

"Dr. Houser, I do believe I could jump twenty feet in the air on a pogo stick and this baby would not move," I told him.

As Dr. Houser studied my skin, I couldn't wait to hear when he thought he might do the surgery. I was so tired of changing my bra several times a day, trying to get relief. Sports bras were the most comfortable. I wore my underwire invention only when I was going away.

"I honestly don't think you need much of a lift on your right breast," he informed me. I smiled.

"Dr. Houser, I am almost fifty years old. I feel proud. And now I know, you truly are my favorite doctor."

"Women like you could put me out of business," he said with a chuckle. He rolled back on his stool with wheels, smacking his legs in deep thought.

"When, Dr. Houser? When can I have my surgery?"

"Hmmmm, How about …"

"When? Oh when?" I pleaded as I fastened my bra and waited for his answer.

"The soonest I think we should do it is October. Your skin has healed and done well from the radiation. But we don't want to do it too soon or you could have trouble healing, and we don't want to have to take it out."

"How 'bout a little eye lift, too? And why don't you have coupons in the waiting room for buy one lipo and get one free?"

We laughed and I headed out with a promise from Dr. Houser that he would make my breast beautiful on October 11, just four days from a year when I received that shocking telephone call that I had breast cancer. I thought my world had crumbled.

And as I headed out the door to meet a friend for lunch, I thought about how time truly had flown by. So many tests, needles, ultrasounds, mammograms, blood draws, and doctor appointments. Oh, and so many tears wrapped in worry about death. Unlike that cold, damp, rainy fall evening, this particular day was full of warmth and sunshine.

And my world did not crumble. I smiled as I climbed into my car to head north.

49
Advantages

As I counted down the days until the surgery to get my expander out, I kept busy. My brain continued to be full of cobwebs, and I assumed it was from the chemo. I constantly wrote myself notes. My forgetfulness was frustrating, but I also loved using it as an excuse to be humorous at times.

"You mean I forgot to cook dinner?"

"And you are? Amber? Katie?"

The kids loved to tease me about calling them the wrong names.

"Katie, Amber has senior night tonight for soccer. Are you coming?"

"You mean, Katie, Mom. I am Amber. Katie is playing soccer. I played soccer one year. I hated it. I graduated in '98."

There are some advantages to getting sick. "The Big C" makes friends and family think about the possibility of death. Just when I thought the healthy world of my friends was movin' on, gifts, phone calls, cards, and the surprises would pop up.

My friend Sandi flew in from Iowa to spend a weekend with my family and me. I hadn't seen her in twenty years, but we'd never lost contact. An immediate bond formed when we worked together so many years ago. She was eight years older than me, a true hippie, and married to John Cougar Mellencamp's brother, and I found her so very cool in my inexperienced young, tender life.

Sandi was always blunt, humorous, and outspoken; I respected her and never forgot all our great times back in the late seventies. By the nineties, she had divorced Joe, who was also a great musician. David and I drove to Iowa for Sandi's wedding when she remarried. It was the last time I saw her until 2005, but we called each other periodically, and Christmas cards were exchanged each year.

E-mail helped make our correspondence more frequent. She had never met my kids but had received pictures of them in the mail for more than twenty years, and then over the Internet.

"Oh, Sandi! It is soooo wonderful to see you," I said. I saw the young woman whom I had worked with daily for three years, looking gently older and thinner. Her spirit, enthusiasm for life, and humor were the same.

"Well, when I heard you had breast cancer, I knew if I didn't make a trip to Ohio to see you and you died, I would never forgive myself," she said as she grinned.

"Oh, I get it! This is a selfish motive," I said as we hugged and laughed.

That weekend was the best. We cooked a huge meal and she finally put real faces with the pictures I had mailed for all those years, as she met the kids. Allie was even present, and Sandi loved her talkative, friendly nature.

We sat up through the night, talking and reminiscing about the good old days.

I hated it when she had to leave, but I promised a trip back to Iowa.

"Good God, if we wait another twenty years, when you get to Iowa, one of us might wander around, trying to remember where in the hell we are. Or we'll be blind or deaf," she said as we hugged and tears fell.

Delaware, my hometown, is famous for the Little Brown Jug horserace. It is a loyal horse town full of expensive standard-bred racehorses, harness/sulky drivers, and avid horse fans. Once a year during the county fair, our entire town looks forward to the race. The motels, restaurants, shops, and bars stock up as thousands travel in to spend the week at races. People surround the half-mile track, watching, betting, drinking, and socializing.

It had always been a big part of my life. For twenty-five years, I had worked special duty on the emergency squad, standing by during the horseraces. The squad was parked in the paddock area, where the horses went out to race and returned after their mile run. I got to know many famous drivers. I loved watching the horses. I knew so many people who worked with the horses. Diane, an outrider for the race, was always a friend I looked forward to visiting.

Every year, my family and I took off work and had a tradition of going to the races. And every year, Dad swore he was never going again after he lost one bet after another. I remember one year as the races ended, Dad threw his horse program on the ground, cussing and kicking it as he walked toward the exit. "I am never coming back to this damn place. They can give all those damn horses to the glue factory."

So every year, Dad still goes, we still bet on horses, and rarely do any of us win. We sit in the same section, seeing the same people once a year. We reunite with our Canadian friends who love to rekindle friendships and bet on each race.

One year, as I sat by one of our Canadian friends, he slumped over in his seat, his horse program resting on his chest. I noticed him snoring loudly and drooling.

"Hey, you all right?" I immediately knew he was having some kind of reaction and needed medical help. It was my day off, but my mind was always keen to medical emergencies. I repositioned his head to open his airway.

"He got stung by a bee a few minutes ago. It hurt but he seemed OK," said his friend, who was sitting next to him. The race distracted him as he turned his head back and forth, watching me trying to help his friend.

"Do you know if he is allergic to bees?" I asked as I shook him, hollering, trying to rouse him. We summoned 911, knowing the squad was on the grounds.

My co-workers arrived, and he was treated on the scene and given a shot of epinephrine, a fast-acting drug for allergic reactions.

He slowly regained consciousness. As they were loading him onto the cot to take him to the local hospital, he began digging into his pocket. I wondered if he might have had some medicine he needed to take. I also wondered if he possibly had a Medic Alert bracelet in his pocket and maybe it wasn't the bee that had caused his problem. He was still not very alert, so I assumed he was confused, as the epi was slowly improving his health. We hooked him up to the heart monitor.

He continued digging into his pocket in a sloppy stupor.

"Hey, while I am gone, would someone put twenty dollars on horse three in the next race?" he said, pulling a twenty-dollar bill out of his pocket as the medics continued to load him for transportation to the hospital. "I'll be back."

We all laughed.

He was treated at the hospital and returned to the races.

So every year, I look forward to seeing him and his generous Canadian buddies. The liquor is abundant, and they celebrate even when a horse breaks stride.

I was skeptical about going after being sick and still not full of my usual energy. But I had that itch to try my luck on winning a perfecta. The Canadians would look for us. Opey, the funny, crazy one, always scanned the entrance gate, watching for Margi and me in my Bug. These men had endless energy for men in their sixties and seventies, and spent a lot of money to come to Delaware. They'd all worked together and were all retired. Opey owned racehorses in Canada. Charlie and Bill, more reserved, would sit in their lawn chairs, laughing as Opey teased and harassed Margi and me. They jabbed at each other as they threw insults at each other, drinking more Crown Royal and heading to the betting window for another bet. They were all harmless, fun men who shared strong friendships with youthful spirits. It was our fourteenth year to see them once a year.

My biggest fear was the crowd. I was just three weeks from getting the expander out. My breast continued to hurt ever so badly. I worried about someone falling into me or bumping me. People were arm-to-arm, and many were intoxicated. The heat affected me. I sometimes thought that damn saline cooked under my skin.

It was a beautiful, sunny September day. The temperature was warm but not too hot, with no threat of rain. I lost one bet after another. Mom, Dad, Cathy, Wayne, Tina, and Wayne's new girlfriend were there. It was so wonderful to see Wayne happy and full of romance. Shelley, my favorite niece, and her friend Hope were at the races too. None of us had made any big wins, but we continued foolishly going to the windows to pick horses.

My cell phone rang as we watched another race begin.

"Hey, Connie ... what ya doing?"

"I'm bettin' on these damn horses. Who is this?" I asked.

"It's me. Diane Winters. Get over to the paddock area by race fourteen. We have you a ride in the starter gate."

"You are shittin' me," I squealed. "Whose idea was this? Yours? Oh my God! You mean I get to be in the starter gate when the horses come out to race?" I asked as I wiggled in my chair and threw my hands around in an excited gesture.

"Our buddy Paul set this up for you. We all know you love the races and we know you have had a rough year. Get your butt over here, OK?"

And so it was ... my special day at the Little Brown Jug. It all happened in seconds as the horses approached the starter gate. I was sitting backwards in the start car, with the man operating the buttons, microphone, and start-gate controls to my left. The driver's back was directly behind me, going around the track.

I watched the horses coming closer. The pace of their feet was amplified as they grew nearer. It sounded like the rhythm of drums as their feet paced forward in unison.

Their eyes amazed me, as they seemed mesmerized, approaching and staring at the gate to begin the race as the car continued down the track, heading for the start spot. Their carotid arteries pulsated on their sweaty necks as their hooves hit the clay track. Their nostrils flared.

I could have almost reached out and touched them as they charged into the gate without missing a perfect stride. In mere seconds, the gate slowly went up as the horses paced away from the starter gate and the driver drove back toward the paddock area. I turned and watched them as they paced ahead, doing what they were bred to do.

As they ran like the wind, my heart raced. It was much more exciting than hitting a perfecta.

"See what friends do for you when you've been sick?" I said as I climbed out of the starter car. "They think you are going to die! Isn't it great?"

Diane and Paul stood smiling as I ran over to hug them and to thank them for all they had done for me. Gems, true gems, are how I describe my friends.

50
Mental Agony

October 6, just nine days shy of a year after I found out I had breast cancer, I was heading to an appointment to have my annual mammogram. For the rest of my life, I would have only my right breast checked, and I was scared as hell. I couldn't believe a year had gone by.

Five days later, I was scheduled to have the surgery to have the expander taken out. Woohoo to that! But what if I had cancer in my right breast? What if they had to change the orders and do another mastectomy?

I dreamed about seeing Dr. Linda pushing Dr. Houser out of her way as she walked toward me lying on the surgery table to remove my last breast. Her gloves were on and she held her hands up as she approached the surgery table.

My hair was thick, healthy, and growing daily. I could finally feel water drip off my hair and land on my face when I shampooed it. What if they wanted me to do chemo again? Could I stand having it again? Being bald was so emotionally hard on me as I thought back. I joked, I had fun with the wigs, and I learned a million ways to accessorize with hats and scarves. But I did not feel strong enough for a setback, and my joking had been therapeutic in helping me up that mountain.

I wanted to stay atop that mountain. I told very few friends and family that I had a checkup. I didn't want them to worry. I also thought that IF I got bad news, I wouldn't be pressured by those who loved me. I wasn't sure I wanted to fight again. I hated chemo more than I had ever hated anything in my life.

The mammogram technician had my entire medical record for the last year. She had all my ultrasounds, mammograms, and MRIs. I assumed she had looked them over and was aware of my expander and lymph node dissection five months earlier.

I was quiet, nervous, and scared. I walked up to the mammogram machine in my cotton wrap, like I had so many times for years. I listened to her as she directed me on how to rest my breast in the machine. I pushed in closer as she advised me. My left breast was shielded in the cotton garb.

Without a warning, she jerked my left arm upward to move it away for a better angle of my right side. I flinched and moaned. I wanted to smack her.

"Could you kind of hold your left breast and pull it slightly back," she asked.

"Honey, this baby is not going anywhere. It is as hard as this machine. Even if I could move it, I couldn't because it hurts to touch it."

Duh! She then figured it out. She had lost my trust in her.

As I walked out, I hoped she was more alert about the mammogram then she had been about my medical record.

The actual test was nothing compared to the four days of torment I had in waiting for the test results. It seemed I always had a weekend to get through as I waited for doctors, news, and test results.

By Monday morning, I was sure the results were in. They had put a rush on them to get the news prior to my expander surgery. I took that to assume that the game plan might change and I would see Dr. Linda just like I did in that damn dream if they found more cancer. I had already decided that the expander was coming out, come hell or high water, even if she did have to be present and do a mastectomy or lumpectomy on the other side.

In eighth grade I remember cleaning out my locker. I knew I would never have to wear that monkey suit, as we called, it for gym class ever, ever again. I was not wearing that darn thing one more day, I thought as I threw it in the wastebasket. That expander needed to be disposed of in the same way.

I knew my mammogram results were on Dr. Linda's desk. By Monday afternoon, I was literally sick to my stomach. I jumped each time the telephone rang. I was growing furious and feeling like Dr. Linda was being insensitive in not reading my mammogram and calling me quickly. I wanted to feel special and forget she had other patients who required her attention.

I called twice. Each time the receptionist told me that she was with patients and would probably read the results during her lunch break. By 3:00 PM, I was sure she was putting off calling me, knowing I would go psycho when she told me I tested positive for more cancer.

I had made everything up in my mind. "Think positive," is what Tammy said to me on the phone.

"And Miss Tammy, how do I turn on that switch, may I ask you?"

By 3:20, I called Dr. Houser, whose office was just down the hall from Dr. Linda's.

When Beth, the office manager, answered the phone, I told her my concerns.

"I have waited all day for Dr. Linda to call me. I know she is busy. But I am so close to tears. My entire day as been ruined with all this worry and sitting glued to the phone."

"Oh, Connie ... I can understand how you feel."

"Well, I have my surgery tomorrow," I told her. "I know Dr. Linda and Dr. Houser wanted to find out the results prior to my surgery."

"You give me ten minutes," she said. "I am walking down to her office right now. I'll call you back."

"Oh, thank you, thank you so much," I said as I hung up.

I paced back and forth. I watched the clock creep as I waited for the telephone to ring. When it rang, my heart raced.

"Connie? It is Beth at Dr. Houser's office. Negative! It was negative. Now, breathe," she said.

I breathed and then I cried tears of joy.

I had just hung up when the phone rang again. It was Lisa at Dr. Linda's office.

"Connie Curry. Don't you ever send someone down here to our office," she said laughing.

"Lisa! I am sorry, but you know I am an impatient patient. I waited all day. Is Dr. Linda mad at me?"

"No, silly. She doesn't even know we walked into her office to read your results. She has been so busy today. We won't tell her what you pulled this time," she said. "You know she calls you her poster child, don't you?"

"Well, I feel honored and special, even if I did have to wait all day to get my good news," I said. "Thank you, Lisa, honey. I'll be in soon to show off my new boob," I said as we hung up.

I jumped for joy and turned on the radio. Melissa Etheridge was playing. How cool. My woman. My inspiration. We were bald together and were diagnosed days apart.

She would never know how much drive she gave me as I watched her perform at the Grammy Awards, stylin' her bold, bald look. I remember crying uncontrollably during those steroid days when she sang.

I listened to her interview with Barbara Walters about her battle with breast cancer. I related so with this rock-and-roll icon as I cried more.

"Let's rock on, Melissa," I said as I listened to her sing, "I Run for Life."

I started supper.

51
Serenity

I remember being extremely afraid, just thinking about the possibility of surgery. EMS days had scarred me. When I was in medic school, doing my required clinical hours in the hospital, a young intensive-care nurse had been our instructor as we did clinical hours.

She was a young mom working full time, and a great nurse. Then she had a sudden onset of gall bladder problems and found herself being the patient. She was to have a reasonably simple surgery. In recovery, she had horrid side effects from the anesthesia. An anti-nausea drug was given to her (another routine, common procedure). She had a severe reaction to the drug and went into cardiac arrest.

The nurse who had been such a great teacher to the medic students had become a critical patient in the unit where she worked. She was on a ventilator and had severe brain damage. Her nurse co-worker/friends cried. They cared for her for months in the ICU. Her husband came daily to be by her side. He brought their young children, in hopes she felt their presence. Each day, she deteriorated and slipped closer to death. It was months before she died. I always recall how sad it was for this young family.

When I worked my clinical hours in obstetrics, I saw a crack addict admitted when she went into premature labor. She was in her second trimester. I watched the entire delivery, and I won't ever forget the poor attitude of the OB doctor and his incompetence during the entire ordeal.

I was just a student, *green*, as they say. I was there *only* to observe. The young woman's legs were placed in the stirrups. Her buttock was on the edge of the delivery table. A kick bucket was below the bed. The nurses were gloved, gowned, and standing around the patient.

"Push."

"Push."

I heard this command several times. My thought was *why are they telling her to push? The doctor is not in position to assist in the delivery.*

"Push."

I glanced at the doctor. He seemed to move in slow motion, as he was snapping and pulling gloves on. He had a scolding look on his face. I remember thinking ... *that baby is going to come out and it will fall.*

Just as he was a step from her, again I heard, "Push!"

The mother bore down with her eyes closed and pushed.

I learned what an explosive delivery was that day. Because the baby was so small and the woman pushed extremely hard, the baby flew across the delivery room. I watched it slide across the floor. My heart raced. The entire delivery team was quiet as their eyes located the baby lying on the cold floor. I knew they wondered if the mother knew her baby had fallen to the floor, and they all reacted quietly but quickly to try to hide this huge error. The baby was so small, there was no sound when it landed on the floor.

Then we heard a whimper.

"Where's my baby? Is it on the floor, for God's sake?" the mother said as she leaned upward.

A nurse ran over to the floor and picked the baby up. It was so small, the nurse held it in the palm of one hand. The mother tried to sit up as she turned her head side to side, trying to locate her baby.

"Get it out of here," the doctor said as he kicked the bucket out of his way.

The respiratory team took over and the baby was taken away. I later learned the baby was life-flighted out to Children's Hospital. It was a fifteen-ounce baby boy who lived two days.

After that horrible incident, I knew the medical team discussed this total screw-up. They certainly knew the doctor did a horrendous job. The reality is that the baby probably would have died, regardless. But …

My presence as an observer was a problem. I saw things I was not supposed to see. I was an obstacle.

I was furious. How could this doctor be so insensitive? That baby did not ask to be conceived by a crack mother with no prenatal care. And why wasn't the doctor doing his job properly? Who was he to assume this baby would be stillborn? What right did he have to do a half-assed job? He was an older man … burned out, I suspected. He just didn't seem to care.

I walked out of the clinic that day and went to my paramedic instructor. I reported what I had witnessed. I couldn't and wouldn't cover for this doctor and staff. The only person I respected that day in delivery was the nurse who was brave enough to walk over to pick the baby up. I hated myself for not reacting and doing what she did.

And so, I set out to try to make things right. There were incident reports written, investigations undertaken, and the doctor was forced into retirement. I suppose that was a slap on the wrist for this man. I also would like to think he was once a good doctor with compassion and was professional to his patients.

That I would never know. I just knew I had witnessed incompetence, and the patient had no control. But I do believe that baby is now an angel.

Several years later, when I had my tubal ligation, I begged my doctor to do it under a local. I feared everything about surgery. I wanted to be in control of my mind and body.

My attitude has changed. When I was diagnosed with breast cancer, I slowly started to trust. Dr. Linda continually laughed at my skeptical attitude and how I questioned her authority and intelligence.

I continued to be concerned when I was put under, but I felt a little braver each time. Every time the IV was started, the anesthesiologist asked me many questions about my medical history. My doctor would come in to talk to me, and the anesthesiologist would say, "We are giving you something to help you relax," which translates into, "We are going to knock your ass out."

And just like the snap of fingers, I was in recovery. Time had no time. Surgery seemed not to have a middle. The beginning and the end tied into what seems like seconds. I discovered that being put under was a bonus, and time only stood still for my loved ones who waited. The end meant I could put my lips on the rim of a coffee cup, smell that scrumptious aroma, and get my fix! There was no waiting and suffering. The middle was gone.

Apprehension can last for days prior to surgery. I had many of those each time. The eve of my mastectomy was the worst. I held my breast in my hand throughout the night as I tweaked my nipple back and forth. It was so sick with cancer but so alive with sense. David kissed it goodbye.

The day my expander was taken out, I was not as apprehensive as I had been from the prior surgeries. I was sooooo ready to rid my chest of that uncomfortable device. Under clothes and inside my bra, it looked perky and full. Naked, I could see how unnatural it looked. It sat too high, even for a twenty-year-old. The rock-hardness was a brutal feeling. And just to touch it hurt so badly. Yes, I was ready to dance in for this surgery.

After the fifth surgery in less than a year, David and I pulled into the driveway at home. It brought extra enthusiasm, an adrenaline rush, and a second wind. Nothing looked sweeter than home. Peace of mind swept through me. And most of all, I felt safe again.

My bed felt like what heaven must feel like. I always took in the smells of the sheets and the pillowcase. The warmth of the blankets made me snuggle and feel comfortable. Even in pain, I still had all those wonderful feelings that far outweighed the discomfort. I wouldn't feel tired. My mind raced and I just found rest in being home, alive, warm, and safe.

It's over. I am alive. Nothing bad happened to me while I was under the anesthesia.

And when I lay supine, my left chest area felt sore, but the expander was gone and I didn't have that sharp poke downward to my sternum.

"Christmas comes in three days," Dr. Houser said as I was being wheeled out to go home.

"Huh? What ya mean?" I asked.

"You have to leave the bandage on for three days and you can't shower until Thursday," he replied. "Christmas comes when you can see it."

"Oh, Dr. Houser ... you KNOW I HATE rules. And you know how excited I have been to get this. Three days?"

So as we pulled into the driveway, I had already started trying to peek into the gauze dressing, pulling on the tape to release a teeny corner.

"Connie, you heard Dr. Houser. Leave it alone," David said.

And like in recovery, I continued to hurt like hell. I assumed this surgery would be a cakewalk. After having the expander in for five long months, I thought the silicone implant would be like holding marshmallows. My skin would welcome it easily. Oh, I was wrong. It felt like barbed wire wrapped around a basketball and scuffed into my chest cavity.

As soon as my feet hit the driveway, nausea hit me instantly. I was lightheaded and dizzy, and I puked.

David helped me into the house. Graham, my goldie, wiggled his tail. And as quickly as I saw my bed, I felt that instant safe feeling.

I was home.

52
Deidre

Three days after my silicone implant surgery, as we were about to have dinner, the phone rang.

"Connie?"

"Yes?" I said as I recognized Dr. Linda's voice. My heart raced. When would I ever not freak out when she called?

"How's the girls?" she asked me with a chuckle.

"Dr. Linda, I am tellin' ya, this is like having a new Porsche in the garage and you still can't drive it. It hurts!"

"Just think of all that horsepower you are going to have, though, when it heals," she said.

I bellowed in the phone, laughing, and I think I snorted.

"Oh, Connie ... it is so good to hear you laugh," she said.

"Well, yeah! Usually when you call me, you are the bearer of bad news," I snapped back kiddingly.

"I need a favor from you," Dr. Linda said. "Can you do something for me?"

"Sure," I said, wondering what she wanted.

"I have a new patient," she said. "Her circumstances are so much like yours. She is beautiful, with beautiful breasts like you had ... very youthful and firm."

"Huh? Repeat that, I didn't hear you," I said as I snickered.

"She has pretty breasts like you had and you WILL have again, Connie," Dr. Linda said in a gentle, sincere voice. "She also went to get a second opinion at the same facility you did. She needs a mastectomy. She'll be going to see Dr. Houser also."

"What do you want me to do?" I asked her as I walked over to the door to let Graham in. The autumn air was crisp, the trees full of vibrant colors.

"I want you to talk to her. You always lay it right out there. She is so upset. She had concerns and asked many of the same kind of questions you asked. I will save her areola like I did for you. I told her I was giving you her number. Can you call her?"

"Sure, I'll call her. How old is she? What's her name?"

"Her name is Deidre Woolum. She's forty-two, a mother of four. She looks much younger."

"Well, I'm forty-nine, and with this new boob, I look thirty-five," I told her as I walked over to the oven to check dinner. Katie walked in the door from football practice.

"Oh, no, Connie, you look thirty-two."

"Oh yeah, now you're talkin'," I said as we laughed some more.

Then it made me think of presurgery night, when I called my high school buddy, Bob, father of British Open champ Ben Curtis. I had to share my humorous tale with Dr. Linda about this new boob theory and aging.

My surgery was on October 11, and I knew that date seemed familiar to me. I thought of Bob, whom I had known since first grade. For some odd reason, it hit me that October 11 might be Bob's birthday. I picked up the phone to call him on the tenth.

His answering machine came on so I left a detailed message.

"Bob, this is Connie. I have been thinking, and if my poor memory serves me right, you will be fifty tomorrow. I can't call you tomorrow because I will be out of commission for a while. I'll be in the hospital getting my new boob. So when you get up tomorrow and look in the mirror, wondering if you look fifty, think of me. I will look thirty-five because I will have my new boob. Haaaaaappy birthday, Bobby!"

An hour later, Bob called me back.

"Yep, you are right. I will be fifty. And good luck tomorrow with your surgery," he said. We talked and caught up as I again wished him a happy big 5-0.

Dr. Linda laughed as I shared the story with her.

As I hung up, I thought about this new breast cancer patient. I felt sympathy and compassion for her. I wondered if she was as scared as I had been a year ago. *That poor woman,* I kept thinking. *I hope I can help her to feel better,* I thought as I laid her phone number down on the coffee table.

That evening, I called her. She didn't answer, so I left a message explaining that I was the patient Dr. Linda had mentioned and I would love to talk to her.

"Call me anytime, Deidre," I said and hung up wondering if she would ring me back.

It was three days before she returned my call. I will never understand how breast cancer patients can have such an immediate bond, but I had watched it happen since I got sick. And Deidre was like each of us when we are first given this horrific news. She was terrified.

"Nights are the worst for me, when my kids are in bed and all is quiet. My mind wanders and I am so scared," she said as I heard her sniffle.

"Do you like to read?" I asked her.

"I do, but I never have time with the kids."

"Well, instead of lying in bed worrying, with your imagination going crazy, get a good book. Read until your eyes won't stay open. There is nothing like a good book that takes you far away," I told her. "I am a writer, and I have always loved books. Reading and writing helped me so much. When I was taking the steroids, I would go nights with little sleep. My writing and books was my salvation."

She listened.

"Another great thing ... when you take the steroids, you will feel like you are on speed for the three days when you are on them. You will clean things, organize closets, and fix stuff that you have not done in years!"

"This house needs it." She laughed and said, "Guess what, Connie. I have a degree in journalism and I hate to write."

"Oh my gosh, you do? What I would give to have that," I told her.

"I wish I could give it to you. I would."

"Dr. Linda told me that you are beautiful. I am sincere, Deidre, when I tell you that you can win this battle, and Dr. Houser and Dr. Linda will make your new breast beautiful. They truly are the best."

I continued on as she listened.

"I assume you will have chemo. I am not going to lie to you. It is not easy to lose your hair and be bald. But rest assured that your hair will grow back, and the wigs are very natural-looking. I have three, and you can have them," I told her. "You'll learn so many ways to accessorize with scarves, too. It is rather fun."

"Connie, I guess I should tell you. I am African American."

"Oh. Well. I guess the blonde bombshell wig won't work for you," I said.

Deidre and I talked for about an hour. We laughed. We cried. We laughed some more as I shared stories with her. She asked me many questions, some very personal.

"I feel so blessed that Dr. Han [Linda] hooked me up with you, Connie. I feel so much better since we talked. I just want this stuff out of me. Thanks so much for helping me. I feel like I owe you lunch."

"Oh, Deidre, you don't owe me anything," I replied. "But I think it would be fun to meet. How is your schedule next week?" I asked.

"Let's do meet! I have so many doctor appointments coming up, but you check your calendar for next Thursday and I will call you the first of the week," Deidre suggested.

I was about to help a cancer soldier who didn't realize how she was helping me, too.

53
Bosom Buddies

I had my annual pap smear at a new doctor. I didn't like having to build a new relationship with a new obstetrician/gynecologist, but my faith in Dr. Wagner had been shattered.

Deidre and I decided to meet that day for lunch, since my appointment was in the morning and south of me, near Deidre's home. She chose the restaurant, a classy Italian one, and I was eager to meet her.

I took her a breast cancer pin and decided to bring along some of my Pam scarves for her to borrow.

I purposely wore a slightly low-cut top with a hint of cleavage showing. I knew her curiosity would let her eyes travel down to my chest. I wanted to assure her that I had cleavage and looked feminine.

I arrived at the restaurant a few minutes early, so I got us a seat, telling the hostess to watch for a tiny black woman named Deidre who would be arriving soon. I tried to picture her in my mind.

I saw her from a distance as the hostess was escorting her back to our table. She was beautiful, just as Dr. Linda had said, and dressed very classy and stylish in a tight spandex tank top, also showing a little cleavage. She immediately smiled as I jumped up from my chair.

I noticed her breasts, and they were very round and perky. I immediately understood her sadness.

It came so natural as we hugged tightly and felt such happiness in meeting. We immediately began talking, questioning, and sharing our feelings about breast cancer, doctors, treatment, and life.

We shared pictures of our children. Her kids were beautiful. I showed her various snapshots that I had brought along of my various hairstyles, from long to bald.

"You know, Connie ... it is very trendy now for black women to shave their heads."

"Well, there you go! You will look marvelous," I told her. "Look at your beautiful face. Hair camouflages beauty. You will look so sexy," I told her. I handed her the scarves. "These are great for warmth, too. Your head will get cold."

I didn't tell her they came from Whitney, whose mom had lost her battle to cancer. But they warmed my heart and head for many weeks, and I hoped the vibes would go to Deidre.

She had gone to many of her appointments alone because her husband worked out of town a lot. "But he is wonderful about this and very supportive," she told me. "He doesn't care what the cost is; he just wants me well. My mom has been ill, and I don't want to worry her with it."

"Do your kids know?"

"They know something is wrong, but I have not told them," she replied.

She told me the order of events, from how she had a bloody discharge coming out of her nipple to how she ran out of one doctor's office, crying and angry at how blunt they were in announcing to her she needed a mastectomy. Her cancer was evasive lobular carcinoma like mine.

"That is exactly how Doctor Number Two made me feel, and is another reason why I left him and found Dr. Linda," I told her. "I don't think they mean to be so callous. They see breast cancer and deal with it on a daily basis. I do wish they would remember that it is new to us and we are frightened," I continued as I took a drink of my water and skimmed the menu.

"Connie, this nurse came in whistling, all happy, and there I was all upset. She handed me a photo album to look at. In it were mastectomy patients with breasts of all shapes and sizes. The mastectomies looked awful."

The waiter came over to see if we were ready to order. We had talked nonstop and asked him to give us a few minutes.

"Deidre, I am telling you. Trust me when I say that Dr. Houser will start the reconstruction the same day as your mastectomy. It will take a several weeks to complete it, but you will come out of surgery with cleavage. It won't look like the slaughtered mess in those pictures you saw."

"My grandmother and mom had breast cancer," she said. "I have two sisters, but so far it was me who was given this disease. I do think I have eaten poorly for years. I had not had a night of uninterrupted sleep in ten years either."

"Well, you will never know why you got it. You can wonder, and blame it on diet, but chances are that it was genetics for you, unlike me," I told her. "It isn't important anymore how you got it. It is important that you beat it and get it out of you, and you will."

It was then that the waiter came over and we both ordered healthy foods. "Lots of greens," I told her. "Eat as many green vegetables as you can."

"I have a question for you, Connie."

"What ... ask away," I told her.

"Have you got a nipple yet?"

"Well," I said. "You know that tune, *All I want for Christmas is my two front teeth, my two front teeth.* My song for this season is, *All I want for Christmas is my left nipple, my left nipple.* No, I don't have a nipple yet. But I do have my areola, and it looks so much better at least in having that."

The waiter brought our salads.

"I see Dr. Houser next week for my follow-up from surgery. I am sure curious what he thinks, and I'm sure he'll give me an idea on when he plans on making the nipple," I told her as I unwrapped my napkin and placed it on my lap. "Deidre, if it will make you feel better, I can show it to you. I truly don't mind. But not here," I said as we both looked around and laughed.

"I do want to see it, Connie. I do."

"Well, when we finish eating, we can go in the bathroom and I'll show you," I told her. We smiled and talked more about our kids, and I told her tales about Allie and Katie, who was winding down her senior year with style and success on the football team.

"My mom never got it again and is still living. My grandma lived to be eighty. I keep reminding myself of this over and over. That helps," Deidre said as she picked through her salad, about to cry.

"Yes, you hold on to that. Your children need you, and you can kick this."

She started to grin. "My husband has always wished I had bigger breasts. Can this Dr. Houser make me bigger ones?"

"Heck yes! If you choose to get a double mastectomy, yours will look better than mine. They'll be exactly alike. If you wish to just have one mastectomy, he should be able to add to the other one just like women who get bust jobs. Just ask him when you go in next week. He is sooooo damned cute, too. I keep telling him that after he finishes my breast and starts on my crow's feet, he'll want me when he is done. He always shakes his head at me and laughs. You'll love him, I am tellin' ya!"

Deidre insisted on buying my lunch. We walked away from our table and headed to the bathroom.

The stalls were empty. I walked into the spacious handicapped stall as she followed me. I felt weird hiding in a toilet stall. Actually lifting my top didn't bother me. I wondered what women might think if they walked in and saw two sets of feet in the handicapped stall with neither pair of feet facing outward in front of the commode, but side by side, near the door.

But I also visualized me lifting my top near the door and someone walking in and seeing me flashing another woman.

"Now remember. I just had surgery ten days ago, and it is still swollen and a little hard. You might see some sutures, and remember it will look much better as each day goes by," I said as I lifted my top.

"Oh, Connie ... it doesn't look bad at all. Can I touch it?"

"Sure. Touch it," I told her. (Homophobic I am not.)

I pulled my top down as we headed out of the bathroom.

As we headed to the parking lot, she told me, "I'll call you next week. You make me feel so much better."

"You do that. Call me anytime, and thanks for lunch. Stay strong, Deidre. It'll all be OK."

I headed north. She headed south. She had kids due home from school soon. She had a new friend in me.

I had a new friend, too.

54
I Missed My Nipple

The morning of Deidre's appointment, I woke up thinking about her. Two days later, I would have my appointment with Dr. Houser. He was my favorite doctor to go visit, because he didn't give bad news, just art and hope.

I wanted to find out if it was normal for my breast to still hurt so badly. But most of all, I couldn't wait to find out when he might make my nipple.

I missed my nipple. A lot.

When I crashed and burned from my hot flashes and the fan hit my glistening skin (we women glisten, we don't sweat), I become cold. My right nipple reacted. When I walked by mirrors and saw just one hard nipple, it freaked me out. I had spent years with hard nipples because of my cold-blooded body.

Many women opt to have a breast reconstructed without having a nipple made. I think I figured out why they don't want a fake nipple. I'd read that plastic surgeons make nipples that look hard.

Men love seeing hard nipples. They tell jokes and are entertained by them. They brighten their days. *Cold toes, warm heart, and hard nipples!*

"Looks like you are happy to see me," my fire buddy Don used to say as his eyes zoomed in on my chest.

Some women put Band-Aids over their hard nipples to hide them under their clothing. I wanted two nipples, and I didn't want to hide them.

For financial reasons, some women don't have nipples made. They may not have medical insurance.

I felt so thankful each day that I had two medical insurance policies. I didn't have to spend any out-of-pocket money. Within a week of my surgery, the itemized statement came showing the cost alone for my one day of surgery when I got the implant. Fourteen thousand dollars was the cost JUST for that one day in surgery. That didn't include doctor appointments, consultations, follow-up, medicine, etc.

Fourteen thousand dollars! And a year of all the other treatments, doctor visits, and tests put my coverage far higher. I thought about adding up all my EOBs that had come in the mail, just to see what all the costs added up to.

Thank the Lord I have insurance. I thought this each time I studied the bills or insurance statements showing the coverages for the last year.

I skimmed the itemized statement. Silicone implant: $3,952.00; operating room service: $6,789.00; and $837.00 just to knock my butt out by the anesthesia. Across the bottom of it read: THIS IS NOT A BILL.

Whew and thank you for insurance!

My job had fallen through the hoop of poor management, and the company was about to go bankrupt. I missed my job, the patients, and the nurses I had built such a wonderful relationship with. I was so relieved I would always have my retirement and insurance from my county job.

Claire called me and invited me out for lunch to our favorite Mexican restaurant.

The waiter looked at us as he handed us our menus. "Would you like something to drink?'

Claire gave me that look, wondering if we should have a margarita.

"Excuse me, but I am drinking Diet Coke," I told her as we both snickered, recalling that summer day when they had gone down too smooth and Tom had to rescue us. The waiter left us with our menus.

"And look at your hair," she said with much excitement as she reached across and touched it. "It is so curly and I like it," she said kindly.

We talked about her health, too. The esophagus scare that she had was better. The precancerous cells would be watched and checked closely by her doctor.

We planned more margaritas in our golden years. But only on Tom's days off.

The following day, I headed to see Dr. Houser. I purposely wore a low-cut silky brown top with spaghetti straps. The jagged long length hid my hips well as it hung over my low-cut jeans. I added a cool, beady, sparkling necklace and topped the outfit with a denim jacket.

I decided it would be fun to show some cleavage. Besides, an artist hangs his work in galleries to share, so why not show off Dr. Houser's work? I was struttin' the stuff.

As he knocked to come in, I stood. "Well ... what ya think?" I asked him as I stuck my chest out.

"You look pretty darn good, Connie. How does it feel?"

As he palpated my chest, he explained to me about the edema and forewarned me that the slight swelling might last a couple of months.

"Look at this, Dr. Houser." I lifted my right breast slightly to show him that I thought I just might need a little lift in it. "It makes my nipples line up when I push it up a little. We need these lined up even, don't you think? What about my nipple? I really want it. I look like a new car with a headlight kicked out. When can you do the nipple?" I pulled the spaghetti strap up as I waited for his reply.

"Connie, you were so borderline in needing a lift on the right side. We need to wait and see how it looks in the next few months, and then we will talk about tuning things up."

"I want to know one thing. It has been bugging me. Gravity pulls downward. I want you to tell me the truth." He looked at me, puzzled and wondering what bizarre question I was about to ask.

"Do you stand or tilt patients upward on the surgery table? I have thought so much about this. You can't know how a woman's breast hangs unless she is up. So do tell. I have this visual of my head drooped down with a ET tube hanging out of my mouth as you sit me up to compare my two breasts. What an ugly visual that is," I said as I grinned.

"We do tilt you up forty-five degrees. That is the most the anesthesiologist will allow us to do because of his protection of your airway."

"I knew it! I knew you have to do something like that," I said as I jumped down off the examination table.

"I push downward on the breast to simulate the gravity pull," he told me. "We have ways of telling," he said without going into detail. "I heard you have been advertising for me."

"Yep, just call me your PR woman. I assume you mean Deidre? I told her she would love you. She is a wonderful girl. We met. Did you know that? Dr. Linda hooked us up."

I continued on. "Yep, I even showed her my breast. See, we went to this Italian restaurant and … "

"You did not show your breast in the restaurant, did you?" he immediately interrupted and asked.

"Dr. Houser! No. I have more class than that. I took her to the bathroom and we squeezed into a handicapped stall."

We both laughed as I headed out the door and up to the receptionist area to make my appointment for two months later: Christmas. It would be Christmas before I got my new nipple. But it was OK and I had learned how to wait. Time had a way of flying by, and I was heading down the big hill I had climbed.

56

Toes Rock

When kids become seniors in high school, they are in constant need of money—$165.00 to keep her football jersey, a souvenir that she was determined she couldn't live without; $416.00 for senior pictures; $150.00 for Christmas break basketball camp; school fees; a prom dress in the spring. My God, the costs never stop.

Off to college, and the expenses escalate. Short of selling my flawed body, I prayed for a scholarship.

Continually, Katie heard me whining, "We can't afford it," or, "No, Katie, we are short of cash and Christmas is coming."

Christmas stresses me out. It's too commercial and too expensive, and the reason for the season is lost under Visa payments, wrapping papers, clothes that teens don't like or ever wear, and new electronic toys that encourage them to be couch taters. I feel obligated to purchase gifts. I find more joy in buying things for family and friends when I spy the perfect gift and can give it to them on no particular occasion. I grumble every October when I see the stores stocking shelves for Christmas.

My magazine stories weren't selling fast enough, and although I loved to stay busy, we seemed to always be short of cash. And Christmas was coming. Ugh to that.

But I had one foot in the door of my local newspaper and was going to start writing human-interest stories. I was excited to begin.

"Katie, we have dinner here that I cooked. You don't need to eat out," I would remind her. "Invite Shannon here. She is welcome to eat with us."

Katie hung out in high school with some wealthy friends. It was tough trying to keep up with them. No way could we compete. She always needed something, and I wanted to please her and be able to give.

"But, Mom, I need dress clothes for basketball. Coach Fraker wants us dressing up on home game days."

"OK. Fine. But, we are going to the thrift store," I warned her.

I'll always remember that Saturday in November, jumping in my car with Katie and heading to town. Even if I had bitched about not having any money, I needed to improve my mood. The heck with worrying about the late electric bill and being behind on a college loan. The checkbook was in the overdraft, too.

I felt ugly. My curls made me crazy. My back ached and I felt fat. Hell, I was fat.

I fretted daily about the visit I had coming soon with Dr. Rhoades. I assumed he would be ordering an entire body scan on me. I feared it. My body ached daily and it seemed I was always tired. I wanted to believe it was Tamoxiphen that was making me achy. I hoped it was the reason for my tiredness. *Please, Dear God, don't let me have bone cancer.*

It had been eight months since my last chemo. My arm continued to hurt from the intravenous chemotherapy. The vein was ruined, gone ... destroyed.

And just maybe I was turning into a hypochondriac. We cancer patients feel like hypochondriacs for a while after the first big blow.

Katie and I headed to town.

"Why we going this way?" she asked.

"I have a surprise," I told her.

"For me? What is it, Mom?"

"I told you. It is a surprise. After the surprise, we will go to the thrift store."

She became so excited, guessing and looking around, trying to determine our destination.

"This is probably a surprise for you," Katie said.

"How the heck could it be a surprise for me?" I asked as I stopped at the red light. "A surprise is unexpected, unknown. I know where I am going and what we are going to do." I turned west and passed the hospital.

"C'mon, Mom. Tell me," she said as I pulled into the strip mall.

She skimmed the parking lot. "Are we going tanning? To that bar?" she said as she looked at the tanning salon and sports bar. "I am not old enough to drink."

"No, Katie. Follow me," I said, as she was one bouncing step behind me.

As I put my hand on the door of the manicure shop, I announced to her, "We are getting pedicures."

"Oh Mom, I can't do that. They can't see my nasty feet. I have calluses from basketball, and my feet are ugly."

"Katie Belle [that is what I call her when I am being firm], they have seen so many ugly feet and feet much worse than yours. They'll take this little file and sand your calluses down. And the whirlpool and massage feels soooo good," I told her. "They have every color of polish under the sun. You can pick any color you want."

"I thought we were broke," she said as we walked in.

"We are," I said with a laugh. "Don't you worry about it."

And so that day we sat side by side, wiggling our toes, relaxing, feeling like rich bitches, as I used my Visa card and decided it was worth every penny.

A friend once told me that if we have any regrets in life, it should be about things we did, and not regretting things we wished we had done.

And I knew that someday if I was in a nursing home, sitting on the porch in my piss-stained nightgown, I wouldn't think about the late electric bill or my checking book overdraft.

I would smile and remember our pretty toes. Katie's purple and mine ... bold red.

57
Detailing The Headlight

I had my hair trimmed, because it looked like the seventies big-hair days. After the bald gig, I became very paranoid about haircuts. Watching it hit the floor, I imagined my hair screaming to me—*Hey, I fought hard to come back—why are you doing this?*

Fifteen months had gone by since the beginning of this tour of duty with breast cancer. I had one last thing to do to come full circle and feel completed as a woman.

It was nipple day with Dr. Houser, and as I drove south, I still had not started wearing my seat belt again. I looked in the mirror at my new "do," and I liked it. The curls were slowly leaving traces of no return. I was playing my Sheryl Crow CD, thinking about her recent diagnosis with breast cancer.

I wondered what the nipple reconstruction would be like, but I had no fear. My adrenaline was pumped and I was excited. I was curious about the tattoo artist who would be working on me. I pictured a Harley-looking babe with body piercing and connected tattoos up each arm.

I rushed through the door right on schedule. I signed in and peeked in at the Houser staff. "I'm having a great hair day and I'm getting a nipple," I sang to the girls after I had slid open the glass peek-a-boo window. "I'm getting a nipple! I'm getting a nipple!" I danced as I sang.

I noticed a new face and guessed. "You must be the tattoo artist," I said as I looked at a woman about my age. She was very pleasant looking, dressed simply, with a cute figure. Elaine had been a registered nurse for years and found an interest in cosmetic tattooing and traveled all over Ohio to many doctors' offices.

After we shared some laughs, I went into the examination room. Elaine followed me, and I noticed her Black and Decker toolbox on wheels. In it were various paints and supplies to begin working on my breast.

I immediately removed the top half of my clothes and put on a cotton gown as she directed me. "Open it in the front, please."

I thought about all the times I had heard that comment.

I heard a cheery voice and a small knock. Knowing it would be Dr. Houser, I flipped open my gown to flash him again. This had become my trademark, and I certainly didn't want to change my attribute.

"Well, are you ready?" Dr. Houser asked as he walked toward me, smiling. "Elaine, this is Connie. She is not one you will forget."

"Ready? I have been ready. You know, Dr. Houser ... I have been waiting months for this day. I want to end my book. The conclusion has been waiting for this special day even if Dr. Linda did steal my headlight."

"I am going on *Oprah* with you," he warned me.

"Well, of course you are. You know you are my favorite doctor."

As he got out his handy-dandy marker to draw on my areola, Elaine and he began discussing their goals. I was fortunate because I had an areola and he was going to utilize part of it, skillfully turning a piece of it into nipple.

Elaine snapped a picture of my breasts. As Dr. Houser finishing consulting with Elaine, he patted me on the shoulder.

"You've missed me, haven't you?" I proclaimed with a giggle.

"You know ... I have," he said as his dimples radiated with his warm smile.

"Wait. Don't go yet," I said to Dr. Houser. "I have a stupid question." I paused and he stopped as he always did, giving me time and never making me feel he was rushed.

"I am always horny and I am always cold. SO! My nipple is hard the majority of the time. Are you going to make me a hard nipple to match this one?" I asked, pointing at my right breast.

"Well ... " He laughed as he paused. "Today is your lucky day. I am happy for you because you ARE getting a hard nipple."

"Cool, so cool," I said as he started out of the room.

"Elaine will begin and I will be back."

There were three phases to complete the task. Elaine prepped my chest, cleaning it as we talked. We shared some of our personal life, and she told me about her new marriage. She showed me her new wedding ring. It was a rock. I missed those exciting days when marriage is so fresh and exciting.

"Oh, we debated about getting married. I have three kids from a previous marriage, and he has four." She tested her ink machine, and it hummed. "I am a country girl who grew up training horses, and he is a city boy," she said as she began mixing colors, constantly looking at my right areola and nipple to get a good color match.

As she worked, our conversation continued. I asked questions about her profession.

"See my lips?" she said. "They are tattooed. I never have to worrying about putting on lipstick."

"You are kidding," I said as I stared at her beautiful, slightly pink defined lips. "What if you decide you want to wear a different color?" I asked.

As I studied them more, I realized that the subtle color gave her the option of adding real lipstick over the lightness if she wished to darken the color.

I asked so many questions; she walked over to show me pictures of clients that she had worked on. I saw faces before and after. Tattooed eyeliner, eyebrows, and scars were camouflaged with coloring. Her work was amazing. I was fascinated.

"If you want ... when I come back in a month to check your tattoo after the color has settled, I can tattoo your mastectomy scar," she said. "It is entirely up to you."

As she injected Xylocaine into my breast area, I turned away. Although I had a strong stomach after all the trauma I had seen in EMS, I didn't want to watch anything with sharp objects going in my chest. I feared flinching, and Lord knows, I might end up with a nipple on my belly button. So as I turned away, I heard her tattoo gun buzz again.

"You shouldn't feel this," she said as she began the artwork. Without warning, tears fell down from my eyes. My emotions were delicate, and I was filled with appreciation for life and being a woman.

I thought about all the wonderful medical people who had come into my life. I truly felt that they didn't help put me back together just for making money. Each one made me feel special and I sensed their loyalty to their job and the strong desires to do the best job they could. My trust lay behind my tears as my cheeks became wet and my areola was getting color.

The next step was Dr. Houser's job.

"I will go get Dr. Houser, and I have another client here to work on," she said.

"Oh, is someone else getting a new nipple?" I asked.

"Oh no. I have another nipple later today here. But this is an eyelash permanent I am doing."

"Say what? Did I hear you right?" I asked as I sat up.

"Yes. Some women with long eyelashes like curl. The permanent lasts about three months, which is the life of eyelashes before they shed like all hair on the human body."

Some women have too much time and money on their hands, I thought as Dr. Houser appeared to begin step two.

I turned away again, deciding I didn't want to watch him create my new nipple. I felt pulling, tugging, and pressure. But I continued looking away as we talked and shared many stories. We laughed as he twisted, tweaked, and sutured.

He had cut a small piece of my areola, forming it into a nipple. Sutures were placed on the new addition. I visualized the stitches working like an anchor to redirect to the middle of my breast.

Elaine came back in, cranked on her power tool, and began injecting more color into the pink, fresh tissue to match it to my right nipple. Titty pink, or boobie brown, I wondered as she put the color back into my physical appearance.

She finished.

"You can look now," Dr. Houser said. "It isn't yours! Don't touch it!"

We laughed as I peered over to see a nipple standing up, looking so perfect. It made me think of a lit candle standing erect, bright, and glowing so radiantly.

The tears slowly slipped down my face. I fought to keep my headlight, and although I took the long road and lost it, I got a new one after all.

"You have a nipple, Connie," Dr. Houser said. "Now ... go finish that book."

Epilogue

It's been almost three years since I went through breast cancer. I am alive and well. I still go to various doctors for checkups, and I continue to get scared as I wait for test results. I never got a boob lift on my right side. I was content and thankful learning how to age gracefully. Life was for living, and not sitting in waiting rooms. I had a lot of celebrating of life to do.

I learned to love short hair and wear it short, sassy, and dark. De was glad I let go of the fake blonde stuff.

The kids tested us continually and brought us sadness, financial burden, and anger. But in their huge struggles in maturing, they also gave us hope, love, and patience to deal with their stumbling blocks.

Ryan continued to stay away a lot. He worked, lived with a friend, and paid his bills. He was a weekend partier and spent his weekend days sleeping the drunkenness away. In November 2005, he was arrested for DUI. The day he was to go to jail for three days, he cried tears of humiliation, fright, and disappointment in himself and for us.

I wasn't brave enough to take him to jail, so David took him. As I hugged him, I told him I'd be there to pick him up.

"I promise I will never drink and drive again and I will never go to jail again," he said as he climbed into the car, unshaved and ragged-looking after serving his time.

The arrest was the best thing that could have happened to Ryan. "Hmm, freedom," he said as I drove him home. "I can't wait to shower."

I watched him turn his life around mentally and physically as he joined a gym and volunteered to take counseling to learn why he drank so much. "Mom, they said everything you have said to me over the years. I should have listened. You were right," he said. "I thought I knew everything, and I thought you were overreacting. I'm sorry, Mom," he said as he cried and hugged me one day.

Those two words—"I'm sorry"—spoke volumes to me, and Ryan quit doing the disappearing act. He always comes home to visit, continues to work hard, and always wraps his big, strong arms around me with a hug and kiss. He tells me he loves me as he heads for his home with a plate of leftovers to take to work for lunch.

Instead of drinking all weekend, he gets up early and hits the golf courses. He advises his buddies about drinking but never pushes them too hard. He offers them all rides when they drink, and he hopes that in time they will learn how destructive, dangerous, and expensive drinking is.

After repeated invitations from one of his best friends to go out after work for a beer, his friend said, "What are you, a beer queer now?"

"Nope. But I won't ever drink and drive again."

He has stuck to that oath, and his friends have slowly learned to accept the changed Ryan. He has learned what a social drink is and admits that it's more fun to get up on the weekends feeling constructive and good.

He still can't find the perfect girlfriend, but knows that looking in a bar is not the answer. He loves to cook and eats healthy again. He is kind, respectful, hard-working, and responsible. Although he never finished college, he continues to seek a passion in the work world that will draw him. With his exceptionally good credit, he talks about investing money and saving to buy a house, and he looks wonderfully healthy and handsome. He has a six-pack now, but it isn't in the fridge.

On May 20, two years to the exact day after I'd had my mastectomy; Amber was involved in an automobile wreck that gave her a second chance at life. When I received the call from the emergency room at 4:00 AM that my daughter was injured in a car wreck and had asked for me, my first question was if she was alive. I knew in my heart before I asked that she'd been drinking. She'd split up with her boyfriend, and she and Allie had moved back home. It was tough taking them back in, but we knew we had to do it for Allie. I hoped I could help Amber find her way. She struggled and continually dated worthless men. I was so sad and worried for Allie. Disappointment in Amber weighed on my heart, but I loved her so and knew somehow we could help her turn her life around.

As I drove to the hospital, my emotions were mixed. I was scared, mad, and thankful Allie was with her dad and not involved in the wreck, too. I was apprehensive about what her injuries were. When I got to the hospital, it was obvious that she had been drinking. Her alcohol level was twice the legal limit, and her injuries were severe.

As I literally helped hold her head together as the doctor put staples in her head, I knew we had another bump in the road of life to deal with. After she was X-rayed, it was apparent that she needed to be transported to a trauma hospital. She crushed her right foot, her pelvis was fractured in four places, her left leg had compound fractures, and her knee was damaged from the tibia and fibula bones that had literally jammed up into the knee.

After two weeks in a trauma hospital, two months in a nursing home, and five surgeries, David built a ramp on our front porch for her wheelchair as we prepared to bring her home. We bought a hard mattress for the bed in the spare bedroom to aid in comforting her unstable pelvis.

I visited her every day in the nursing home. Rehab was tough on her, as the physical therapists worked with her daily. Each day, she slowly got better. The pain she endured for months was tremendous. I truly believe that because of her strong physical strength and her bullheadedness, she recovered much more quickly.

Katie was about to graduate high school with honors and had made us so proud. I had a graduation party to plan as I ran from hospital to nursing home daily through Amber's ordeal. I resented

Amber for disrupting our lives and Allie's and Katie's special time.

Just two weeks before she had crashed, as I observed her behavior, I told her, "Amber, you cannot live the lifestyle you are without hurting yourself or someone else. I fear someday you will get killed or kill someone else. I picture you in jail." Each day, I wished for her to be the mother to Allie I expected. Her childhood had been so wonderful, and I wanted Allie to have some kind of normalcy. Shared parenting continued, and I still didn't agree with it. It gave Amber too much idle free time.

As I sat at the nursing home with her one day, my cell phone rang. Amber was having a bad day and was in a lot of pain. As I answered my cell phone, I immediately panicked when I heard Dr. Linda's voice on the phone. In between all the running and nurturing of my adult kids, I had taken time to have my routine bone scan.

Dr. Linda was holding the results in her hand as I jumped up from my chair by Amber's bed and ran out the door.

"Connie, it is not good news," she said.

I continued walking fast and slammed out the door of the nursing home. I needed air.

"Your cancer has spread. I am so sorry," she said. "It is in your bones ... your back," she continued.

My neck got stiff and my throat dry just like the day the doctor had called me to tell me I had breast cancer.

"It is in your back," she said.

"Nooooo, this can't be true," I said as I cried and tried to talk in between sobs. "You don't understand," I told her. "Katie is graduating and about to go off to college. I am at a nursing home right now, Dr. Linda. Amber was in a very bad car wreck. I need to help her get well for Allie," I said.

I felt like someone had kicked me in the stomach. I was instantly overcome with nausea. I feared dying and being a burden and worry to my family and friends.

I dropped to my knees and cried. Becoming an old woman looked bleak. How was I to help Amber to mend and become whole again? How could I function and get through Katie's graduation and not rain on her parade when we had a party to give to celebrate her success? Allie loved me and needed me as she tried to understand why her mom couldn't come home. I wanted my parents to live forever, and they didn't need the sorrow of possibly burying me.

I knew I had to return to Amber's room. I wiped my eyes and headed back to her room. I protected the kids since I'd become a mother. I couldn't hide anymore. When I returned to her room, she looked at me and knew something was dreadfully wrong. I lay down beside her on her bed and cried like a baby. She knew without words spoken that it was bad.

Because I had so much faith in my surgeon, I took Dr. Linda's advice when she suggested I switch to an oncologist closer to my home. His reputation was good. It seemed a logical choice. All my many cancer doctors would now be in the same medical building and work at the same hospital.

I signed the proper forms to have all my medical records copied and sent to the new oncologist. I'd had my first consultation with the doctor and liked his compassion and the time he gave me. The day after Dr. Linda called; I called him for an appointment to go over the bad bone scan results.

I told most of my family except Katie. I told David I didn't want her to know until after her graduation party. It was her time, and there had already been too many showers on her parade. Ryan was no longer the silent, in-denial, inconsiderate son. He was devastated, and like David, he would not believe that I might die.

"The breast cancer has spread near your spine in the L-3 area. It is also in your hip. Without treatment, you probably have eighteen months to live. We can put you on a trial chemo that you probably will have to take for the rest of your life. You'll take fourteen chemo pills orally a day, and every three weeks you'll come in for the trial IV therapy. IF it works, we might be able to give you five to ten years."

Those were the powerful words of my new oncologist as I sat in the office chair and wept.

"If you agree to do the trial chemo, you must sign this form. After signing it, you must start the treatment within five days or the trial can't be used," the male nurse said. "There are strict guidelines. We highly recommend this. The FDA has released this for colon cancer patients, and it has given them a few more years. It has not been released for breast cancer, so we don't have studies on its effect yet. You will be our first patient who fits the parameters to use it. There are some possible side effects."

Out of desperation, I signed the form. I would start the chemo in a week, and Amber was headed back for her third surgery.

With all the information given to me to absorb, my sixth sense kicked in and I started to question this diagnosis. I had many unanswered questions. Having cancer in my L-3 and right hip was too coincidental. I had had many MRIs and a multitude of tests and studies done on my back. My back history had been with me for many years. I was full of arthritis in those areas. Something seemed wrong, but the RN insisted it was cancer and not my arthritis causing a false reading.

Instead of being intimidated by a doctor, I researched, read, and called a friend who has a master's degree in research and who was also a breast cancer survivor. She was full of information, and I was full of questions for my next visit to the doctor.

The day when I was to start my first chemotherapy, I walked into the doctor's office skeptical and hesitant. In one hand I carried the questions I had written down, and at my other hand was my friend Margi, who I knew would support me in whatever decision I made and understand if I decided I would not take chemo again. Having someone not as connected as family was important to me. Although selfish, I thought it had to be my decision and not a desperate plea from family.

I had already read and learned that a bone scan is not as accurate as a PET scan. A radioactive tracer substance is put into the vein for a bone scan. The tracer travels through the body and collects in the bone areas. When the test is read, it looks for hot spots. If the test results are normal, the radioactive tracer distributes evenly though the body.

If a reading is abnormal, like mine was, hot spots are detected. These hot spots do not automatically mean that those areas are cancer. Fractures, old and new, can show up. Bone infections, arthritis, or even Paget's disease, which is an abnormal chronic bone disorder causing abnormal growth, can cause the hot spots.

PET scan, positron emission tomography, is a powerful imaging technique and measures abnormal molecular cells. It pinpoints diseases in the body. Cancer cells are highly metabolic, and the PET scan can detect the cancer from the radioactive glucose (sugar) that is injected into the patient prior to the scan.

PET scanning provides a better, more accurate reading for patients. It gives physicians extra insight, and I was determined, because of my history with arthritis and a bad L-3 disc problem, that *my* insight was going to be used on me before I started a chemo treatment for life. I needed to be sure.

I refused chemo and insisted on a PET scan and Margi and I walked out of the oncologist's office. The male nurse was angry. He had put many hours into the trial test paperwork in preparation for me to be in the study. I didn't give a damn.

"Ya know, I am not a guinea pig," I said. "I am Connie Curry, and not a number in your study," I told him as he pressured me to start the chemo. Margi looked on, starting to side with me on my sixth-sense feeling.

"If you don't start this today, you can't be in the study," he said. He was very angry with me.

"You can stick that paperwork up your butt," I said. "I am not doing it. I demand a PET scan."

And as almost always with my sixth sense, I was right. The bone scan was picking up arthritis in my back, just as I had suspected. The PET scan was able to separate and confirm that the hot spots were not cancer. I won't ever forget how sheepish the male nurse was when he had to tell me on the telephone that the PET scan showed no cancer. I am sure he and the entire office were very embarrassed. I can only hope that the doctor leaned a lesson about taking time to read and compare a patient's medical records. I suspect the bone scan would have showed the same questionable spots on old scans. I am not certified with knowledge on reading scans, and used only common sense and my wonderful sixth sense. It angered me because I took the time to make sure all my records were sent to the new oncologist. He was obviously too busy or careless to learn my medical history. But I was so happy and relieved that I couldn't react negatively to the male nurse on the telephone, and I just wanted to hang up and spread the good cheer. Besides, I was sure he felt bad enough. The thankfulness I felt for being right and not being terminal was a blessing I can't put into words.

The next thing I knew I had to do was call Dr. Rhoades. I'd made a big mistake in leaving him and needed him back as my doctor.

After Dr. Rhoades, my old oncologist, read the tests and reassured me I was just fine, I also took them in to Dawn at the radiation office. My radiation oncologist took the time between patients to reassure me also that he agreed with Dr. Rhoades.

I was cancer-free. I thought about Amber, and although she would have pain for the rest of her life with so many rods and pins in her legs, and she'd never be able to run again, she was blessed too. Her brain and spine were intact. I look at the pictures of her car and wonder how she lived. And every day as she became stronger and went from a wheelchair to crutches, she got to come home. Sadly, days later she went to jail to serve time for the DUI.

Like Ryan, her dad was there to take her. I still did not have the courage to drop her there, but was there for her when she hobbled out. Her wreck and jail were huge wake-up calls. As we drove home, I told her, "You were given a second chance. There is a strong message out there to why you were spared," I said. Tears ran down from her eyes. "Look at you. Even without makeup on, you are beautiful, but you need to learn beauty from within. You have a beautiful daughter who needs you so much. We need you. You've had a long road, and you need to keep climbing upward. Your dad and I are here for you. But you must start living life right. I will not sit back and watch you make bad decisions and date bad men again," I said.

She cried, and unlike the old Amber, she did not mouth me, make excuses, or deny. Jail had been good for her, too.

Amber met a wonderful, self-supporting man who adores her and Allie. I love having a computer engineer about to be in the family. My computer is clean, and life is cleaner for all of us. It's nice to have a guy in her life that we all like and have faith in.

After eighteen months of being unable to work, Amber got her driver's license back and started a great respectable job. She is also a motivational speaker for many schools throughout Ohio, talking about the dangers of drinking and driving. Speaking has been good for her and keeps her grounded. As she shows a slide show that we put together, and relives all the pain and damage she did to herself because of one reckless night, it helps her to heal emotionally.

I have gone to listen to her speak at a few of the high schools. The students listen. One could hear a pin drop as she gives advice. "You are young. You think you are invincible. I thought I was, too. I didn't want to listen to anyone. I ran with the wrong people. You act and become your environment. What I did to myself was bad, but the worst part was how selfish it was and how many lives I affected. I thought I didn't need my family. I do."

I wonder how she speaks so strongly without becoming emotional or nervous. I am yet to listen without crying because it brings back so many bad memories. I am very proud of her. She is well-spoken and determined to send a strong message to teens, and strives to make a difference. The feedback has been amazing, as she speaks more and more at various schools.

Recently, she spoke with Coach Jim Tressel, the Ohio State football coach, and Dimitrius Stanley, a former O.S.U. football player and now commentator for our local TV station. The high school, located in Columbus, Ohio, is a huge school that had been dealing with a lot of alcohol and drug abuse. Like always, Amber felt such self-worth as she spoke, and hoped if even one student listened, she succeeded.

Amber and Ryan were young and lived in a different time than me. I never went to bars as a young woman. My life was my kids, work and trying to keep my family intact. It was later when they were grown and I got the bug for singing that I enjoyed getting out to see old friends and to sing my blues away.

Ryan was in bars drinking and probably looking for women, like most young men do. The alcohol gave him courage. Amber married too young and became a mother before she was ready. I expected and hoped she'd grow up fast for Allie. I remember my dear friend and high school counselor telling me once to hold on tight. Amber would grow up someday and we would be friends. I held on to those words as we struggled and fought through each bump.

David and I married young. We waited four years to have our children. We grew up together, and when our babies came into the world, we were ready and doted over them, giving all our time and love to them. I expected Amber to do the same. Being a single mom, I now know that was impossible and she reminded me of that many times. And I have watched her change and become a good mother and my friend.

I've done the best job I could have raising the kids. I always told Amber as she parented Allie, "Raising kids is the hardest job you will ever have. There is not a book to give you step-by-step how to do it. We all make mistakes along the way. They grow up too fast. You need to stop and smell the roses and enjoy this precious little girl."

Rarely today do I visit a bar. After what we have gone through with Amber and Ryan, I don't have the desire to go. I used to blame myself and question my parenting. I only know that I loved them very much and gave them all of me, to the point where it caused marital problems. Maybe I did too much and gave too much.

All I know is that Katie, being the youngest and observing the pitfalls of her siblings, has sworn to graduate from college with a degree. She is a sophomore in college, and I know she worked hard to obtain a 3.4 her freshman year. I am proud of her. When her school friends are out many weekends, drinking as much alcohol as they can, and I call her, she is usually in her room, studying.

She is very honest and mature, and has so much common sense. She looks so much like Amber as she has grown into adulthood. And her love of sports is still a big part of her life as she plays softball and became the catcher her freshman year for Heidelberg College.

With all the problems, David and I continue to move through life trying to mend our family. He sees the same beauty in me he saw when I was eighteen, and for that I am thankful.

My wonderful friend Dave from the Vinntage Band, who believed in me when he asked me to sing at my high school class reunion, died unexpectedly on Thanksgiving of 2006. Even today, I think of him and miss him very much. His music will live on. When we had our thirtieth reunion and I had my lump, Gary, the other high school friend who came back to play with the old band, was sick too. We just didn't know as we celebrated life with old friends that night that we both had cancer. Gary has also died, and we all attended the funeral just months after that great reunion.

Wayne continues to rebuild his life and finances but has never truly found happiness without his daughters. Parental alienation syndrome, a newly publicized theory on some family split-ups, should be titled, "Wayne's Life."

I wish each day that one of his daughters would come home to him as he fills his life with work to keep his mind less troubled.

Mom and Dad are going strong. We are blessed that Mom is able and still insists on cooking Thanksgiving dinner and being the hostess at all the family gatherings. My parents are a special couple. I have always said if people had half the love and devotion my parents have for each other, no one would divorce. I recently attended the funeral of my neighbor man. He had lived into his golden years but would be missed by so many. I thought a lot about many things as the minister spoke. I am blessed that I still have my parents.

Gene, my neighbor left a huge positive impact on many lives. He was a great man. The minister spoke about how people polish things through life. But a good person polishes hearts of others. He spoke about how a person's birth is etched on paper and a tombstone. His death is etched there, too. It is the dash in between those two dates that is so important. How one lives in between is what is so important. I know many people have polished my life. I also think about my dash and hope someday my in betweens are noteworthy.

I still participate in the Susan G. Komen race and the Relay for Life. Dr. Linda still asks me occasionally to talk with other breast cancer patients. On July 12, 2006, Dr. Linda purchased a personalized marker with my name on it. It was displayed on the eighteenth-hole fairway during the ninth annual Jan Hurley Memorial Pink Ribbon Tournament. I felt blessed that she chose me.

I still love Dr. Houser, and have seen him briefly from time to time. He welcomes me back in his office as we chat and catch up. Recently, he asked me to come into the office because he wanted to have pictures taken of my marvelous new breast reconstruction to show other patients. I still remember the day he called me, when news had traveled to his office that I had bone cancer. I heard him cry as he talked on the phone, when I had not found out yet it was a misdiagnosis. "This shouldn't happen to people like you," he'd said to me. "Fight hard, Connie."

Dawn, my favorite radiologist at the BBQ pit, took another job out of town. We keep in touch by e-mail and continue to be friends. After all that radiation, I no longer have to shave under my left arm pit. The hair follicles were destroyed, I guess.

I lost Deidre. She refused chemo, quit going to our doctors, and walked away from everyone who was involved with cancer. She wouldn't return my phone calls. I think of her and wonder if she survived. I learned to not refer to chemo as rat poison, and accepted it even if it was a tough cocktail. Maybe Deidre found a new doctor and was cured. I hope so.

Jim, who lost his wife to cancer, continues to deal with depression and loneliness. We invite him over occasionally for dinner. He never regained any use of his left arm from the stroke. Whitney, like many young adults, moved back home after realizing living alone is not as easy as it is fun. She is attending college. We talk about Pam a lot, remembering all the good in her.

I took many of the scarves Whitney gave me and patch worked them into an old pair of jeans for a seventies-themed conference that I attended. I had the coolest bell bottoms at the conference. My Susan G. Komen scarves from three races were included in the bright design also.

My other friend, Pam has never gotten over the death of Nicole. Would any loving parent? But I learned what strength she had and how she tries each day to find happiness. And Nicole lives on in all our hearts.

Sue, my chemo partner, and I continue to keep in touch. Her rare cancer seems to have been cured. She is full of life and loving each day with her new grandbabies.

I continue with Dr. Rhoades for my oncology checkups. He was so forgiving of me for leaving him when I had that routine bone scan that turned to hell. I have so much faith in him even though I still get very frightened as I wait for test results.

I continue to write for my local newspaper and Habitat for Humanity. I never thought in a million years that I could ever work in sales. I guess selling all those 50/50 tickets gave me some sales experience. I remember hearing that if you love the product, it's easy to succeed. I fell in love with Silpada Designs jewelry and have never looked back. It was easy to start building my clientele. I signed up to sell, bought my sign-up kit, and sat down to jot down the names of friends and family who might have a party. I am very lucky to have such a large volume of friends who supported me and helped my business skyrocket. Silpada Designs keeps me motivated and gives me energy to succeed and prosper. It rejuvenates me and each day I love putting on different, beautiful pieces of my jewelry.

My first year, as I went to numerous homes, doing shows for many wonderful women and friends, I earned my Sterling Silver Award, selling $50,000 in beautiful sterling silver jewelry. There are approximately 22,000 representatives in the nation, and I rank in the top 4 percent in sales. My gosh. It is a blast!

I worked hard and was promoted to Star Leader and have a great team working with me. We are Silpada sisters and support each other and have formed great friendships, too.

EMS was the most rewarding job I ever had, but Silpada is the most fun and gives me passion. I make great money and reward women with so much free jewelry. It's a party every time, I say to my hostesses. I love it!

Karen, my cousin was right. Getting cancer did make me stronger. I always knew I had a special family and special friends. I am blessed. What a support team I had. They all helped lift me up.

Last year, while Mom, Amber, Tina, David, Allie, and I visited the local fair, we walked Allie around the pet barn. Numerous farm animals were there with new babies for children to see and pet.

Allie stood very patiently as she watched baby chicks under a light. Cracked eggs were there, too, with the promise of life.

She watched and watched as she leaned down, peeking into the glass. An egg was cracking. Allie was mesmerized as she watched life forming before her eyes. The egg cracked ever so slowly as she stood, motionless and quiet. I stood beside her as she saw a leg struggle to come out. The little wet chick took forever to come out, as the egg slowly cracked wider and wider until it fell apart in two pieces. I heard Allie gasp.

I think she thought it was dead. The little chick didn't move as it was recuperating from its struggle in coming out of the egg.

We talked about how wonderful it was for Allie and us to see this miracle. Jared, my brother-in-law, who has such faith in God and so much logic on life, said something about that birth we witnessed. It has stuck with me: "Think how hard that chick fought to live."

I had not been to church since I was a teen. After my bone scan scare, and when Amber was able to walk again, I asked her to go to church with me. We both had a lot to be thankful for.

I struggle with religion, but there was something about going that Sunday that gave me peace of mind. I felt closer to God and Amber. I put my seat belt on and continue to wear it each time I drive out of the driveway. Life is precious. Oh, and I still have my Bug. She truly is glorious.

But if any woman has long hair, it is glory to her. And I have my glory back.

And like the chick that fought cracks, we continue to trip over cracks.

We just step over them.

Advice when going to surgery:

Remember when your mom always advised you to wear clean, decent under panties? Don't wear panties when you are going to the hospital for surgery. They strip search you! And if you wear them, they make you take them off, anyway.

Do you wear your beautiful sterling silver jewelry with pride and feel pretty with it on? Don't wear jewelry to the hospital, because they will make you take it all off.

Wear lipstick at all times to feel pretty. Forget wearing your mascara to surgery. They will tape your eyes shut during surgery, and you don't want to come out of surgery looking like a hooker. Put your mascara on ASAP after your return from recovery. Redo your lipstick. Don't look down or feel your chest area. Save this for later, when you are feeling stronger, and mentally ready.

Leave your fingernail polish on when you arrive if you want to feel like you are getting a semi-manicure. They have to remove it to get a good reading on the pulse oxygen machine. (This is the little cuff that will go on your index finger and it measures the air you breath.) If you want to be helpful, and please the medical staff, go ahead and remove the fingernail polish prior to admittance.

Take nail polish; polish remover, files and clippers to the hospital. Have a relative give you a pedicure so you can feel pretty. They want to make you happy again.

After you have won this vicious battle, share with other cancer victims. Try to give them upbeat, positive information. Don't feel compelled to share the worst experiences with them. This information is not necessary unless they ask for it.

If you are unblessed with a chemo port for your chemotherapy, give the medical team your input on where to put the port. Don't allow them to place it where the scar will show when clothed. Doesn't it make sense to have it under where your bra strap or tank tops crosses up to your shoulders?

And remember, scars fad, just like your Levis and hair dye. This is a perk for scars, unlike the fading of our hair dye and jeans.

When your hair falls out, buy wigs, scarves, turbans in various colors and styles. Go blonde if you are a natural brunette. Be Cher for a night when you karaoke. Be a sexy redhead when you sing a Reba McIntire hit.

Misbehave, say what you want, sulk, scream, and laugh out loud. Your behavior can be overlooked and excused. Blame it on the chemo, and tell people the side effects can cause these various inappropriate outbursts. You will be excused, and I don't mean literally from the establishment.

If your eyebrows fall out, remember they will come back just like your eyelashes. Depending on your mood for the day, paint on whatever style of eyebrow that fits your mood. Being scared is a normal reaction when you are dealing with cancer, treatments, trips daily for radiation, hair loss, etc. Pencil on a scared look. Want to feel mysterious? One eyebrow can have the lift, arched look.

Ever wish you had long eyelashes? Buy them!

And of course the plus side is, no swimsuit trim job, and no plucking eyebrows for a while. Woohoo!

If a insensitive, stupid man says something off color, such as, "Well, at least you will still have THAT," as he points downward at your pelvis area, simply raise your knee is a quick, forceful gesture, aiming at HIS balls, and kick upward with all your strength. Watch him drop to his knees. (This comment was made to me when discussing my cancer with his compassionate wife, and he felt compelled to share his two cents worth.)

And always remember, sometimes you must cry before you can smile or laugh. You will laugh again and you can win the war.

Photo taken by: Karen Harris

About the Author

Connie E. Curry grew up and continues to reside in Delaware, Ohio with her husband David. A mother of three and grandmother to one, she writes for the local newspaper, The Delaware Gazette. She volunteers for Habitat for Humanity as a writer for their newsletter and is a freelance writer for various magazines.

She has won many writing contest including The James Thurber Humor writing contest and the B + T makeover through Silpada Designs where she is currently employed.

After retiring from emergency medical services, she continued her love of writing and has been published in Country Living Magazine, Official publication of Electric Cooperative, Reunion Magazine, Grit Magazine, Shotgun Sports and Off Lead Magazine.

Several of her humor stories appear in published short story collections, including "I Wanna Be Sedated", "Dance of the Chickens", "Chicken Chisme: The Fine Art of Gossiping", and "Chicken Fluff and Other Stuff". "Romancing The Soul", another short story collection, Curry also contributed to.

Graham, her Golden Retriever and Betty, her Maine Coon cat can always be found at her feet as she writes, turning words into stories.

She is a member of the Write Life Writing Group, Delaware Writing Group and Ohio Writer.

Curry's love of Volkswagens enabled her to buy and become involved in the restoration of her 1974 Volkswagen Bug. Her first publication in "Women with Wheels" told the funny tale about this project and validated the passion she has of vintage cars. Her Bug is her pride and joy and she loves showcasing it in numerous parades, waving and celebrating life and the joy of people.